Game Design Tools

This book provides a series of transdisciplinary tools to help game designers improve their design pipeline and design output. Using approaches from psychology, anthropology, and sociology, it offers practical tools for all the main aspects of game design from conception through to testing.

Drawing on game design theory, the book looks at the relationship between game design and other disciplines to create a toolbox of modern tools for game designers. It covers archetypes, praxeology, behavioural game design, and emotional game design. Covering a wide breadth of content, the book includes chapters on:

- Documentation
- Production
- Evaluation
- Analysis and marketing tools

This book will be of great interest to students on game design courses, as well as early-career game designers and those looking to break into the industry. It will also be of interest to more experienced game designers looking for new game design tools.

Game Design Tools
Cognitive, Psychological, and Practical Approaches

Diego Ricchiuti

CRC Press
Taylor & Francis Group
Boca Raton London New York

CRC Press is an imprint of the
Taylor & Francis Group, an **informa** business

Designed cover image: Enrico Sartini.

First edition published 2023
by CRC Press
6000 Broken Sound Parkway NW, Suite 300, Boca Raton, FL 33487–2742

and by CRC Press
4 Park Square, Milton Park, Abingdon, Oxon, OX14 4RN

CRC Press is an imprint of Taylor & Francis Group, LLC

© 2023 Taylor & Francis Group, LLC

Library of Congress Cataloging-in-Publication Data
Names: Ricchiuti, Diego, author.
Title: Game design tools : cognitive, psychological, and practical approaches / Diego Ricchiuti.
Description: First edition. | Boca Raton, FL : CRC Press, 2023. | Includes bibliographical
   references and index.
Identifiers: LCCN 2022036234 (print) | LCCN 2022036235 (ebook) | ISBN 9781032134802 (hardback) |
   ISBN 9781032134789 (paperback) | ISBN 9781003229438 (ebook)
Subjects: LCSH: Video games—Design | Video games—Psychological aspects.
Classification: LCC GV1469.3 .R49 2023 (print) | LCC GV1469.3 (ebook) |
   DDC 794.8/3—dc23/eng/20220825
LC record available at https://lccn.loc.gov/2022036234
LC ebook record available at https://lccn.loc.gov/2022036235

ISBN: 978-1-032-13480-2 (hbk)
ISBN: 978-1-032-13478-9 (pbk)
ISBN: 978-1-003-22943-8 (ebk)

DOI: 10.1201/9781003229438

Typeset in Times
by Apex CoVantage, LLC

Access the Support Material: www.routledge.com/9781032134789

Dedicated to the people of the game industry,
without whom I would have only lived one life.

Contents

SECTION FIVE   Conclusion 239

20 Games, Cakes, and Love 241

21 The Cake Is Real 245

Foreword by Dominic Butler

There has never been a better time to approach learning game design. The industry has gone through such a massive growth in the last 30 years—this has not only been a surge in potential market (more people are playing games now than ever before) but also in terms of access to learning content and tools. The democratisation of these tools, where anyone with an idea and access to a computer *can* make a game, has led to an explosion of content resulting in an abundantly rich playspace. More than ever before, small teams—even solo developers—can and do build new experiences and successfully bring them to market through mainstream channels such as Itch.io and other early access channels.

At the same time there is a growing amount of tutorials, how-tos, and advice out there for developers (both new and veteran). Something that becomes quickly apparent when going through a lot of this content is that there is no "one way"—no singular ruleset that will ensure your games' success; it's a series of iterative processes. Sid Meier famously described a game as "a series of interesting decisions", and in many ways game design and development is exactly this (while it may not always feel like it at the time). Where to place a platform? Where on the screen to put a HUD element? What options will the player have at a particular point? What will it look like/sound like? How will it *feel*? Developers make countless decisions throughout development to bring their visions to life and to create those experiences for players, and knowing which choice to take is rarely easy.

Players will come to different games for different reasons, e.g., as a form of escapism or seeking some sort of cathartic release. Increasingly it offers players ways to socialise and act as a form of expression—allowing them to try out decisions or behaviours in a controlled space (just as animals learn by playing). Whatever it was that attracted them in the first place, the designer's job is to find ways of engaging players right from the moment they launch the game and then, crucially, to keep them engaged in the long term. Humans are natural mental model builders and our experience with games is no different. No game is real—only the experience is—and that's ok. Players, through their suspension of disbelief, can feel the excitement of a thrilling car chase or the bitter pangs of defeat and the hands of an enemy; they can be moved to tears or driven to anger. They come to games for these experiences and in doing so give their most precious resource—time. As developers we are competing for that time with everything else in their lives—meeting friends, watching a movie, etc. Respecting the player's time requires excellence in design. This is demonstrated through the game experience: how a game approaches onboarding, leverages player affordances, i.e. not wasting the player's time with invisible walls or their equivalent (places where that mental model falls apart, where players continually have to guess without the tools required). It extends to understanding cognitive load, the user experience, and the overall player journey. It means studying ways to meet their needs beyond the immediate audio/visual experience—to do so on a psychological level. This is not to exploit players (we can leave that to the casinos of Las Vegas) but to ensure that the time they spend with the game—whether it is one hour or hundreds, feels well spent—that they can feel good about it. This is how the games industry has grown and will continue to grow.

In this book Diego has outlined a learning approach through iteration and experimentation that addresses that need for clarity and excellence in design. Laying out the principles as he has given the reader a shared vocabulary across a spectrum of topics that occur throughout any project from ideation and brainstorming techniques through to understanding player motivations through the lens of self-determination theory and building mechanics. The result is a strong foundation for both newcomers and experienced developers—even if you were aware of some of the topics before reading, chances are you will find some that are new or offer a fresh perspective.

Foreword by Fawzi Mesmar

I first met Diego in Rome. I think he and I were speaking at the same conference; I was doing a talk about inspiration and was at the time leading the design team at DICE. I remember that it was a funky event; the venue was part of a movie studio on the outskirts of the capital. Around the sound stage where the event was held, there were countless sets of what I was told were the backdrop of a lot of famous moments in Italian cinema and TV. What made the venue even cooler was that the organisers held a section for retro games, a large room where many old-school consoles and CRT TV sets were on plastic tables and all the attendees—myself included—were having some pretty fun, nostalgic times.

Diego brought some of his students along to attend the talks and to get to meet industry professionals; he introduced some of them to me after I was done with my presentation, and they took me outside to try out one of the best sausages I've had to date—nothing beats Italian street food. I was quite moved by how close Diego and his students were; I could tell that they held quite a bit of respect for him and that at the same time he was part of the crew; it was clear that they have learned a lot from him and, observing the writing of his book, I think by now we have documented proof.

As a tutor of game design myself, I have observed that there are two types of students: there are students that thrive in abstract notions—philosophical definitions that they ponder, get an understanding of what that means to them, and then proceed to apply their new-found thought processes to their projects and professional lives beyond. The other type of students are the ones who long for specifics; they want *answers*! They would like to know how things are done and how they can do it themselves. I love that Diego managed to balance both, providing lots of thought-provoking challenges for the reader to ponder on but also giving the reader a set of tools and frameworks that they can immediately whip out of their belt and start cracking. It's quite a varied tool set at that; Diego presented everything from game design theory, to business analysis models, to Richard Bartle's taxonomy, to even psychological concepts, all of which are industry standards that I have seen being used in hallway discussions, design meetings, and pitch decks in stakeholder meetings.

I could almost hear the teacher in Diego call out at me from the pages of the book to pay attention or go back and read things properly again when I skipped a chapter or a paragraph when I should not have. I can also, however, hear the game designer in him that has done time in the trenches of game development in both small and large projects. I can relate to how he wants to bust a common industry myth or a misconception that people from outside the industry have about game design as a profession. Most importantly, the player advocate in him is immediately apparent, as he urges the reader to understand the players they're making games for and to make sure they keep the future in mind whenever they make a design decision.

If you are just curious about game design and want to learn about it without any prior knowledge, then enjoy; you are in for a treat. If you are already deep in the weeds, I found this book to be what the namesake suggests, a reference that the reader will come back to many times. It might be on your bookshelf within arm's reach as you are tackling an issue in your current project—either as a student or a professional—and you need to quickly look up one of those frameworks or tools that are perfectly suited for a situation you are currently facing.

Fawzi Mesmar
Game designer, author, and tutor

Acknowledgments

My first thanks goes to my family; thank you for believing in my desire to make games even when you had no idea what I was talking about, and thank you for believing in me today despite still not knowing how my job works.

You have always cheered for me when I moved to attend university, looked for a job, and travelled all over the continent. Thank you for being my parachute when I fell, for nudging me toward writing this book, for feeding my passion for games since I was a kid, where other families would have ignored it or even gotten in the way. All those times you bought me a game when I was young or played with me while I talked for hours about this dream, you may not remember them, but for me they are the treasure that made me who I am today and who I will be tomorrow.

Thanks to Joseph Kinglake, who, other than being a great source of inspiration and fruitful design talks, was also a spring of motivation: when I first thought about writing this book you were one of the first people I told it to, and I remember you replying that you knew I would have written a book since we first met in university. What you don't know is that those words made me feel a manifest destiny of my goal to share knowledge, and it has given me courage ever since. I hope we will always have such news to share with each other.

Tommaso Bonanni, for all the nights spent talking about design, making theories and developing them while freezing out in the cold. Thank you for helping me plan the game design course at *AIV*, where we formalised the foundations for this book and its pedagogical method. You value just as much as I do the importance of honest and improvement-aimed feedback for the growth of both the students and the industry where our paths had the luck to meet.

To Mattia Beffa, who brought me back on the right track when my words started to feel more like commands rather than explanations: after years of technical documents where the content is more important than the form, one starts to forget about the poetry those same words hold. Thank you for reminding me of their beauty with your romantic way of seeing the world.

Just like any game, a book improves with the feedback it receives, therefore I can't thank enough those who gave me opinions and tips during all the writing phases of what you are holding right now: Dominic Butler, Fawzi Mesmar, Simone Cicchetti, and Roberto Pavan, thank you for sharing with me the vision for this book.

Lastly, thank *you*, the reader, for dedicating your time toward reading my words and for trusting my teaching no matter your level of experience in the game industry. The same way the best game that has ever existed could be out there with no one playing it, this book would have no value if you weren't here absorbing its concepts and bringing its tools with you in your journey. The goal of this book was to share knowledge, to be lent to friends or colleagues—even to be criticised if that means people sharing what once was tacit information—and the fact that someone is reading this right now means everyone can play their role in the improvement of this industry. There is so much I still have to say, but for the time being thank you for being part of this big first step.

About the Author

What is game design? The real question for me is: what isn't game design? I've done various things in my life, and none of them taught me something I couldn't apply to game development.

I've always loved playing games, but when I was younger, I used to buy them only based on their cover; this changed when, at 14 years old, I found a book called *Paid to Play*, a small volume with interviews of some game-related workers. It wasn't particularly detailed or innovative, but it made me fall in love with the other side of the medal: creating games.

The first project I worked on was *Aspectus: Rinascimento Chronicles*, a "garage indie" point-and-click experience made with no game design knowledge, just a lot of passion and will to make games. At that moment, I decided I wanted to dedicate my life to game design.

So, I decided to study game design, but no such school existed in Italy, so I moved from Italy to England and joined the University of Suffolk. After years of hard work, I developed my thesis—*The Vernon Project*, a virtual treasure hunt supported by the city hall that could be played in Holywell Park in Ipswich—with other students that I only could pay in "pizza and compassion". In that moment it became clear to me that we were all doing what we loved.

I then started working in the AAA industry joining Ubisoft Milan with *Tom Clancy's Ghost Recon: Wildlands* and moved to Techland with *Dying Light 2*. While it was great working on such big titles—meeting many people across multiple departments, working for a company with its own game culture—I looked back at how many sacrifices I made to get to that point. Then I realised: "I don't want other people—my future colleagues—to go through the same struggle to get their dream job". Why should you skip meals to pay for your stay or move to a whole different country to find a qualified school? This led me to the next chapter of my life.

I joined the Accademia Italiana Videogiochi—Italian Videogames Academy (or AIV) as a game design lecturer to pursue my goal of making the industry a professionally formed environment where information is free to spread around, to then co-found *affinity project* and creating *Don-Ay*—the first donation game.

To this day I still see myself as a scholar, learning something new every day. Every project I work on feels like a privilege and an opportunity, as each game is different and allows me to discover something more about game design. This also goes for other disciplines, as the next lesson could be around the corner, and this is where the transdisciplinary game design was born.

My best advice is to always be willing to learn something new: the moment you start thinking you know it all is the moment you stop creating. A piano only has 88 keys, but the number of songs you can make is higher than the stars you can count; game design has more than 88 points—we are still discovering new ones today!—so why limit yourself with what you already know?

Precisely because game design is composed of various disciplines, studying it opened my eyes to as many aspects of my life: i.e. understanding the paradox of choice taught me that low expectations are key to enjoying the small things in life. After over 13 years in the industry—both board and digital games—these lessons are still a key trait of myself.

As for the future, I hope a game culture will rise in every part of the world, great games will be created, and students become professionals. These are also the reasons why I teach, as the higher the bar the better the games. Who knows, one day I might play your very own game!

SECTION ONE

Introduction

How to Use This Book

1

This book uses the following structure, but not all parts might be present in all the chapters:

- Every chapter starts with a theoretical part, explaining a concept and how to apply it. To provide a better understanding of each topic, examples are included from game design and other topics.
- After the explanation, a task is presented: while no one is making sure you complete all the tasks, I highly suggest doing so for your own good, as effort is crucial for improvement.

TASK GUIDE

Tasks are exercises located at the end of some design techniques that the reader should do to follow the intended curve of growth as a game designer; each task is different from each other, and each task may need a different format or tool to be carried out.

While their form can change, their objective is the same: helping the readers consolidate their knowledge; while reading and thinking are fundamental parts of the learning process—as well as repeating, taking notes and so on—nothing is as effective as actually doing the thing you are studying and confronting your result with the one you know is procedurally correct—this means it doesn't matter if your tasks went separate ways; the important part is that the process is the same.

Why is practising so important? Because the more you try to do something, the better you will become at doing it, and eventually, your process will be perfect; this has nothing to do with one's talent—you can start from zero, being terrible at game design, and you can practice enough to become better than anyone around you who was more suited than you. The key to becoming a good game designer isn't talent or luck, it's consistency: keep practising, keep learning, keep having a critical eye—also, keep failing—and you will improve your skills day by day. I know it could sound like a hard and long process, but that's exactly how it is: even one year is lived one day at a time, but despite how hard some days are you still live through them, so why shouldn't you do the same with your education?

Now, the practice by itself is not enough: you need the confrontation, this means comparing your results with the ones of someone else—where you know their process

DOI: 10.1201/9781003229438-2

is correct—so that you can understand where you made a mistake and, most of all, learn from it to avoid doing it again in your future: we're like babies touching every object around us; some are soft and easy to hold, others are spiky and could harm us, but once you get hurt the first time you don't touch that object again.

This is also why we need a "parent", this being someone more experienced than us who can show us the right way to do something so that we can compare our way to theirs and understand where we erred.

How do these tasks work? First of all, you don't *have to* do the tasks, I just highly suggest you do so—if you don't, I will never know, so don't worry—but remember that with every opportunity to grow and test yourself that you miss, you are hurting yourself and your career: what if you land your dream job interview, they ask you to perform an *MDA* analysis, and you are not sure how it's done because you didn't do the task and compare the results? That would be a shame, don't you think?

Second, you can do each task alone or in a group, as long as everyone in the group has the theoretical knowledge of the chapter the task is about; doing tasks with other people allows you to start distributing your work, developing your soft skills—this being the way you relate to others, how you behave around people and so on—and, most of all, it makes you understand what working with other people means, because the way you work alone and the way you work with others will be really different things—and that's completely fine!

Once you do—or don't do—a task, you compare it to the one provided on the relative website—the one I did—and you will instantly note something: our tasks will be completely different. How do I know? Because that's just how they work! game design, as we've seen, is 50% science and 50% art, so while our science is the same, the art changes for each one of us, it's something unique; to compare two different tasks, however, you only need to compare the process—therefore the science—and ask yourself if you applied the right theory, process, and mindset: if the answer is "yes", you successfully completed the task.

Nothing stops you from doing the task again to reach the same result I had; it's actually good for your practice or *reverse-engineering* my task to understand what I was thinking, but your goal should always be to test the process and ask yourself the right questions.

At first, this could be hard: maintaining a critical eye while studying your favourite game—or your most hated one—while avoiding our mental biases is a tough challenge, but once you get used to it, you start seeing games for what they are made of instead of for what the all-together product looks like, allowing you to learn something from every game you see or play—and don't worry, you can switch point of view whenever you want.

What happens if I fail a task? First of all, remember that having a different result from mine doesn't mean you failed: if the process is correct, your task is fine; if you, however, misunderstood the theory and made a wrong document, my best advice is to look at mine, understand what design theories I used, and do the task again, with those theories in mind. No task will be perfect; you are here to learn, after all, so don't despair: keep your morale up and try again, even if the task is fine but you are not satisfied, and always remember that hard work always pays off—you just need to grab the opportunities that come to you.

CHAPTER GUIDE

You are almost ready to start your journey, but, before you go, here's a quick summary of what you are going to encounter in each chapter of this book—it's better to be prepared when exploring new territory.

Introduction

This chapter works as a preface, focusing on the modern design philosophy, exploring what it means to be a game designer in the current days, the differences between being a designer and being an author, design as manipulation, and as a pact with the players. Game design evolved in time; what once wasn't a proper job now is a core part of the industry, therefore we need to examine what brought this evolution; it's important to note that this book wants you to look at the future and therefore does not talk about game design history or what a game designer was but rather about what a game designer *is* and *will be*.

Research Tools

The first disciplines chapter talks about research, looking at what the common elements are between the research team and the game design team; we look at what it has to offer to us game designers, how data is applied—and has to be applied—to both disciplines to obtain similar results—but used in two completely different ways, and, last but not least, how research teaches us how to divide our audience into slices we can better understand by using corporate research techniques for data analysis.

Game Design Tools

This is the heart of the book, exploring modern design methodologies, destroying the creativity myth, covering brainstorming techniques to improve your team creativity, and at last, the main game design techniques. Being the core of the book, it is crucial that you carefully read and understand each one of the topics you'll meet, doing the tasks and comparing the results with the examples—more than for any other chapter.

Documentation

The documentation chapter is a more technical one compared to the previous ones; you will see the technical modern documentation used by AAA studios, allowing you to speak the same language as the industry—and I can't stress how important this is; you often can tell a well-prepared designer from an improvised one from the language they use, and while it might be a cruel judgement, it's crucial to use the right word for each element.

Now that you have your guide, you can start your journey. It's not going to be easy, but always remember that hard work pays off: all the reading and the tasks you are doing are aimed at one clear goal. Which goal is it, you are asking? It's different for everyone. You have to think about why you first wanted to be a game designer: think about the moment you realised this job was just *right*: the right job, and right for you; once you remember that—it might not be easy—your goal is going to be clearer than ever.

You have your guide, you have your objective too, what are you missing? Of course, the tools. Don't worry, they're scattered around the pages of this book, you'll know when you'll find one—and, when you do, remember to put it in your tool bag, or you might leave it behind you.

Enough with the chit-chat now, good luck.

Book Introduction

2

MODERN GAME DESIGN

As with every other discipline, game design grows and changes over time; let's take architecture as an example: since its first essay—*De Architectura* by Marco Vitruvio Pollione[1]—many things have changed—the styles, materials, trends, and so on. This, however, isn't true for architecture only: every medium evolves with time, as the customer's needs shift and new ones arise; the more years it takes to create one product, the slower the change will be—centuries for architecture, a lot faster for videogames.

The videogame world changes fast: 30 years ago no such role as the "game designer" existed—we didn't have the same definition of specific roles we have now; whoever wanted to make games did everything by themself. Then the democratisation came in and roles got divided—at first there were artists and programmers, then designers and specific roles were born.

The first designers provided programmers with a huge book describing each game's element and how it was supposed to work, while creating new ways to make games—each one different from the others.

As we said, things changed quickly, and the main reasons are that the game design field is heavily tech driven and fragmented. What does this mean? Being tech driven, new games are created as soon as a new technology is born, while the fragmentation denies the creation of a group of experts that can choose the direction of a "dominant design" for new games for the following years—it's the audience that, playing certain games, creates trends that companies have to follow.

The purpose of this book, however, is not to teach game design history—it is important to avoid repeating past mistakes but not in a historical way. We won't discuss the "when" something happened; we will rather focus on the "what" and the "why" so that you can learn from others' mistakes even while working on a different project. The goal is to teach the development of videogames, therefore it covers only the last five years of design processes—which in this field is actually a lot, as it is much younger than other media such as TV or movies. Long story short, anyone who works in the industry is fundamentally using—or will start using—the principles taught in this book.

DOI: 10.1201/9781003229438-3

WHAT IS GAME DESIGN?

During your career—or your studies—you probably have asked yourself, "what is game design?"; well, there is no right answer. Every designer—from Jesse Schell to Eric Zimmerman, from Brenda Romero to Raph Koster—asked themself this question, and everyone had a different definition.

BOX 2.1   A SPACE FOR THE READER TO WRITE DOWN THEIR DEFINITION OF GAME DESIGN

What is game design for you? Write down your definition, and remember: there is no right or wrong answer:

....

....

Let me tell you right now, the definition is irrelevant: it is the mirror of each designer's soul; from one's definition you can understand what type of designer you are: a data-based design will produce a more consistent game, while a stronger creative vision will result in a bigger identity—neither of which is better than the other! And for every answer, there are thousands of games that just don't fit it—and that's okay. I spent my whole life playing different games and I still can't think of a way to define them all; games—therefore game design—are as complex as life itself, and you can't really define life either, it's up to the way you live it. For me, game design is the science of choices, but—like all the other definitions—it can easily be refuted.

The only sure thing is that game design is a transmedial discipline, as it is born from the union of other sciences that sometimes it can hold and others just fit partially. It expands and contracts based on the product and the necessities of each game, therefore there is not a single winning process or idea that always works.

How can we design winning games then? It may sound scary, but we actually have some safe ground: game design is 50% science and 50% art, as any product is born from the research of a design expanding its knowledge based on the final result. As an example, while working on *Ghost Recon: Wildlands*, we analysed and studied the military pairs system: core principle consisting in never doing anything alone but always with a partner—to provide higher safety in an emergency situation. I had no idea that it existed, so I learned about it: we—the design team—did research on how military strategy works, and Ubisoft provided us with study material we needed to use in order to understand real fights—which are nothing like the ones you see in movies, and I had no idea of such differences until that moment!

The design expands and contracts itself depending on the needs of the product; it's completely normal not to know an aspect of the design—you can always learn new things—the important part is using the 50% science to create a stable ground for your design to be built on—like building a house. You plan the construction, test the land, set up the foundations, and then you start by putting in one piece at a time, brick by brick. Maybe you will need more concrete than you thought, maybe you will use fewer tiles—and it's fine to adapt! The important part is that the walls you are in—your science—are safe and sustain the weight of everything: your belongings, your roof, and yourself—your ego won't fit, be advised.

There are affirmed theories all designers can agree on—the concept of agency, gameplay principles, etc—but those are the basis: from there, everyone develops their set of knowledge and tools to use in their career. It's also true that, sometimes, you break those rules and go against the dominant design: it could be to create a unique experience, to arouse specific feelings—sometimes negative, such as discomfort—and so on; however it's crucial that, before breaking those laws, you understand them at their best: you need to learn how to ride a bike before doing wheelies. While many tools can be the same, the results will always be different: from the 50% science part we know certain parts should work, but each game has an artistic side up for personal interpretation.

It's like baking: you start from a recipe—the scientific part, as a bakery needs to be followed precisely—and you obtain the product—theoretically perfect. Your audience might like it or not depending on their taste—the artistic part, as it differs from one person to another—so you iterate the recipe and you get a product more similar to what your audience wants—the audience, as they will purchase and hopefully enjoy your product. Science assures the cake—this being the solid part, the solid ground that you will always get following the recipe—while art allows you to add, for example, some sugar—meaning finding the right way to provide it to your audience the way they like it.

Why is this 50/50? Because designers, starting from the same scientific theories, reach completely different creative visions. Give the same mandate to five groups and you will end up with five different games—the 50% art comes from them. You might think, "Isn't it scary? Having 50% art means a 50% chance of failing!"; that's true, it can be scary sometimes, but remember that without the art, our job wouldn't exist, as it could be automated and done by a machine. So yes, it is a high risk, but always remember your vision, the game you always wanted to make, and, most of all, its essence. Without the essence you find, the game couldn't exist, and no machine could ever find it in a game, as the game's essence is part of our own.

THE BEST COMPROMISE

While we can't define game design itself uniquely, we can understand its component—like a soup, you can't really tell what a soup *is*, but you can list what it is *made of*. Game design is, other than 50% science and 50% art, the best possible compromise (Figure 2.1).

There are two types of design: theoretical and real; the theoretical design is done without an actual product in mind; it is a game on paper—you do all the research and document everything—but there is nothing playable.

Why does this design exist? Maybe for no reason, maybe for thousands: you may want to target a niche, test your designing skills, or express yourself as an author. Just because it

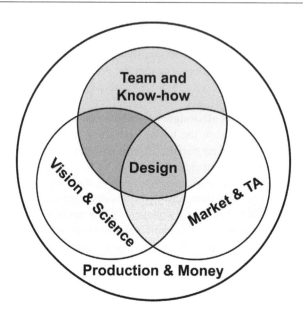

FIGURE 2.1   A scheme showing the meaning of "best compromise".

Source: Author.

doesn't actually exist doesn't mean it is not valuable work. It's important to note that, while this design is purely abstract, it's not based on design theory only: its elements can come from previous experiences and tacit knowledge as well, they just haven't met their limits yet: as long as it's a theoretical design, they never will—that's the best part!

Then we have a real design, done to create a product that will be published and played by others—which is the focus of this book, as every part of the industry is oriented to deliver the best possible product.

What's the main difference between those two designs? Theoretical projects are impossible because of how the development process works: you have timelines, costs, limits—technical, human, economic, and so on—that you need to respect, or your game won't be shipped. Real games are made with all these aspects—and many more—in mind; they are made thinking about which is the best compromise among all those limits. This is why students must work on practical projects if they want to learn: theoretical design is—and always will be—important to learn, but there are aspects that can't be taught—you need to deal with it yourself; don't worry, though, you have a whole team by your side.

It's also the reason why tasks are included in this book: I can't make you work on a project, but I can provide you with tasks to test your knowledge and skills, all while allowing you to compare the results; comparison is a key aspect of learning: we all learn from our mistakes, but only if we can see them.

Four circles: an outer bigger circle with the caption "Production & Money", containing three smaller circles, "Team and Know-how", "Markert & TA", "Vision & Science". The point where all the three smaller circles overlap says "Design".

A good designer is not someone who does all the research and provides the team with a whole vision—that is the worst one. The best designer is the one that, starting from the problem, does research, applies scientific theories, and compares the results with the best possible compromise within all the limits he/she/they finds.

While you may think this doesn't apply for AAA games, it actually does even more: while the budget is higher, so are the costs, the development time for each feature, and the complexity of coordinating hundreds of people across multiple departments—so the design needs to be an even better compromise.

I know the word "compromise" sounds like a bad thing, but we are talking about the best compromise available, the best possible situation for your game to succeed and for your audience to enjoy it at its best; it's not about just cutting parts to fit with budgets and deadlines, it's about understanding what can be optimised to deliver the desired experience at the least possible cost. It's about using the limits to come up with better and smarter solutions, thus the game design theory is crucial to problem-solving.

DESIGNER AND AUTHOR

People often introduce themselves as designers when they are actually authors. What's the difference, you ask? First of all, a designer and an author are two very different people; if you are 100% author, you can't be a designer—and there is nothing wrong about it, they are just different roles. Let me explain: when you create something—anything, from a game to a painting—it is composed of three main factors: commerciality, authoriality, and social value.

Commerciality tells how much the work can sell, authoriality indicates how deeply it represents the author—and how much it allowed him/her/them to express him/her/themself—and the social value conveys a social critic or analysis from the author of the society.

Why are these so important? Because every work can be a combination of all three, but it can't be 100% each one of them. Imagine you have a glass and three different bottles, one with sugared water, one with angostura bitter, and one with bourbon; you can have a glass of bourbon neat, or you can mix the three fluids to create a classic old-fashioned! Every different ratio between the elements will produce a different result, with different consistency and taste. You can't, however, fill the glass more than it allows you to: it will overflow, as you only have that space to fill. This isn't necessarily a bad thing—if you make a 100% commercial game, it's not worth any less than a 100% authorial game—but it makes you need a clear objective for what you are working on, and that's the reason many authors were poor in their time—they made works to express themself, not to be sold.

It is crucial to understand this difference, though, as if you want to be a game designer you need to love the process—which will be the majority of your work—and not the final result only: most of us start for an authorial call—we want to express ourselves—but we fall in love with the process along the way; sometimes you will have to work on a game with no authorial space, but if you enjoy doing it you won't miss it.

I like to talk about a friend of mine—and one of the best designers out there—Bradley Smith: he always had a strong authorial component and worked on games that respected this view; in the last years, however, he started looking for other ways of expression, as working on a project with less "creative freedom" just wasn't right for him. This means that you can still love developing a game but need some extra space to work on a project closer to yourself—and that's completely fine, it's part of being creative.

Of course, you can still create your indie studio and develop your own game swimming against the tide—some of the most iconic masterpieces were born this way—but be aware that for every successful company of this kind there are ten that fail.

DESIGN AND MANIPULATION

The first thing I want to make clear, and I can't stress this enough, is that design—any design—means manipulation: while it sounds bad—as it is associated with people in a toxic way—it is our strongest tool; manipulating the users allows us to provide them with the best possible experience. Take a website: if you want to log in, the button should be visible and easy to find because that is what you want; if the web designer did their job right, you will be manipulated into finding it with no problems, but it wasn't a *bad* manipulation. What if the same button was hidden at the bottom of the page, maybe in the same colour of the background? That would be a terrible experience for the customers. How many times couldn't you find what you were looking for on any website? That is a bad manipulation and leads to frustration, anxiety, anger, and discomfort, and that is the opposite of what we want.

Manipulating our players means using the design tools we have to direct users into the best possible experience—our ideal design; this can go from adding a VFX effect to better show an interactable item, to creating a whole system to make the players live everything the game has to offer. Players are constantly manipulated to behave as they should: take Soraka from *League Of Legends*—one of her core functions is healing her teammates—when allies are low, they have an icon standing above their head; while this also has something to do with her passive ability, this icon instantly shows the user playing Soraka which teammate needs her help, allowing a quicker response time by said user, meaning a better team collaboration and a higher chance of winning the game—of course, this is only one of the many manipulations going on during a game that can lead to the victory.

The ideal manipulation is a win-win situation, where you get what you want and the designer successfully provided you with the best possible experience.

Take a door: when you see a door and you understand how it is going to open, you feel relieved, because the door allows you to understand how it works—this is called affordance: "a relationship between the properties of an object and the capabilities of the agent that determine just how the object could possibly be used".[2] Now think of a door you didn't know had to be pushed or pulled, so you had to try both actions: that has a terrible affordance, and a bad design.

How do you know if your prediction was right? With experimentation—by trying. Experimenting can lead to a positive dynamic—you accomplish an action—or a negative one—you fail to perform the action, or you break the door.

If something goes wrong, as long as you are designing, you can use the iterative process to understand what went wrong and why, in order to provide a better experience the next time—a plate to say "push" or a handle to say "pull".

That is exactly how game design works: you have an idea, develop a concept—by designing it—make a prototype, you see where people don't perform as you expected—where your design failed—and you fix it. Always remember: no game is born perfect, they just get tested and fixed enough—it's just the iterative process.

Game design allows each player to live unique experiences and feel uncommon or rare emotions that other media might struggle to arouse—guilt over killing a colossus, jealousy for a friend who has a better village than yours. In order to do so, the player needs to be controlled—from disabling the input for a second to more subtle ways—or no game would feel this special.

Gears of Wars gave a bonus to every player every 24 hours: they had higher stats until they got their first kill; why is that? Because no one wants to open a game to die and feel like a *noob*; we all want to feel cool and stronger than our opponents. That bonus allowed each player to enter the game and not die as they spawned, get a kill, and feel confident enough to keep playing and getting more kills—thus playing more. Players, however, weren't told about this power: in order to be manipulated, your target needs to be unaware of the manipulation—you wouldn't allow a thief to steal your wallet if someone told you "I am now going to rob you"; to quote John Nesky, "The whole point of cameras is to focus attention on something other than themselves, they're most noticeable when they fail[3]".

Why should we never feel bad for manipulating our players? Because we are doing so only to make them live the best possible experience, what they paid for—we would be worse people not giving them what they wanted rather than manipulating them into the ideal gameplay; they paid for it after all. Don't worry about manipulating someone, as long as you are doing it for their good—it's our job. Every designer, however, sees this in a different way. Joe Kinglake—an excellent designer and dear friend of mine—has a really unique point of view on the topic:

I believe that as game designers, we are the custodians of the players' time. Every game makes a promise on an emotion, a tone or an experience in return for borrowing time from our players' lives. As designers, it is our job to deliver on those promises, ensuring that the transaction of a player's time for our experience is fulfilled, fair and treated with respect while it is very different from what I see as manipulation, his goal, too, is to create the best possible experience for the player, and therefore it is just as right as an argument—no bad point of view exists as long as it works for you and your game!

Of course, you can also manipulate players in a less moral way, for example by creating money-spending habits. In this book, however, we won't talk about morals: I am giving you the tools to perform the best possible job; it's up to you if they should be used for good or not, but as designers, always remember we should allow people to live their wildest fantasies, unite with friends, create memories, and bring them back to when they were kids—we are almost their parents when they play.

THE FORBIDDEN WORDS

As a designer, there are many rules you need to follow; some are older and well-consolidated, such as using a specific set of tools to analyse a piece of a game; others are less known even if often more important, especially for a professional game designer. During this book, you will read a ton of words specific to a subject that you will use to communicate with other designers, letting them know since the very first interaction that you know what you are talking about, just like a badge or a secret code; there are, however, some words that you must not use for the very same reason: these are words that don't communicate anything, and, as such, they are a designer's kryptonite—more accurately, they are like a virus: someone uses one of these words, infecting a colleague who will say it too to someone else, and the cycle goes on. To stop this cycle, you need to be the one blocking those words from spreading any longer, like a wall protecting your designers-successors and making sure that the virus dies.

These words, as I mentioned, are words that *can't* communicate something, because they are purely subjective: what one means with that word is not what someone else means. You will encounter many of them during your career, but the most common ones are *fun*, *immersive*, and *entertaining*—pay special attention to the first one, the *f word*—in our field it's worse than the other, more known *f word*.

Why do some designers use those? Well, it's pretty simple, they've been saying them as players for years, they are used to them, so it can be very hard to quit, but it's one of those efforts that really shows one's level of professionalism, especially in the early stages of one's career where a single word can be the difference between an interview and a job.

"Wait, are you saying players have been using these forbidden terms for years?" No, not at all: players are allowed to use them because they are players; they don't need to know which specific emotion is linked to an action every time they perform it, they just want to *enjoy* the game and *have fun*: what game did you think about reading that last bit? Maybe you thought of a horror or a grinding-based one; the player I imagined is too scared of horrors and hates grinding, in fact they were thinking about a strategy game. "How could I have known that?" you are probably thinking, and, to be fair, you *couldn't*, that's why those words are useless to a designer: what is *fun* for you may not be *fun* for me, what *entertains* me can be boring to someone else, and so on. Imagine you bake a raspberry cake for a friend; they taste it and "it's not *good*"; you bake another one, this time with less sugar; they take a bite but "still not *good*", one more, this time more raspberry, "that's even worse!" You are in too deep, after spending a whole afternoon baking you *must* understand why they don't like it, so you ask them "what is the element that is ruining the cake the most? Is it too dry? Maybe too sweet?" They look at you, take a brief pause, and say, "I hate raspberry, man".

When you ask for feedback, players will give you their *personal* feedback, using words that absorb a meaning depending on who is using them, like a sponge; good, bad, fun, boring, they all mean nothing by themselves, and if you don't ask the right questions or analyse a feedback under the right lens, you will never have a helpful answer.

If designers talked to each other like players do, no game would be done because every sentence could be interpreted in 20 different ways. For this reason, the best way to describe your game to another designer is by naming the type of experience you are designing, with what mechanics, to generate which emotions, for instance "this game aims to satisfy the audience's need for sudden jump scares, created with appearing gore-based mutants and loud noises, used to generate *fear* and *impersonation* aesthetics"; there are parts that may sound tricky, but don't worry, you will read everything you need to know about them to get started in the next chapters—your designer vocabulary is about to get heavy.

Note that, just because certain words don't mean anything to us, it doesn't mean they can't be used with non-designer people: when talking to your players, with the press, and generally people who don't and shouldn't care about "finding the right words", you are free to use them. A player likes to read a review that says "I never had this much fun in my life, 10/10" written by some big newspaper, placed on the main page of your game; it's not like you have to take it down and tell the person who wrote it "You can't say that", because that's how players communicate with one another—that's how we all communicated before entering the design side of games. The important thing is that you don't use such words with other designers and on your internal documents, and when you come across vague words while reading the players' feedback, you use the right tool to understand what they meant—it's very much like decrypting a code: you try different ciphers at first, but as you get more experienced you learn to recognise which one is the right one very quickly in 90% of the cases.

NOTES

1 Pollione, M. V. (15 b.c.), *De architectura*.
2 Norman, D. A. (2013), *The Design of Everyday Things: Revised and Expanded Edition*. New York: Doubleday.
3 *50 Game Camera Mistakes*, John Nesky, GDC 2014: www.youtube.com/watch?v= C7307qRmlMI

SECTION TWO

Analysis Tools

Design and Analysis

3

Why do we—as designers—need to talk about analysis tools? Because combined with design, they provide the ground for analysis to be built on: a project needs multiple pillars to be built on, and analysis—mixed with marketing—is one of the pillars that helps present the product at its best. Each pillar you choose for your building needs to be functional, to be connected to the others, and to have a specific purpose, otherwise, your foundations won't hold up the weight of the building itself. Think of the Pantheon; it has hundreds of pillars, but if you take one down the whole thing falls into pieces—each design element you use must be like one of those pillars: perfect even by itself but fundamental for the whole structure. There are various definitions of "analysis", but the one I find the most fitting when related to game design is this: "a detailed examination of anything complex in order to understand its nature or to determine its essential features". While it doesn't really say what analysis *is*, it tells us what it *does*: understand the nature and essential features of something—while it's the production team that creates the value behind those features. Once you know the core feature of a product, you can use your marketing to present it to the audience.

First, marketing—as the product itself—is bound to the client: without a client, you don't have a product. Second, it presents value. This is connected to another key aspect of the game design: the value perceived by the customer—or, in our case, the player.

You might bake the best cake in the world, but if nobody thinks it's worth it, you are not going to sell it—and no one is going to appreciate it! Luckily or not, it doesn't matter how *good* something in this field is but how appreciated it gets.

To sum it up, both design and analysis/marketing talk about value, but the first one creates it based on the client, and the second one presents it based on what values are important for the audience.

Take, for example, a bulb: you don't think about buying one the same way you might wish to get a car, but when it burns out you have to pick a new one; there are many factors to consider, depending on what your interests are: consumption, brightness, colours, and many more. How do companies advertise their bulb to convince you it is the solution to your problem? They focus on just a few key elements: maybe it has the lowest power usage, or it has all the possible colours, or it connects to your smart assistant. Depending on what your priorities are, you are going to choose one over another.

The right analysis has the power to convert a problem into an opportunity to satisfy your needs, even ones you didn't think about. Maybe you only cared about a bulb brightness but ended up buying one that has light effects and can be controlled through your phone—and makes you think that they are bonus features you will need when you only wanted a bright bulb.

DOI: 10.1201/9781003229438-5

THE IMPORTANCE OF ANALYSIS IN GAME DESIGN

The reason for us designers to use analysis tools is simple but fundamental: design is the best compromise among many factors—as you've seen in Chapter 1. One of these is the players—thus the clients. While in other disciplines the key clients are the stakeholders—those who have an interest in the project—in videogames the core stakeholders are the players, as games are a consumer good—we still have actual stakeholders, but players come first. Games, in fact, need to be bought and played. Why is being played such an important element of the game? First, there is the refund matter: take *No Man's Sky* or the more recent *Cyberpunk 2077*, at their release date; customers weren't happy, copies were refunded and games were temporarily removed from stores. This generated unhappiness among investors and—most of all—players, other than huge loss of money and face by the companies. This means your objective can't just be to *sell* the game; it should actually be to have players *enjoy* it.

The second, most important element is the gameplay, where the value comes from: a piece of every game's value is in it being played as if your audience enjoys the product; it creates more selling opportunities—for example for sequels, season passes, DLCs, and transmedia products—other than the game itself.

This is the main difference between a game and, say, a cake: while with a cake you need to convince a potential buyer to purchase it—and if they enjoy it, you're good—with a game you need to be sure they do enjoy it but also that they keep eating it, assuring his/her/their satisfaction while also making him/her/them want more. If no one likes your cake, chances are you will not bake it again: this doesn't mean it wasn't *right* for your audience.

In this phase of the development, you shouldn't be focusing on what makes a game *enjoyable* per se—which, as you know, means nothing said this way—but on making sure that your game is *being enjoyed* and developing—and using—the right tools to make sure it will be this way in the long run.

How does this relate to videogames? It's quite simple: games need to be sold—we've established that—but they also need to have a value meaningful in time; AAA games, for example, can last hundreds—or thousands—of hours. How can you use analysis, combined of course with marketing, to sell 100 hours' worth of value with a trailer, some banners, and ads here and there? Luckily, in big companies, the marketing team or publisher takes care of that, but note that videogames advertising is different from most products: we need—or use—early playthrough, closed and open alphas and betas, banners, trailers, forums, and much more. Why that much stuff? you might ask yourself, and the main reason is that we are selling an experience: it's not something you watch, it's not something you use, it's something you *live*—potentially, countless hours will go in your game, so you need your audience to see all the game has to offer.

You probably started to see where this is going—if not, don't worry—analysis and design have a common goal: understanding who your client is. This makes further questions arise about the audience: what drives them? What do they want? And—most of all—what is right for them?

BOX 3.1   AN INSIGHT ON THE UNCOMPLETED GAMES ISSUE

According to a *Kotaku* article,[1] nine out of ten people don't finish the game they are playing—and this is a huge problem. We—as designers—don't understand the value to present to our audience and keep creating products that don't get completed—we are not talking about 100% completion, but just about finishing the game; this represents an enormous loss for the development teams, who need to better understand their audience in order to create games that don't get abandoned halfway through.

You need to ask yourself—and your team—these questions as soon as possible, because if you don't know your audience, they are not going to know your product. Countless other questions help you track a better projection of your product's niche, but the one they all need to answer is: how can the game better satisfy our players?

It is also very important to have a clear path for your game—knowing which people are going to be in that path and which aren't. One of the most common errors is not knowing if your game is meat or fish: they can both be amazing, but it sure can't be both. In this case, you need to pick one and stick with it; maybe you will find out it was the wrong decision, but you would have never known if you hadn't chosen.

Let's take cakes, once more, as an example—I know what you are thinking, game design and cakes have a lot more in common than what you thought—say you are baking two cakes, a low-fat one and a sweet one. The sweet one satisfies gluttony: it's sweet, yummy, and makes your brain release endorphins; the diet one, on the other side, is healthier, can be eaten while on a diet, and is lighter. Both are cakes, but they are two opposite worlds: if you give the wrong one to the wrong audience, neither of the two groups are going to like it—but they might be amazing cakes! To sum it up, the same element to different audiences evokes different emotions.

SATISFYING YOUR AUDIENCE

The designer needs to know their audience to provide them with the most suitable product, tailor-made to fit its needs and expectation toward the product itself—and the experience coming from it.

Doing so, each of us can develop a successful game that respects an implicit mandate unconsciously dictated by its future players—your target isn't the game, it's the audience; we use analysis to concretise and better define an idea we have, soon enough to be fixed if it is not what your target wants.

Marketing relates to design more than you would think, because they both satisfy users' needs but in two different ways: the first offers a product—that already exists—in the best possible way. Sometimes it is put as an "extra"—an item or service you know you don't need but that is tempting for the status it provides because it's trending or due to the "cool factor", which doesn't actually mean anything besides making you think "cool!"—other times, however, it is presented as the solution to a problem.

How can marketing do this? Because—as we've said—they already have the product, so they know what necessities it is able to satisfy, and they know their audience's needs, what you expect from the product itself, and how to surprise you—as if you needed all the features they present. Any item can have hundreds of aspects someone can be interested in, but the key is presenting specific ones you know your target wants; marketing needs to know which needs—or problems—their object/service solves.

While it is not easy for "standard" products—sunglasses, bulbs, washing machines—it is even harder for artistic ones—games, movies, books—because the needs are more complex. Why? Because we work with emotions: imagine a book, your favourite one if you will; what does it give to the audience? Knowledge? Growth? A good story? Maybe it has hundreds of aspects you love, but if you had to pitch it to a friend, you'd only get to choose a few—otherwise, they will get bored or, even worse, forget what you said.

BOX 3.2 A DESIGN TECHNIQUE THAT IS USED TO SOLVE MAJOR PROBLEMS THE AUDIENCE ENCOUNTERS IN THE GAME

One tool we need to use to better engage with our audience is the design thinking method; it's based on two points, *define* and *empathise*:

> Defining means isolating the problem, understanding its causes and consequences, to be fixed during the iteration process.
>
> Empathising with your audience is key to metabolising their emotions, their point of view, and how they see the game.
>
> The combination of these two steps, if well iterated, allows us to decrease the number and importance of problems in our game, to provide the audience with a better experience they will be more likely to complete.

As an example, a few years ago, a company was developing products for near-sighted people; to better understand their problems—and needs—every person working on the project was provided with a pair of glasses that simulated myopia.

This allowed the team to empathise with their audience by living their same problems—this being *empathising*—and understanding what they needed—*defining*—creating solutions specifically designed to fix those problems.

This—to find unique aspects our audience will love—is our responsibility too: we have a set of tools lent from marketing that we need to use as they are part of our comprehension of the audience—our audience.

During your career—and this book too—you will find yourself with many tools from different disciplines; it could seem like a burden at first—having to learn different techniques, how certain things work, and so on—but it's actually a resource: designers can take the best working elements from other media and use it in their own: one day you might need a hammer, and there it is! The next day a saw, there you have it! They are all in your tool bag, so don't forget to carry it with you wherever you go—you never know when the rustiest tool in the bag can be just the right one for the job.

**BOX 3.3   HOW MASLOW'S HIERARCHY OF
NEEDS APPLIES TO VIDEOGAMES**

As designers, we need to understand and satisfy complex and specific needs from the top part of Maslow's Hierarchy of Needs—Figure 3.1. We can't help players with physiological needs—we can't provide them with food, for example—safety needs, or love-related ones, although we can simulate part of those. Our focus, therefore, is esteem and self-actualization: we can make the user feel good at what they do, help them live their wildest fantasies, or allow them to achieve high goals. While designing a game, we need to keep this in mind to identify our customer's needs and really understand how to satisfy them.

FIGURE 3.1   Maslow's Hierarchy of Needs is represented as a pyramid.

Source: Author.

THE IMPORTANCE OF DATA

As you've seen, there are many tools we can choose from, but how do you know when to use which one? When talking about marketing and design, there are two main cases we can encounter:

Case 1, you don't know what the user wants that you can use to create value.
Case 2, you created something and need to present it to the audience.

The most important tool, for both cases, is data gathering: "Without data, you're just another person with an opinion", said W. Edwards Deming, and this is crucial because everyone has an opinion, it comes from what we think, want, our experience and our *tacit knowledge*. What's that? It's our gut feeling, our intuition, that little voice in the back of your head that tells you whether something is a good idea or not, even if you just heard of it. It grows with our experience and becomes more and more precise—but be careful, it's not always right! This knowledge represents our authorial part, which eventually needs to be confronted with the data: data never lies, but we also need to know how to use it. If you understand how to use it to fix your vision, you are on the right track with your game—you are using the 50% science to adjust your 50% art.

Let me explain it with an example: when I was working on *Don-ay*—which is a Tamagotchi game—I did a lot of research on similar games—our competitors, if you will—and I found out that washing your character has no mechanical value; it is a mechanically meaningless action, so we removed it from the design to have a cleaner game and reduce the costs. Smart move, right? Well, not really, but let me explain why:

> On our first playtest, we had kids—our audience—playing the game to gather feedback—as you would normally do with any game. The main response, contrary to what I thought—thus my opinion—was that all kids wanted to clean their pet, wash it, brush it, and so on. So, instead of taking it personally because I made a mistake, we asked the testers "Why do you want to do something with no mechanical value?" and, combining their responses with some anthropological studies, the answer surprised me: apparently there is this concept called *grooming*, which creates a strong psychophysical bond between two subjects; only then I realised it: it wasn't about the progression in the game, it was all about the emotional bond, that was the piece I was missing, and, with that in mind, I focused the design on creating and increasing said bond.
>
> This is the strength of data: we start with an opinion, collect the data, confront why our opinion differed from it, find the cause, and design a solution for the problem. But beware, not all data is the same.

There are two types of data: quantitative and qualitative:

> Quantitative data is statistical, mathematical, and answers questions such as "how much?", "how often?", and so on—these being answers that can be expressed in numbers and/or measured and tested.
>
> This is data we can collect and, say, display on a chart—for example, heatmaps—and is useful because this data is treated mathematically: we can confront different results to have a piece of objective information or insight.
>
> Qualitative data is not representable with maths; it answers questions from the point of view of the user, such as "why?", "how?"—these show emotions and human behaviours.

This data, on the contrary, comes from questions we ask to reach the source of a problem; they involve the emotive part of the test and focus on aspects such as "How does that make you feel?" and "Why?". It doesn't provide objective information, but it creates a gash on the player's armour that allows us to see their emotions; it might be not crystal clear, but it needs to be treated with the best possible respect.

Let me get one thing clear, no data is superior to the other—they have different objectives and yes, you need both: one gives objective knowledge, the other personal; they need to be related and compared to each other. Also, keep in mind that data can be misleading; there will be times where you might think two pieces of information are connected, while it is only a coincidence: when such a situation happens—and you don't know if to trust your gut or not—always ask yourself why, until you get to an objective answer.

How can a designer not get tricked by data? After gathering all the pieces of information you need, use the *9 Whys technique*: you'll read about it in the very next chapter, but, for now, know that asking the right question is often a more powerful tool than having the right answer.

NOTE

1 Kotaku, *Nine Out of 10 Will Not Finish the Game They Are Playing*: https://kotaku.com/nine-out-of-10-will-not-finish-the-game-they-are-playin-5832450

Target Audience Tools

4

9 WHYS TECHNIQUE

The 9 Whys technique comes from *Liberating Structures*,[1] a platform focused on brainstorming strategies: it was born from a group of people who worked as brainstorming experts for the majority of their lives and found out that, most times, brainstorming is useless for countless different reasons—from the lack of a clear goal, to the wrong focus in the meeting, to simply getting carried away with one topic.

Those people developed processes to make each session more valuable and functional: this technique, specifically, focuses on reaching the true origin of a problem, without stopping at the easiest or more convenient answer. It finds its core in the idea of a child: children are ignorant; they don't know many things—and it's perfectly fine this way—so, they are curious: when they don't understand something; they start asking "why?" without stopping at the first response. For example, if a kid asks "why is the sky blue?" and you answer "it's because of each drop of water's refraction: when light travels from air into water, it slows down, causing it to change direction slightly", they are going to ask why refraction works in that way, and they'll keep asking questions until you provide an answer easy enough for them to understand and connect all the previous answers together—for a kid, nothing is obvious, and we should always keep this in mind during our career: never get rid of your inner kid, that part of you that truly enjoys life, that is always curious, that never takes something for granted. As we grow old, we do take things for granted; we start to lose our magic, and that's why we need to keep asking questions—to ourselves and to others. Some answers will be simple, others will be far deeper, but the important thing is keeping this big sense of "why?" in our lives—your inner kid, what keeps you truly young.

A common mistake people make while searching for a solution is taking an answer for granted, saying "ok that's it" to something instead of digging deeper down for a better answer; don't get me wrong, this is completely fine in our everyday life—if we started to ask so many questions for everything we see, we'd never have time to do anything else—but when searching for the true cause of a problem, it's our job to find the real cause.

This technique is the easiest one you'll face, as it only involves you and another person. Theoretically, it can be done alone, but it's less precise—we tend to ask questions we already know the answer for without thinking, and here thinking is crucial: we need questions you would never think of, hard ones and strange ones. The best way to do this is to

DOI: 10.1201/9781003229438-6

pretend to be someone else, take a famous character—possibly an odd one—and pretend to be him/her/them: what questions would he/she/they ask? What is going on in his/her/their mind?

What would Batman say? He would ask very different questions than, say, your friend Tom, because he has a totally different mindset, a different way of seeing the world. Maybe he would look for the danger in any situation, trying to see what could go wrong as if it was a master plan of one of his enemies.

Doing this identification alone is still, of course, less precise than doing this exercise between two people, but it's a step forward.

Let's just get into it:

One person plays the role of the child—asking the questions—while the other is the parent—giving the answers.
First, the adult shows the child a problem: for example, "Players didn't like *this* feature".
Then, the kid analyses—this is really important—the problem and asks a question—starting with "why"—related to the previous statement: "Why didn't players like *that* feature?"

The adult thinks about it and answers, and the process keeps going five to nine—or more—times. It's important that the adult really thinks about the answer, not just giving the easiest one and the child analyses the answer, not just asking "why" followed from the previous sentence: try to understand the problem as if you were living it yourself; think of what could be the cause of each answer to ask the next question, and the further you go the more specific each question should be; you start looking in the sea, and you need to end up searching in a puddle.

If you get to an answer you think is the right one before the fifth "why", it's probably not the right one: it may surprise you how unrelated two elements could seem until you ask yourself the right question—and how many times the problem you started with isn't actually the real problem. Once you get to the core of a problem, you start seeing things clearly: how things relate to each other, how unexpectedly connected two elements might be, and, most of all, you wake up your inner child, as it is your inner child who can see better than anybody else, who is not afraid to think outside the box and create unique connections.

Why is this strategy present among the audience tools? First of all, as we've seen, marketing and design are related by the same goal: solving users' needs—one does so by presenting value, the other one by creating value. Second, it often allows us to find a correlation between quantitative and qualitative data, providing connections and unique insights: quantitative data allows you to set the ground—it shows the big problems without telling you why they are happening—while qualitative data gives you a brief view in the player's mind; combining those two let you see what the problem is and how it makes your audience feel, allowing you to find the problem's origin—it's like reverse-engineering the human mind.

The right time to use this technique is as soon as you have any data and any problem—and, trust me, you'll have plenty of those. Nothing stops you from using it before you have any problem or any data at all, but all your answers will be purely theoretical and—as we've seen—they will eventually face reality: maybe you got it right, or maybe you wasted your—and your colleagues'—time; while it's a good thing to prevent problems, the fact that—as designers—we manipulate people makes it extremely hard to predict how they are going to behave. The resources you have during the development of a game are limited—especially the time—so it's more convenient to solve human problems—technical ones can be prevented—as they arise rather than trying to prevent them all—which, let me tell you, is impossible, no matter the size of the project. My best advice is not to be in a hurry, and use this technique when the right time comes.

BOX 4.1   THE 9 WHYS TASK BOX, ANALYSING THE PROGRESSION'S CURVE OF *BIOSHOCK INFINITE* (FIGURE 4.1)

9 WHYS TASK

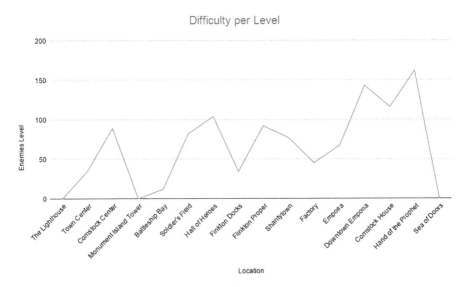

FIGURE 4.1   A chart showing *Bioshock: Infinite* enemy presence over level.

Source: Author.

As we've seen, the point of the 9 Whys technique is to identify the source of a problem; in this case, what you have to do is ask yourself enough "Why" to understand why the curve follows this specific trend, and, therefore, why it works with our target audience.

Why Does This Curve Work for Our Target Audience?

Grab yourself a document and start answering this question, following it with another question, then answering, and so on, until you have an answer you think is the reason for this curve's trend.

While, in this case, we are not talking about a problem but about something that worked instead, if you apply the right process you can consider your task passed. Let me tell you right now, we are not going to give the same answers or ask the same questions—it's just mathematically improbable—so think about the process instead.

That being said, this is your first task, so I wish you the best of luck: it's the first step on your journey; don't come back until you are victorious—just kidding, you will always be welcome in the pages of this book, but, if you succeed, we could talk about your first task when you'll let me play your game in a few years from now.

BARTLE'S ARCHETYPES

Before we get to the model itself, we need to understand the bigger concept that this—and the other following—model relates to: target audience.

The target audience comes from the concept that—as we've seen—when you create a product, it is intended to be used by someone specific—and this goes not only for commercial products but for authorial and social ones too. That "someone specific" is your audience, this being who will spend time, energy, and resources to use your product—or, in our case, who will play your game.

Sometimes the target audience of a product is so wide that it becomes basically the whole of humanity—or a large part of it—take, for example, forks: most cultures—not all—use them, so the audience is wider than, say, a sports drink; there are, however, different types of forks for different audiences: Haute cuisine uses different ones than the ones you have at home—unless you are an enthusiast or an expert, in which case you would be an even smaller audience—each fork has its own specific use.

What differentiates Haute cuisine's fork from the standard ones? Some characteristics, as well as their presentation, are completely different—as is their price—and that is because, in order to target a different audience, you need to pull different strings: while at home most of us only need a fork—any fork, as long as it works—in a *3 Michelin star* restaurant you need to use the *right* fork, or your experience could be ruined.

The same goes for a person who doesn't care about food, put in such an environment: they might not have a pleasant experience, not understand what fork to use, or, even worse, see other people enjoying the dinner while they struggle to do so, resulting in a sense of being out of place.

How does this relate to game design? you might ask, and the answer is closer than you might expect: if you target the wrong audience or provide the right audience with the wrong tools, chances are they are not going to like your game, and, most of all, they will have a bad experience, no matter how *good* the game is because it's just not *right* for them—and we don't want people spending their time on our game to feel bad; that's the total opposite of our goal.

We have seen two types of audiences so far: the one where the audience is not relevant—forks in general—and the one where the audience matters—Haute cuisine ones. The question comes spontaneously: where are games placed? Although you could think they have audiences so wide they don't matter, it's actually the second option: the audience in videogames, as in any other entertainment product, is crucial for their success; what is entertaining for me might not be so for you.

Take a look at sports' core "mechanic": throw something, kick something, shoot something, and so on; I might enjoy seeing a ball getting kicked around a field, while you prefer seeing a ball being thrown—both have a ball, both have people interacting with it, but the outcoming sport is completely different.

This happens because everyone has different tastes; they're something unique to each one of us: while the actual tastes are the same, we all have a different combination of them.

I see what you are thinking now: "it's impossible to satisfy everyone's needs in our target audience if tastes are so unique!", but don't worry, there is a catch: tastes are this different only when inspecting a person through a microscope; once you start "zooming out", you will see patterns arising.

People in similar groups tend to have similar interests, and while with a microscope they enjoy different things, if seen as a group the genre of their likings is solid, and you can see the patterns: males are more prone to competition than women, the West-centric culture sees value in capitalism and individualism while the East-centric one prefers the vision of the society as a whole and not the individual; the more we speak of a "society" instead of an "individual", the more things in common we discover.

There are pieces of information that affect these trends—date of birth, income, gender, and many more—and while in the past we only looked at social-demographic elements—name, age, relationship status, and so on—in the last years, thanks to big data, the amount of information we have on our audience is immense.

There are countless examples of how said data is gained: from Google asking if you were in a specific store because your location said so, to talking about something and seeing ads of that very item on Facebook—or any other social. We are giving away huge pieces of information about ourselves, our lifestyle, our tastes, and much more without even realising it; all of this is used to create our *digital shadow*—this being the footprint we leave behind when walking on the internet. Companies then buy said data—of millions of people—for unspeakable prices, to then target us with specific ads and marketing techniques—we are their target audience. There is a quote from Richard Serra who said "If something is free, you are the product"[2]; this was said in 1973; imagine how more true this sentence has become in the last 50 years.

There is, however, an upside to all of this: this availability of information opened the target audience's world more than ever: data is now more precise and closer to the truth; this allowed creation of "models" of each product's customers—and it happened in videogames too.

Models are not always true—not 100% at least—but they help better target an audience and even create more suitable products for said audience: it means more user satisfaction, therefore more sales, therefore a better product the next time around—it's a virtuous cycle. It allows you to create and discover products your audience will love but that at the same time are selling too: you know that audience X will buy product X at price X, and they will be happy—that's key for a functional business.

The goal of the target audience is to unify your customers' tastes to create a product that can fulfil their needs while having a profitable company, and having so much data allows you to do exactly that.

Now that you know what the target audience is and why it is so important, it's time to understand what player types are: player types are the game design models for our players, ideal archetypes each customer can be represented as.

BOX 4.2   AN INTRODUCTION TO THE *DAEDALUS PROJECT*, GROUND FOR BARTLE'S ARCHETYPES TAXONOMY

The first type of model comes from Richard Bartle and Nick Yee's *Daedalus Project*,[3] a study about MMO games that worked as foundations for Bartle's four archetypes: it's the first—and to this day valid—model of target audience creation using target audience-like models.

Yee's studies revealed—among many key elements for us designers—five main factors for user motivations:

Achievement: the desire to become powerful in the context of the virtual environment through the achievement of goals and accumulation of items that confer power.

Relationship: the desire of users to interact with other users.

Immersion: the desire to be in a fantasy world, as well as being "someone else".

Escapism: the desire to temporarily avoid, forget about, and escape from real-life stress and problems using the virtual world.

Manipulation: the desire to objectify other users and manipulate them for personal gains and satisfaction.

All of these don't fall far from Bartle's player types; at first Yee only identified three main "components"—what we now call archetypes—that were Achievement, Social, and Immersion. Each one of those had subcomponents—Progress, Self-Disclosure, and many more—that are now identified as Aesthetics—as we'll see later in the book—the core of multiple game design tools used to identify an audience and create a coherent and cohesive experience in games.

Yee also analysed—among other parameters—the age range and gender of the players, identifying one of the first documented target audiences in the game design field.

While Bartle's archetypes are older than other archetypes used in modern game design, they are extremely important, both by themself and as they are the foundations for all the other archetypes to be built on: when studying other models, you will often see a comparison between that model and Bartle's one, therefore knowing it is a key factor in becoming a modern designer.

This model is also one of the most used as it proved itself reliable and applicable to both small and wide audiences; it is, undoubtedly, quite older and more limited than more recent ones—just consider that it developed around an audience of MMO games players—but its goal isn't to be always up to date or perfect: no model will ever cover every aspect of your players. Its goal is to understand how to categorise and describe all the different people in your audience, for instance, "This player is a Socializer with a 20% part of visceral killer aesthetics", which gives you way more details than "He is a socializer".

My piece of advice is to use different models to describe your "perfect player", because to communicate it to your team or even with yourself, you need to express in words what is just a concept at first: "I want a player who loves *this* feeling" becomes "The ideal player is polarised in this way, mainly belonging to this archetype, but with part of this other taxonomy"; sure you won't be able to describe *everything* about them—the human essence is just too complex to be put into words—but, combining different models, you can describe most of someone's defining aspects as an audience.

One of Yee's studies discussed the *Proteus effect*,[4] analysing how the user's self-representation changes and how our behaviour changes back in return. It is thanks to research such as this that we now know so much about players, their behaviour, and social dynamics taking place in our games.

While it is true that these studies were applied on a specific type of game and were based on data from almost two decades ago, many of Yee's writings—as shown by the support of the data—are still true to this day; of course some elements have changed, but their ground is more than solid.

Bartle divides the players into four models: Killers, Achievers, Explorers, and Socializers. Let's take a look at each one of them.

Killer: Acting on the Players

Killers want to act and dominate other players—or NPCs, but the feeling is stronger if applied to real people—they want to be the source of change; they are called "Killers" because they dominate others, like a killer imposes his/her/their wish on his/her/their victims—my freedom ends where yours begins.

Killers want to cause distress and uneasiness to others, mostly if the victim knows they are the cause of it; they are not afraid to be feared or hated, and in some cases, these feelings would even increase their motivation. Creating a situation that the killer likes but others don't is part of the core experience of a killer: being the impostor in *Among Us*, creating fear and stress in the other players, or trolling others to generate a feeling of frustration when they can't play the game the way it is supposed to be played. The challenge for them is not the goal; the goal is the result of said challenge—if a killer asks to *1V1* you, he/she/they doesn't care about the fighting but only about the humiliation they can cause you; their win is not enough if no domination or hard feelings arose. They also are the worst losers, as they only see competition as a way to dominate and feel/provoke strong emotions.

Killers love visceral feelings, loud explosions, the thrill of being chased, and similar emotions, as those come from your survival instinct—the need to be better than someone else otherwise you will die—they come from your guts.

These players, as you might have already understood, love strong and visceral horror games—fear is one of the most powerful emotions, especially for a killer—competitive games where they can humiliate their opponents—take *tea begging* as an example: if there is no way to dominate the opponents or to show you are better than them, killers are not interested—and games where they can cause chaos among other players or NPCs while being recognized as the source of that chaos.

As they like to manipulate others, social games that include bluffing and lying are on their list, as long as the feeling coming from manipulating someone is the goal and not a tool to win.

It may seem like a bad image for a player, but no player type is better than another: while it's true killers can be unfair opponents, it's also true they are the most frenetic players of all: they love each moment of a thrilling scene, where other players could be waiting for it to be over, as well as being devoted to the game if it allows them to crush their enemies. Killers are the ones that push your game's—and players'—limit the most, creating gameplay moments—take the "funny moments" videos—and momentum that other players will eventually follow. They are like a hand grenade: dangerous, of course, but it makes you feel alive like nothing else.

Achiever: Acting on the World

Achievers are focused on the game world and themselves: they love challenges, resource gathering/stacking, collecting wins, and they seek security. They want trophies and badges that show their progress to themselves and other players; status is very important— as it shows one's progress and hard work—and they won't drop a game until it's 100% completed, even if they don't like it: their reward is in the completion of the game— these, however, are pure achievers, which are a smaller chunk of the achiever player type. Achievers are interested in a challenge *as* a challenge; the win is just a consequence of their skills—the important part is testing themselves, showing off their abilities—due to their tendency to accumulate—this also includes accumulating strategies—and they are the best winners as an undeserved win is not a win for them—again, winning is the consequence of their abilities.

Achievers want to be mathematically better than others—this means having higher stats (KDA ratio, win ratio, etc.) and titles. This seeking for a better position drives them to improve themselves, especially in competitive games: ranking up from *Bronze* to *Challenger* in *League of Legends* provides achievers with a constant sense of progression for their skills; badges such as the *Mastery Emote* and the *Eternals* are yet another proof of their skills gained by playing—showing off these badges after killing an opponent, however, is part of the humiliation process belonging to the Killer player type.

When a game gets hard, achievers don't quit, they start improving themselves run after run; achievers quit when they lack a sense of progress or challenge during the game, the reason for their liking of grinding: every time they kill a mob, they know they are gaining resources, advancing in experience, and getting better at the game.

When designing a game for achievers, there are a few things that must be present, other than progression and status demonstration: they need to be able to seek security— this being adopting specific strategies to be safer or collecting resources to use in case things go south—as well as having their action being recognized—rewarding safe behaviours, sustaining items collection, and so on.

It sounds like the friendliest player type so far, but they're one of the easiest to lose: if you don't show them you care about their achievements, if they don't feel a sense of progress, or if your game is missing the right challenges, they are going to drop it without blinking an eye: they want to feel the challenge and they will improve themselves until they can beat it, not living up to the game is not an answer for them.

Explorer: Interacting with the World

Explorers are interested in exploring—both literally and metaphorically—the game world: seeing places, roaming around the map in carefree ways, discovering secrets. They need to have the tools to do such things at every time and in every place, without being punished for not minding the game storyline or desired gameplay—make sure your world's rules allow this. They love to test new things, understand existing things—the world's rules— and ask themselves the question "What happens if. . . ?" They don't care about the success or failure of their idea; their reward is having discovered what would have happened: the goal isn't the result, it's the process, the knowledge. Think about a scientist: they make an experiment not to show they are right but to understand the world better and see what happens; if it fails or goes right it's not important; the important part is having understood a new "world rule". For this reason, explorers tend to be less social: playing with others distracts them from their goal; they take their time and do things their own way—they don't care about how something is *supposed* to be done; they do it how they want it to be done.

The challenge—and therefore winning—are important but secondary: the core of their experience is the journey they live and the events they discover. Take, for instance, the YouTube video *What happens if Tidus kills the Water Flan in Besaid?* by Warrior Of Light:[5] he spent over 100 hours on *Final Fantasy X* to see what would have happened if you kill the first monster without using magic—which is the opposite of what the game expects to happen—only to find out that nothing changes; the game plays the same dialogue as if you didn't kill it. Was it bad news for him? Not at all! His goal wasn't to defeat the monster itself; it was to discover what would have changed if he "tricked" the game, and so he did.

When designing a game for explorers, the goal of your game shouldn't be "what *should* the player do?" but "what *can* the player do?", because they are going to test every possible combination of events your game has to offer, even if you didn't know it existed.

Socializers: Interacting with the Players

Socializers take part in a game as a social element, not only with other people but also with simulated people and relationships, socialising with NPCs or actual players—while having a different impact—is part of the same goal. They are interested in multiplayer to interact with other people: it's like going to a bar with your friends, you don't go there for the place itself but to spend time with the people you love—that's the goal of the experience for a socializer.

They are interested in games with other people—GDR, board games, and so on—to interact with people in the way they want to—cooperation, strong experiences, X cards (a tool that allows you to "ban" a certain topic from your game session), etc. While there are many different ways to interact with each other, none of those is superior to the other: some groups of people may love black humour in their games while others hate it; "better than" doesn't exist, there is only "more suitable for your group". Another important element for socializers is simulated human relationships: the *The Sims* saga is based on NPCs interacting with one another in the way players want them to, as the player can empathise with the simulated relations and live said simulation—sometimes it could even be an unhealthy one, but as long as the player cares for the NPC, it will keep going on. Think of marrying someone in *Stardew Valley*: once you get married, your husband/wife will spend the rest of his/her life taking care of the farm, and many players would stop giving them gifts once they are married; that's not the life you live with your partner, but it works well game-wise. An in-game romance I remember particularly well is the one from *Dragon Age: Inquisition*: there are many companions the player has to choose from, each one with multiple characteristics—mechanics, story, background and appearance— and you can also have a romance with some of them; depending on what the player cares about, they will choose a different character—for example, they picked the one with their favourite gameplay, or story, or look—and, in my case, I picked Dorian: I didn't like the gameplay, but he was my boyfriend, so how could I not pick him? In this case, my attachment to the NPC brought me to pick him, even though other characters could have had a better mechanical value.

It's important to clarify that just because relationships are simulated, it doesn't mean they are all the best relationship a player could wish for: socializers like to live experiences outside of their comfort zone as long as there is a bond, even if the theme is a strong one; in *That Dragon, Cancer*, the player lives a positive relationship—between a loving family and son—in a dark and extremely strong theme—the son has brain cancer. This setting is something you would never want to live in real life, but users enjoy the game as it provides them with a compelling and engaging story that makes them bond with the characters.

The last important element characterising a socializer is the "viewer effect"—this being situations where the player isn't the protagonist, but he/she/they see the story as an external or secondary character—like watching a movie you are not part of but still caring about the story and the characters.

In these situations, users are not the protagonist of the story and they don't need to empathise with him/her/them; they just care about seeing what happens while acting to support the main character's goal.

The difference between a "player as centre" game and a "story as centre" one can be seen in *Detroit: Become Human*—we'll call it *Detroit* for short—and *Beyond Two Souls*—this will be *Beyond*—in *Detroit*, you live as the main characters of a story: while able to change its outcome, the story is about you; in *Beyond*, on the other hand, you are not the main character: you see the story, you can act upon it, but it is not about you—you are a secondary character. While *Detroit* has relationships between NPCs too—choices you have to make to save other characters—your goal is not *someone*, but *something*: the story; in *Beyond*, the main bond you have is with the actual main character, and it's not your job to complete the story, your job is to support the main character, who will be the hero of the experience.

One last element we need to talk about when considering socializers is what happened during the COVID-19 pandemic: many people discovered gaming as a tool to communicate and stay in touch with loved ones, to strengthen bonds, and to meet new people; people found in gaming what we thought was—at the time—impossible to have: contact. They could meet their friends, hang out, and have adventures in simulated worlds, party games and much more, enjoying being with people without any sanitary risk to their health. This brought many new players into the videogame world, with casual and funny games to play with friends and forget—even for a brief moment—about the global pandemic that was happening all around the world—and around them.

How could this affect most of us, even non-socializers? This leads us to the next point: no one is only one player type: each one of us is a combination of all four types, but we have one or two main categories we fit in, and the other two occupy a small part of ourselves.

You are probably wondering how can someone be, for example, a killer acting on the player and an achiever acting on the world at the same time; it's simpler than it sounds: everyone likes certain feelings or emotions, feelings that arise when specific events happen, and each one of these emotions can be led back to one of the player types. This means that a person can like, let's say, out of 100–150 killer emotions, 40 achiever ones, 6 of socializers, and 4 of explorers; there are, of course, fits harder to manage than others— think of a killer socializer who loves meeting people to then destroy them—but no fit is impossible. It's also the goal of this tool: knowing your players, their likes and dislikes, to create the best possible experience for them; sometimes, players that don't really fit in with the target player type still want to play the game, and this is when designers manipulate players—almost temporarily redirecting their player type—to let them play the game and have a positive experience.

How to Use These Player Types

First of all, you need to identify your audience by analysing your competitors—similar games a user could choose instead of yours—and understanding their audience: interviews, players' comments, and reviews analysis—what they liked and what they didn't like about the game—making surveys and making an MDA analysis—which we'll see later on. Once we know how the audience is divided—their ages, what they love and hate, what they wish the competitors had, and so on—we can create a product that best satisfies our audience; be careful, though, as what worked for a game's audience doesn't necessarily work for yours!

This is why you need to implement or create mechanics that suit your specific target audience, in a way that is coherent with your vision and the overall feeling of the game: adding a mechanic just because the player would like it, while it has nothing to do with the rest of the game, can create a sense of inconsistency among the players.

The target audience tool is a guideline that removes arbitrariness from your design choices: you're using the 50% science we talked about to have a product that will objectively be what your audience wants, but be aware, people often don't know what they really want; this is why you need to analyse their feedback on your competitors—and not just read them—as users speak as non-designers, and it is our job to understand what they really mean—like a diagnosis. Think of a doctor who receives a patient saying "my abdomen hurts": the patient doesn't know what such pain can mean, but neither can the doctor if they don't investigate: which part is hurting? Since when have you had this pain? Do you have any other symptoms? These questions allow the doctor to reduce the scope of the problem, until he/she/they identifies it and can offer the patient a solution. As for videogames, someone could say "this part of the game was too boring", but what does that mean? Was it not challenging enough? Was the progression curve flat? Did it lack "wow moments"? As you read more reviews—or ask more questions—you find out that, while the area is new, it is filled with old enemies that players have already fought tens of times, so you change the enemies and suddenly your users find it a challenging and unique part of your level.

This shows how we—as designers—need to really understand our audience, like a parent with a baby trying to understand what foods he likes and which one he's going to throw back at us with his spoon—the same spoon that feeds them can backfire you, depending on what you put inside. It doesn't matter if *you* don't like the food; if it's best for your baby, you will feed it to him.

QUANTIC FOUNDRY

The quantic foundry model,[6] as Bartle's one, bases itself on the key concept of target audience, so, before going any further, be sure you understood it at its best.

This model differs from the Bartle archetypes as it is more modern and gameplay focused, rather than focusing on the players; it was created by Nik Yee and Nicolas Ducheneaut as a user's diving tool. It was first presented in 2019 GDC,[7] where it was extremely successful, basing its model on over—at the time—400,000 players, from board games to VR ones; it was released as a free tool, for the base format, with the possibility to purchase the in-depth data of the now over 850,000 users for bigger companies—PopCap studios, Wizards of the Coast, and Codename, just to name a few. While this could sound limiting for a smaller studio or solo developer, it's actually a good deal even in the free version: the data it provides us with is valid—as the model itself—and meaningful, therefore while purchasing a copy of the full data is extremely helpful as a large company, it's still useful as a free tool.

The quantic foundry model has a main factor you need to keep in mind: it is different from Bartle's model because it doesn't divide the players, it divides the games. Bartle, starting with the data, segments the audience into clusters, understanding what each cluster likes and dislikes; quantic foundry, instead, cares about understanding the gameplay types, and only then does it place the players into the clusters. While these models are different tools from one another, there isn't a right one for your whole game: you need some—if not all—of them to really understand your audience, as we'll see later on.

There are six types of gameplay, according to this model: action (explosions, chaos, fast pace, and visceral feelings), social (cooperation, playing together, competing, and anything involving the presence of multiple players), mastery (thoughtful processes, improvement, decision making), achievement (always wanting more, *platinating* a game, collecting badges), Immersion (plots, living the story, being part of the game world), and creativity (testing ideas, discovering rules of the game world,

ACTION	SOCIAL	MASTERY	ACHIEVEMENT	IMMERSION	CREATIVITY
"Boom!"	"Let's Play Together"	"Let Me Think"	"I Want More"	"Once Upon a Time"	"What If?"
Destruction Guns. Explosives. Chaos. Mayhem.	**Competition** Duels. Matches. High on Ranking.	**Challenge** Practice. High Difficulty. Challenges.	**Completion** Get All Collectibles. Complete All Missions.	**Fantasy** Being someone else, somewhere else.	**Design** Expression. Customization.
Excitement Fast-Paced. Action. Surprises. Thrill.	**Community** Being on Team. Chatting. Interacting.	**Strategy** Thinking Ahead. Making Decisions.	**Power** Powerful Character. Powerful Equipment.	**Story** Elaborate Plots. Interesting Characters.	**Discovery** Explore. Tinker. Experiment.

FIGURE 4.2   A table showing each category and subcategory of the quantic foundry model.
Source: Author.

creating machineries, and constructions); these elements can, of course, be combined, but we'll get to that later.

Each one of these categories is then divided into two categories—see Figure 4.2 for a scheme:

Action: destruction (guns, explosives, chaos, mayhem) and excitement (fast-paced, action, surprises, thrills).

Social: competition (duels, matches, high on ranking) and community (being on team, chatting, interacting).

Mastery: challenge (practice, high difficulty, challenges) and strategy (thinking ahead, making decisions).

Achievement: completion (get all collectibles, complete all missions) and power (powerful character, powerful equipment).

Immersion: fantasy (being someone else, being somewhere else) and story (elaborate plots, interesting characters).

Creativity: design (expression, customization) and discovery (explore, tinker, experiment)

One of the important elements of this model is its subdivisibility: each one of these subcategories is composed of other elements—for example, design is made of expression and customization—therefore you can choose how in-depth you want to look at an aspect. You can analyse a game's creativity value—talking from a gameplay point of view—while you can go more in-depth and look at its design and discovery values, or you can go even further and analyse every subtopic of both those aspects.

How deep should you go? It depends, you could only analyse a topic from a macro point of view if you're not really interested in it, while looking at each subtopic closely—almost as if you were using a microscope—for the gameplay aspects that really interest you.

Now, it's important to understand how to use this tool: the main factor of the quantic foundry model is that the two subcategories are—theoretically—mutually exclusive—while the macro ones are not—this mean that if a game focusses on design, it will focus less on discovery. Now, this isn't completely true: sometimes you can have both subcategories and, when that happens, there usually is a dominant category and a submissive one; this allows the design team to focus on a key aspect of the game, while having a lower risk of being a product in the middle of two different worlds, not actually being either of the two.

By dividing the gameplay into 12 groups (six macro groups) the quantic foundry model asks the players which are their favourite games, what they like and dislike, to see the creation of players clusters, each one of which likes X but doesn't like Y. For example—and this is purely hypothetical, therefore probably not true in reality—if you know that players that love Destruction hate Story, you can create a game heavily focused on Destruction—so, as we've seen, guns, explosives, chaos, and mayhem—with loud explosions, *gunporn*—this being a game with a focus on the satisfaction coming from using the guns, as well as just looking at them, their animations and their details—vehicles exploding like they were in a Hollywood action movie, knowing you have to avoid elaborate plots and uniquely characterised characters—therefore allowing you to focus your design and budget on the first elements—to create a successful product in that market segment.

Why is this interesting? First of all, a modern model based on over 850,000 players is truly incredible: the *Daedalus Project* was based on a fraction of this size, and it still is one of the best and most reliable models existing to this day. Second, the quantic foundry model can be applied to any game—let me repeat it, *any* game; this allows us to better iterate our analysis on multiple games, creating a unified document containing data from thousands of games from hundreds of genres.

It's important to understand that, while Bartle's Archetypes analyse the audience to then understand the game, this model analyses the game to understand the audience: in the quantic foundry model, instead of talking about *players*, we talk about *gameplay*. They are, of course, strictly connected to each other—there is no gameplay without a player and vice versa—but in one case you study the person to understand what the game should look like—Bartle's—while in the other you study the game to understand which are the audience's likes and dislikes—quantic foundry's.

This model can be used in two different ways:

> First, to analyse one or more games of the same genre: you take the model, an Excel file—or equivalent—and start assigning a value between 0 and X—depending on how precise you want it to be—to each one of the model's categories. If you need less accurate data you will only analyse the macro category—for example, action, social, mastery and so on—while if you need a higher accuracy you will evaluate each one of the sub topics—guns, explosives, and so on. You need to iterate this process for each one of your competitors; of course the more you analyse the more accurate the results will be.

This type of analysis is extremely relevant and modern, as, after the research phase—yes, you still have to do research first—you can analyse your competitors to see if there is any market whole you can use to fit your game in or to find the dominant design and follow it to use an already existing and established audience—none of these two is superior to the other; they are just different techniques and depend, of course, on your project's needs. This can be applied, as we've said before, from a macro level to a micro one: the more in

BOX 4.3   AN EXAMPLE OF THE QUANTIC FOUNDRY
MODEL IN ACTION, IN THIS CASE WITH *IT TAKES TWO*

We are taking Hazelight Studios' *It Takes Two* as an example, where another designer and I gave a vote to each one of the categories, then used the average of the two values as the data entered in the table; the macro category value comes from the sum of the sub categories elements.

Note that those are based on personal perceptions, therefore you might disagree—this just means that our comparison points are different.

ACTION	SOCIAL	MASTERY	ACHIEVEMENT	IMMERSION	CREATIVITY
6.5	9	2.5	4	8.75	4.25
Destruction	Competition	Challenge	Completion	Fantasy	Design
7	8.5	4	4	8	2
Excitement	Community	Strategy	Power	Story	Discovery
6	9.5	1	4	9.5	7.5

If you want to, you can go more in depth by analysing each component of each sub topic (for example, destruction is composed of guns, explosives, chaos, mayhem). Once you have all the scores of each category, add them together and divide them by the number of elements—for example, action is destruction plus excitement divided by two, if we break down destruction into guns, explosives, chaos, and mayhem, we would need to divide the value of destruction by four, then add it to excitement and divide the result by two to have the value of action.

Each vote doesn't represent *how good* something was but how *present* it was; maybe you hated the story, but you can't say—as a designer with a critical eye—it wasn't present. We can see how *It Takes Two* has strong social and immersion elements, therefore, if we wanted to make a competitor targeting the same audience, we would make a game with similar values in those categories—while the others could change based on the style and identity of the game we are making.

depth you go, the more precise results you'll have, but the higher the required time for the analysis will be—as always, you need to find the right balance for your team/game.

The second way is to analyse your own product: once you have a demo—or a vertical slice—it's possible to share it with playtesters, or actual future players, and, once the playtest session is over, ask the players to give a score to each one of the categories and subcategories, to see how the game is perceived by the players.

Explain to them that the score is not about how much they liked each aspect but about how present it was in the game; they won't, of course, have our critical eye, so be sure they understand the task properly. Once you have their results, you then ask the same task to your team—that has to answer *without* playing the game, to test their vision versus the player perception—and there are three possible outcomes:

First, the players' score and your team's one are the same: this means that your vision and their perception is on the same page, therefore what you are doing is creatively correct and is well passed to the players—congratulations!

Second, the player's score is slightly different from your team's: this can be due to many reasons—bugs, technical/budget/time limitations, a slight loss of vision by the team, or maybe your publisher pushed certain decisions on your game that weren't originally included. This mean that the game has changed, and while it's not necessarily a bad thing, there is a slight discrepancy between what you have in mind and what the players perceive, therefore this tool allows you to identify where the problem lies and then fix it, or the team can embrace this new version of the game and fix their vision to sustain it more—there is no right answer, it depends how willing you are to sacrifice the original vision to accommodate the players.

Last case, there is a big difference between your team's vision and your audience perception: there are, of course, many causes for this issue—the game was tested too early, it had too many bugs, the design wasn't ready, and so on—but, whatever the cause is, this is a problem: your team doesn't know what they are doing; it doesn't matter *who* is the cause—never, never look for a person to blame: you are all on the same ship, if it goes down, everyone on it goes down too—the important part is *what* is the cause, so you need to adopt communicative solutions—meetings, confrontations, Q&A, etc.—to make sure everyone—let me repeat that, *everyone*—has the same clear vision of the game you are developing. There is, however, a second possible cause for this problem: the players didn't understand the game. While it may sound like the easiest solution, it's actually the worst one: while in the previous scenario the problem is inside the team, therefore fixable with enough communication, in this case the problem isn't the players—never blame the players, they have no fault—it's the way the game was presented: your team gave out the wrong idea about the game, therefore you now need to recreate the game's perceived identity from scratch, before the game comes out, or you will face a terrible scenario.

Take Hello Games' *No Man's Sky*, we all know what happened—the game was hyped as a revolutionary product, never seen before, with procedural worlds, creatures and much more, but after the release it faced a terrible crash, leading to refunds, a bad reputation, and unhappy players—but many people don't know *why* it happened: the biggest mistake made by the team was presenting an indie game at E3, where AAA games are usually presented; this led the players to think it had the scope, team, and resources of the biggest games out there, when it wasn't even close to being a product of that size.

How do you avoid such situations? By working closely with your marketing team, ensuring they understand both your game and your players, not misunderstanding the audience or the scope: you don't bring a wedding cake to a birthday party, the same way you don't bring a birthday cake to a wedding—they're just for two different situations.

BOX 4.4   THE QUANTIC FOUNDRY TASK, THIS TIME
THE GAMES ARE DECIDED BY THE READER

QUANTIC FOUNDRY TASK

Take three games from a similar genre and analyse them using the quantic foundry model, creating a table with all the categories and assigning each one a value—as we did with *It Takes Two*; you can choose how in-depth to go, just remember that a more focused analysis gives more accurate results, but it requires more time.

Once you have the compiled table for a game, briefly describe what insights it gives, how it relates to the other games—what do they have in common? What are the differences? What do they mean?—and what it tells you about the audience.

End the document with a concise conclusion, saying what you learned from the information you gathered—as if you were reporting to a colleague who asked you to perform such analysis.

Remember that the games you choose are—statistically—going to be different from mine, so don't focus on the games themselves but rather on using the same process and understanding what you did wrong or could have done better—or what you did better than me; that's the best part of game design: you never stop learning from others, no matter their experience.

You can use the format you prefer: if you like the one I used, feel free to take it, while if it doesn't suit you, don't be afraid to experiment—as long as the result is a professional and informative document.

BIG FIVE

The Big Five model—Big Five Personality Traits—is a taxonomy model for personality traits used in psychology, first created in 1961 by Ernest Tupes and Raymond Christal—then further developed by other psychologists, reaching an academic audience in the 1980s; just know that, as the model is open source—meaning anyone can contribute—it's always in further development, as experts from all around the world are testing and expanding its limits with new discoveries. As Bartle's model divides the audience in different groups, the Big Five Ocean model measures everyone's personality into five dimensions:

Openness: based on aspects like imagination and intuition, a high value on this scale indicates a wide range of interests, a curiosity in the world and other people, as well as the desire to live and try new interests. On the opposite side, a low value in openness means a more traditionalist person poor in abstract thinking, reluctant to change and innovative ideas.

Conscientiousness: the sense of duty, the ability to respect everything you say; a high level indicates a person able to control his/her/their impulses, with behaviours aimed at reaching a clear goal, organised and with a keen eye for details. This type of person always thinks ahead and respects deadlines without any problem. A low value on this scale, however, characterises an unorganised, procrastinating person who has severe problems when focusing on bigger tasks.

Extroversion: excitability and sociability; people with a high extroversion value gain energy when around other people; they feel energised and want to take part in social events. A low value indicates a private person, who often dislikes social situations and needs alone time to gain the energy back.

Agreeableness: trust, altruism; an agreeable person is trustworthy, kind, loving, and has prosocial behaviours. On the other hand, an unpleasant person is more competitive and can often be manipulative with the people around him/her/them.

Neuroticism: sadness, emotional instability and bad mood; the higher the value on this scale, the more anxious and frustrated the person will be. The lower the value, the more emotionally stable the person is, while being able to be in a good mood even in negative situations.

Recently, as the model was brought outside the US, a new trait has been discovered: Honesty-Humility, a trait opposite to the Dark Triad that indicates narcissism and psychopathy—another personality test you can take a look at. This discovery led researchers to change "extroversion" in the acronym into an "X" and rename "Neuroticism" as "Emotionality", transforming the "Ocean" model's acronym into the "Hexacom" model.

These traits are universal—they don't change between different cultures—while they however have biological, social, and ambiental situations; they tend to be relatively stable in the adult age, but some traits tend to change when getting older—for example, extroversion lowers and agreeableness increases.

While it can be scary to measure our whole personality on a test,[8] it's actually really helpful when trying to better understand ourselves, why we behave in certain ways, and it can help us to find our optimal job. For example, a person with a really high value of extroversion would feel tortured in a cubicle, working eight hours a day alone with no interaction; a more suitable job for this individual would be, say, in sales: talking to clients, meeting them in person, using their charm and their ability to make people open up with them to create a connection are all aspects that would make such person feel alive and passionate about what they do.

This is also true with relationships: if you're looking for a long-term partner, it's a good idea to be with someone who has traits similar to yours; if you're an extreme extrovert dating an extreme introvert, you will often argue about how often you should go out, with how many friends, and so on. While these are not *fights*, you may find your partner forcing themselves into someone they are not—and the same goes for you. This doesn't mean you should date someone *exactly* like you, small differences can actually be helpful: if you have a slightly low value on Openness, while you partner has a slightly high value, you partner can help you get outside of your comfort zone, trying new experiences and finding new hobbies—of course, one step at a time—just be careful when the differences between you and your partner are too high. It sounds cynical, I know, but we are not talking about being madly in love with someone you've spent your whole life with; we are looking at dating someone new, when you are often too blinded to see the red flags about your differences.

You might now think that some extremes are better than others, but we have to make it clear that any extreme is bad: it can mean being too controlling, too careless, too trusting, and much more; it's also true that we can't change our personality out of the blue—it requires time, discipline, and effort—but the goal of this tool isn't about hating yourself for how you are; it's knowing yourself better to help you deal with your life: if you realise you are too conscious, you can try to set some pauses every X hours of work, while not feeling guilty for "doing nothing"—and, by the way, resting is not "doing nothing", it's as important as the work itself.

BOX 4.5   A BOX BRIEFLY EXPLAINING HOW NORMAL DISTRIBUTION WORKS

One of the most important parts of the Big Five theory is that it follows a normal distribution;[9] this means that you are going to have average values in most of the options—thus these traits don't characterise you—while others are going to be strongly above or below average: these are the traits that define who you are, what you like, and what you hate.

The normal distribution is used in many fields—from statistics to finance—to prove that, when evaluating something, the majority of people will be located in the middle section, and, for the Big Five model, these are the irrelevant values: what makes you *you* are the off-chart values, the uncommon ones, as those are the ones that distinguish you from the rest of the people.

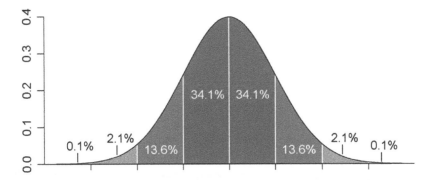

FIGURE 4.3   A visual representation of a Normal Distribution curve.

Source: Author.

Take a look at Figure 4.3, and let's say we are—once again—talking about cakes: this chart represents how much people like cakes or candies. The more you go on the right, the more you like cakes and hate candies, while on the left you love candies and hate cake:

34.1% of the population—we are talking about the whole audience, not our target audience now—doesn't really care about cakes but is slightly positively polarised toward cakes rather than candies.

13.6% likes cakes and will probably buy ours—if presented in the right way—instead of buying candies.

2.1% love cakes; they will buy our cake and it will be an amazing experience for them.

0.1% of the population will have their life changed by our cake; they will praise it as the best cake ever baked and will never find something like that.

On the other side, the exact opposite happens:

34.1% of the population doesn't really care about cakes but is slightly negatively polarised toward it—they prefer candies.

13.6% doesn't like cakes and probably won't buy our cake—they'll purchase candies instead.

2.1% hates cakes, not only will they not buy our cake, but they'll probably talk people out of buying it for themselves.

0.1% hates our cake so much they will create a hating group, pointing to everything wrong with our cake and convincing everyone they know in the central 65% to never buy our cake and, instead, to buy candies.

How does all of this relate to game design? As we've seen before, each one of us is unique, but can also be clustered with people with similar interests—when we "zoom out"—and this is where the Big Five model comes in handy: it shows each cluster's uncommon values, the ones that define them.

While the Bartle model shows what motivates us and the quantic foundry model shows what the key gameplay elements are, the Big Five model shows what polarises us: what makes you *you*, your—statistically speaking—flaws and your tendencies. Let me explain better with an example: take your favourite game and imagine a sequel—if it already has a sequel think of a different sequel—that never came out—or hasn't come out yet—now imagine they added, let's say, competitive multiplayer; would you still play it? What if they added loot boxes? Still interested? What about it being an MMO? Stealth only? With a lot of grinding? What about vehicles?

One—or more—of those questions made you think "no, I couldn't stand it", and that answer comes from your polarisation, that one thing that makes you give up on the sequel of your favourite game, because you just can't take it—don't feel bad, I don't think that a stealth-only MMO with grinding and loot boxes would have been a great game; maybe it's for the best it doesn't exist. Some of the options may have interested you, therefore this polarises you positively—making you want the product or even making you buy it at day one—while you didn't really care about other ones—these are non-polarising values, meaning you are in the average cluster of those.

It's really important to understand both how to attract and to turn audiences away, because you need to interest your target audience, while moving away those players that wouldn't like the game, creating bad experiences for others or just not enjoying it— wasting their time and money; always remember that you made a pact with the players: you provide them with games they will like, and they will spend their time and money on them. If you break this pact by delivering to the wrong audience, it's not their fault for not having understood the game, it's your fault for not making it clear that the game wasn't for them—and if we break that pact, what else do we have bonding us with our players?

Before going any further, I highly suggest you to do the previously mentioned test, in order to see where you place yourself for each category; this also allows you to become a better designer, by seeing what you like and dislike coming from your personality, you can then see—when you are designing—if you pitch an idea because you think it's good for the game or because your personality is polarised toward that type of idea. Let's say you *love* grinding, from the bottom of your heart, and you are designing an open world game for explorers: you may want to insert it because you think that "it's cool", but always remember that "being cool" isn't an emotion; you can't force it on someone with different tastes from yours; what you can do is, analysing Jason VandenBerghe's archetypes—we'll talk about him in a second, understand if this particular element fits the liking of your audience. Explorers don't like grinding as achievers do, so it's prob- ably a good idea not to insert it in the game; I know you are probably wondering "Why did you talk about achievers and explorers—which come from Bartle's model—in the Big Five section?" and the answer is that, while they are different lenses, they are not isolated from one another. They are like the old red and blue 3D glasses: if you look through the red lens, you will see something, while if you look through the blue one, you will see something else, but the best way to use them is by looking at the same thing from both the lenses at the same time—and so it is how we should look at the players, but we'll talk about it later.

Looking at Figure 4.3, you can see how almost 70% of the population is located in the central area; this means that 70% of the population finds most elements non-polaris- ing—therefore they won't be interested in purchasing a game with such elements. The audience cluster you'll want to target is the next 26%—those people finding the element slightly polarising—the 4% with a polarisation for the elements and, even though they are a really small chunk of the population, the last 0.2% who find those elements extremely polarising.

Of course, this means that, if you target the "first half" of the chart—excluding the main 70% who don't really care, you have a 13% of not-so-caring people, a 2% who will buy the game for sure, and a 0.1% that—no matter what—will always praise your game to others. This leaves you with around 15% of polarised people interested in your game, 15% of polarised people who *won't* buy your game—the other half of the chart—and almost 70% of people who don't really care about your game. While it sounds bad at first, the 15% of a whole audience, who will statistically like your game, is an excellent result: if your audience is the whole PS4 audience—around 80 million players—up to 12 millions players—15%— will buy your game, and that is anything but bad for me. Now, this isn't completely true: not *everyone* in those percentages will purchase your game—the most relatable chunk is the 0.1%—they will just be positively polarized toward it; on the same train of thought, the

70% of people who don't care about your game are not completely gone: 35% of them are not really interested, while the other 35% are slightly interested. This means that, while they don't really care about your game, they don't have a negative opinion either: you can, by studying their interests and implementing them in your design, get the attention of some of them to your game—meaning a higher chance of them playing it.

At first, this model wasn't really relevant to videogames, until Jason VandenBerghe—amused by this model—dedicated himself to convert it to games; he was fascinated by this model, so he made studies—I highly suggest you look at them yourself—to convert said model to videogames. He took four of the five—we'll talk about this later—dimensions and found a game design equivalent for each one of them:

Openness equals novelty, conscientiousness equals challenge, extraversion equals stimulation, and agreeableness equals harmony; as you notice, neuroticism doesn't have an equivalent, according to Jason.

Each one of these dimensions is made of six different aspects, for example, looking at Figure 4.4, you can see how "Openness To Experience" is composed by six lines, each one with two options at each extreme; the closer your results from the Big Five test are to an extreme, the more similar to that aspect you are: if you have a high score in "Liberalism", you are less "Traditionalist" and vice versa, for each one of the six lines.

How does Jason convert these to game design? Let's take a look at Figure 4.5 to see the equivalent of each extreme.

Before taking a look at specific elements, let's put every dimension—and its extremes—in a table each, with both the Big Five structure and their gaming equivalent:

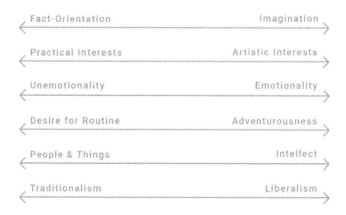

Openness To Experience

Fact-Orientation	Imagination
Practical Interests	Artistic Interests
Unemotionality	Emotionality
Desire for Routine	Adventurousness
People & Things	Intellect
Traditionalism	Liberalism

FIGURE 4.4 A scheme showing how each dimension is composed of six values, each one within two extremes.

Source: Author.

FIGURE 4.5   A scheme converting the values from Figure 4.4 to game design according to Jason VandenBerghe.

Source: Author.

OPENNESS TO EXPERIENCE		NOVELTY	
BIG FIVE		GAME TRANSLATION	
Fact-Orientation	Imagination	Realism	Fantasy
Practical Interests	Artistic Interests	"Technical Artistry"	Artistry
Unemotionality	Emotionality	Melodrama	
Desire for Routine	Adventurousness	Cultivation	Exploration
People & Things	Intellect	Puzzles	
Traditionalism	Liberalism	(nothing)	

Most words, if you are familiar with the terms, are self-explanatory but cultivation: this means seeing things grow and improve from the same place—just like a vegetable grows; one other element it's important to discuss is "Liberalism". Jason couldn't find a game design equivalent, but, from my point of view, it can be associated with the game's franchise: if you are more traditionalist, you will not want to see the games a certain studio makes change, for example when *Final Fantasy* went from being turn-based to being a faster-paced game, you would have hated this change—and the studio behind the game for this decision; if, however, you are a liberalist, you love to see your game develop and try new things, therefore, in the previous example, you would have been happy for the change the game took.

CONSCIENTIOUSNESS		CHALLENGE	
BIG FIVE		GAME TRANSLATION	
Un-Self-Efficacy	Self-Efficacy	"Easy"	"Hard"
Disorganisation	Orderliness	Set Completion	
Resistance	Dutifulness	Social Freedom	"Guilding"
Contentment	Achievement-Striving	Achievements	
Procrastination	Self-Discipline	Grinding	
Impulsiveness	Cautiousness	Run-And-Gun	Precision

The Challenge dimension takes a lot of parameters from the Achiever player type from Bartle's model, however there is a key difference: this dimension doesn't say you *like* those elements, it just measures how much you are oriented toward them. Take, for instance, achievements: a true achiever would be on the far right of the table—meaning this player loves achievements in games—but someone who hates them would be on the far left. Remember that this tool measures your polarisation toward multiple elements per dimension, meaning that your real archetype would be composed of 6 parameters per dimension, 24 in total—these are way too many if we have to study a whole audience, but we'll talk about this later.

EXTRAVERSION		STIMULATION	
BIG FIVE		GAME TRANSLATION	
Reservedness	Friendliness	Communication	
Non-Gregariousness	Gregariousness	1–4 Players	Larger Groups
Receptiveness	Assertiveness	Follower	Leadership
Activity Level (low)	Activity Level (high)	"Size of the task list"	
Excitement-Aversion	Excitement-Seeking	Calmness	Thrill-Rides
Inexpressiveness	Cheerfulness	Joy-Expression	

The Stimulation spectrum of the model is what led to the creation of Light MMOs—this being MMOs with a smaller number of players—as Non-Gregarious people—therefore made for smaller groups—enjoyed playing an MMO, but their experience was ruined by being in large groups that characterise this game genre.

As for Joy-Expression, it indicates how much the product allows you to express at a social level—is there a dance you can do? Can you type in chat? And so on.

AGREEABLENESS		HARMONY	
BIG FIVE		GAME TRANSLATION	
Scepticism	Trust	Cheating (you)	
Guardedness	Straightforwardness	Cheating (me)	

Non-Altruism	Altruism	Rogues	Healers
Competition	Accommodation	ME vs Players	US vs Players
Immodesty	Modesty	Rank	
Indifference	Sympathy	Characters (Real and Virtual)	

Harmony is dictated by the presence—or absence—of fights: as President Ronald Regan said, "Peace is not absence of conflict, it is the ability to handle conflict by peaceful means[10]". The best possible example is any typical healer in videogames: they can usually harm other players, but their goal is to cure the teammates; it solves the conflict by sustaining—peacefully—the players who will defeat the enemies—those aren't peaceful, but they aren't healers either.

You might think that a game with a high harmony is a peaceful game, where there are no enemies, but the true harmony is in the collaboration and sharing among players; it can be a PvP game, as well as a PvE one, but, as long as there is a high degree of cooperation and need of every player, the harmony will be high.

The next big step Jason takes with this model is placing each dimension on a Cartesian plane, then used to create archetypes; according to Jason, each player has one archetype on each of the four dimensions—neuroticism isn't present as it's impossible to create a relatable taxonomy (Figure 4.6 and 4.7); we're now going to take a look at the archetypes generated from these parameters, with both a non-game-related person and a game example:

> As we've said, there are 24 parameters total per player, but, since it would take too much time and data to collect all of them, Jason simplifies each dimension into two main parameters, one on each axis of the taste map—note that these definitions came from Jason VandenBerghe's 2013 GDC talk[11]

While with Bartle's model you had to identify yourself in one of the archetypes, in this model you need to take the results of your Big Five test and "translate" them into their game version; it uses archetypes, just as Bartle, but it's more precise, as it's based on four different sub-archetypes (Figure 4.8 and 4.9). It's an extremely useful tool, for it can be used in two different ways:

> First, you can take the test with your team, to see which are your mental biases—a distortion of how we see certain things; once you know what they are, you can be careful not to be tricked by them: let's say you love competitive games, but you are designing a casual single-player platformer. You might think that the game isn't fast-paced enough or that it's *too* casual, but once you look at the users' feedback, they love it. How can it be possible? Did your own players understand the game better than you? Not at all, you just had the wrong perception of what the game should have looked like due to a mental bias; now, let's say you take the Big Five test and find out about this bias: you start asking yourself—and your team—if the game is actually not fast-paced enough, or if you are just picturing it wrong in your head, therefore you can remember to think about the game your players want, not you. After all, once you know what controls you, it's pretty easy to stop its hold on you, and with your 50% science, you can always fix your 50% art.

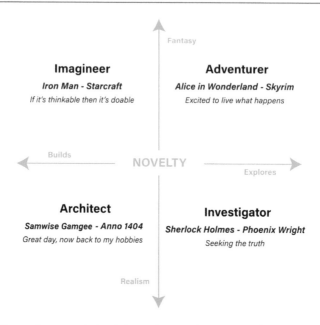

FIGURE 4.6 The archetypes derived from the novelty aspect of the Big Five model, with examples for each one.

Source: Author.

FIGURE 4.7 The archetypes derived from the challenge aspect of the Big Five model, with examples for each one.

Source: Author.

FIGURE 4.8 The archetypes derived from the stimulation aspect of the Big Five model, with examples for each one.

Source: Author.

FIGURE 4.9 The archetypes derived from the harmony aspect of the Big Five model, with examples for each one.

Source: Author.

Second, it's useful to collect feedback: before asking your players any feedback, ask them to take the Big Five test, then collect the results from both the test and the game. Now you can filter what your players are saying based on their test results: if they say the game is too easy but they are not your audience, is the game really too easy, or are they just the wrong players? Maybe you find out they are all *masterers* in every game they play, while you intended your game to be played by a more casual audience. This can be extremely helpful in avoiding making changes for the wrong reason because once you make sure whether that is your right audience or not, you can weigh their opinions accordingly.

Jason takes another important step for the game design world: starting from the normal distribution curve, he creates a *taste map* to understand the players' polarisation. (Figure 4.10)

BOX 4.6   AN EXPLANATION OF TASTE MAPS WITH A PICTURE FOR AN EASIER UNDERSTANDING

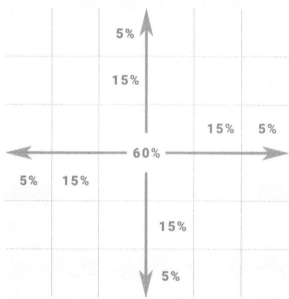

FIGURE 4.10   A taste map showing the ranges of interest based on the location on the chart.

Source: Author.

Taste Maps are a tool that allows you to visualise player's likes and dislikes on a Cartesian graph, where one extreme excludes the other, meaning that the 5% of players who like the square on the far left won't like the one on the far right; this segments your audience, letting you decide where to put the focus—and the resources—of your game.

This map is used to understand where the product is polarising for the players—as we've previously said—therefore showing us which part of the audience would be interested in certain aspects of the game.

To create such a map, you need to ask yourself a question for each one of the rings:

For the central box, "Does my game have this feature?", if the answer is *yes*, you can colour the box—therefore knowing you have the attention of that part of the audience—while if it's *no*, you leave it empty—thus not targeting that audience.

For the second ring, the question is "Is this feature part of the game? Is it good enough for players to like the game even just for this feature?" as before, depending on the answer you will or will not colour that box.

For the outer ring, ask yourself "Is this experience among the best in the world?" and apply the same process as before.

The goal is not to colour all the boxes—that would require a tremendous amount of money, time, and skill—the goal is understanding which part of the game should be so important to polarise the audience; by colouring each box, you are making a promise—to yourself and the players—about making an aspect *that* good: if you colour one of the 5% boxes—the outer ring—you are committing yourself to make one of the best experiences ever created for that aspect, so be sure you can live up to that expectation.

This tool is extremely useful also to balance your goal with your budget and time: if you check multiple 5% boxes, you need to create something truly amazing in multiple aspects of the game.

How do you compile this map? It's pretty simple: sit down with your team, discuss it, and, while being completely honest—this is crucial—start talking about what boxes you think you can colour—and deliver; since no one has unlimited budget and time, you won't be able to colour them all, and this is why you need to address your focus to what is truly important for your game—and your players.

It's crucial to remember that the further you go colouring the boxes, the more players won't like your game—because they will be negatively polarised by it. It's also important to know that if you have a game made by only central boxes, chances are it won't sell a lot and, most of all, players won't have a special experience—it will be a game like many others, as your audience won't be polarised by the game.

Each one of the 5% boxes creates two types of players: the evangelists—who will literally praise your game, suggest it to friends, and love it from the bottom of their hearts—and the haters—those who, without even playing it, will call it garbage and talk people out of buying it; that's the human nature of polarisation, and, whether you like it or not, you need to accept it and learn how to deal with it in your career.

We need to make an exception, while creating these taste maps, for neuroticism: neuroticism, which is still being studied, is—in my opinion, therefore not coming from Jason's model—the dimension defining all those elements that make you drop the game—which is opposite to all the other dimensions; it's about all the negative feelings generating discomfort and physically or mentally painful events (Figure 4.11). Take, for instance, rugby: I'm too scared to get hurt to play it, so fear alone as an emotion makes me never play rugby in my life; can you see how powerful these emotions are? It's enough to feel one of them at a certain level to never play a game, not even if it was given to you for free. This is by far the

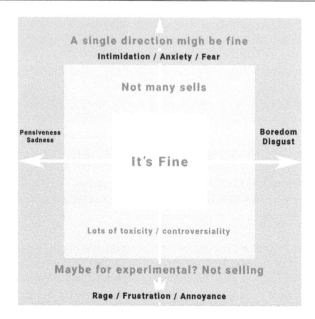

FIGURE 4.11   A graph showing the three rings of neuroticism.

Source: Author.

hardest dimension to measure, as there aren't fixed parameters working for every game: a level of fear acceptable in a horror game couldn't be used in, say, a puzzle game. You need to adapt the scale depending on the game you are making, therefore binding even more your 50% science to your 50% art: if your art really sustains certain negative emotions, you could be able to pull them off even if they were stronger than what they normally are in other games.

We saw how neuroticism is different from the other dimensions, and so is its taste map: the closer you are to the centre, the better it is for your player; every outer ring you move toward, the more likely your players will drop your game, as this generates unpleasant and negative feelings—from disgust to paralysing fear.

This doesn't mean you can't have *any* negative feelings, for example, horror games are based on fear, the *Fiero* emotion comes from frustration, and so on; this just means that, if you decide to step one ring further, you must know what you are doing, or you could ruin the whole experience for the players.

The third ring is, in my opinion, an area you should never touch, with the only exceptions being highly experimental games that want to cause negative feelings in the player and a really brief session of exposure to those emotions—in a horror game, it can be fine to have a single moment of gore to imprint the memory in the players' minds, but if it happens multiple times, the players will soon drop the game: an extreme situation of disgust could be a villain popping someone's eye with their thumb, with blood and fluids flying around; it would be iconic and memorable, but very disturbing for some people that might become afraid of similar scenes happening again.

This model presented two main problems when designed:

First, designers think in groups, while people think by themselves; this is where the taste maps come in handy, allowing us to study the preferences of each cluster of people—remember, the more we zoom out the more unified the opinion inside a cluster will be.

Second, a player's motivation changes over time: you don't keep playing a game for the same reason you first played it; for example, if you open a game to see cool explosions, you will eventually get tired of seeing them—or you'll develop habituation, feeling weaker emotions the more you see the same explosions taking place—and designers can't just add *more explosions*—you would still get tired of them. What we need instead is something that keeps you in a long-term interest: this is where the Self Determination Theory—or SDT—comes to our rescue, but we'll talk about this in a later chapter.

In this chapter, we've seen how each of us is unique but how we can also be clustered to see patterns arise; the Big Five model is based exactly on this assumption: it identifies the extremes of your personality. Your value around 60 will be the same as most people, therefore irrelevant to a designer; what is truly unique about you—and what defines your personality—are the traits out of the ordinary, on the extremes. These values, once converted into the game design version of the model, are the ones that will make you decide whether you love or hate a game before even playing it.

Think about people who practice extreme sports, say base jumping—a sport where you throw yourself in the air from the roof of a building or the top of a cliff with a wingsuit, to glide for some time until you open your parachute; this person will most likely have an extremely high openness—allowing them to try such experiences without being too scared to stay focused during the glide—and an extremely low neuroticism—letting them not panic while performing and enjoying the experience itself.

The same goes for games: your personality traits define if you will love or hate an experience or if you will care at all—as we've said, you won't care about most of the things present in most mass games.

There are many other models we didn't cover—Lazzaro's types of fun, 16 personalities model, Kalios' taxonomy, and many more—not because they are less important or accurate but because they are currently less used in the industry—and we only have so many pages. Is there a model superior to the others? Of course not, each model should be used for its purpose, and multiple models should be used together; the core of each model is showing a different face of the same die which is the player—a really complex die but a beautiful one. The more models you use, the clearer all the die faces will appear. Does this mean you should use all the models? Again, it's quite the opposite: use the models you think will show you unclear parts of the player, as applying a model to your audience requires plenty of time—and time is the only resource we don't get back, so be careful with how you spend it.

Bartle's model analyses players' motivation, the quantic foundry model looks at the gameplay, and the Big Five model focuses on what polarises the players. Your true target audience won't be a perfect Bartle's archetype; it will be partially a Bartle's archetype, partially a quantic foundry's archetype, polarised in ways only the Big Five model can tell you.

New models come out every six years—more or less—for example, a colleague of mine is studying a narrative-based model—which doesn't exist right now. This doesn't mean that you need to throw everything you know away every six years; some models will come out but won't be used for hundreds of different reasons—too time-consuming, not accurate enough, too invasive, and so on—but you still need to be on the lookout for opportunities to expand and improve game design, so, if you see a model you think would be suitable for your product, don't hesitate to learn and apply it.

BOX 4.7 BIG FIVE TASK, ONCE AGAIN THE GAMES ARE CHOSEN BY THE READER

BIG FIVE TASK

Similarly to the quantic foundry task, take three similar games—not the same you chose in that task—compile a taste map for each of the five categories to see what aspects of each dimension they satisfy—remember the question you have to ask yourself to colour each outer ring; then, think about what could be the target audience of the three games. Last but not least, think about what the causes of abandonment could be.

NOTES

1 Liberating Structures, *Nine Whys Technique*: www.liberatingstructures.com/3-nine-whys/
2 TechHq, *If Something Is Free You Are the Product*: https://techhq.com/2018/04/facebook-if-something-is-free-you-are-the-product/
3 Yee, N., *Daedalus Project*: www.nickyee.com/daedalus/archives/001539.php
4 Yee, N. and Bailenson, J. N. (2007), *The Proteus Effect: The Effect of Transformed Self-Representation on Behaviour:* http://web.stanford.edu/~bailenso/papers/proteus%20effect.pdf
5 Warrior of Light, *What Happens if Tidus Kills the Water Flan in Besaid*: www.youtube.com/watch?v=jDsPAmy826Q
6 *Quantic Foundry*: https://quanticfoundry.com
7 Nick Yee at GDC 2019, *A Deep Dive into the 12 Motivations: Findings from 400,000+ Gamers*: www.youtube.com/watch?v=gxJUPfKtg_Q
8 *Big Five Test*: https://bigfive-test.com
9 Normal Distribution, *Wikipedia*: https://en.wikipedia.org/wiki/Normal_distribution
10 Ronald Reagan, *Eureka College, 9th May 1982, Reagan Foundation*: www.reaganfoundation.org/ronald-reagan/reagan-quotes-speeches/commencement-address-eureka-college/
11 Jason VandenBerghe, *GDC 2013*: www.youtube.com/watch?v=6uX6ye66NK0

Data Tools

5

We've broadly talked about the importance of data, and while the target audience tools are aimed to gather information from other sources, we are now taking a look at ways to gather and analyse the information yourself. Do you remember the two types of data we have? Quantitative and qualitative, exactly! Quantitative data is statistical, usually numeric, and can be displayed on a chart—this is the data you can measure, remember? Qualitative data, on the other hand, is what tells us the players' emotions, their thoughts, and, therefore, it's not objectively correct: it's what the players are feeling, which must always be treated with absolute respect.

STAKEHOLDERS

From the software development and marketing world come the stakeholders: these are groups of people bonded to the project by an interest—any type of bond and any type of interest.

There are many possible interests and types of bond: the CEO has a monetary interest, the development team has both a monetary and qualitative interest, while the players have an emotional interest—they are stakeholders too, but we'll get to that.

Outside the videogames world, there are plenty of other interests too: if you buy a medicine, your interest is healing, while if you buy a first-class ticket, you want the comfort it offers.

The stakeholder analysis is aimed to, of course, identify your stakeholders, how much "weight" they have, what their interests are, and what their areas of expertise and power are. What do I mean by weight? A weight is, in this case, anything that can alter the objective of a project: a designer who wants to respect the original vision is a weight. Everyone who works on the project, as we'll see, has some type of interest and a certain amount of power in the project development: the combination of those two is a weight.

This tool is extremely important to understanding who interacts with the game, who has the most power, and where they are hijacking the project's route. Knowing how much power each stakeholder has lets you know—and prevent—bad management for the team and the project: if the 3D art team is made of 20 people, while the programming team only has 5, it's pretty obvious who has the most decisional power.

DOI: 10.1201/9781003229438-7

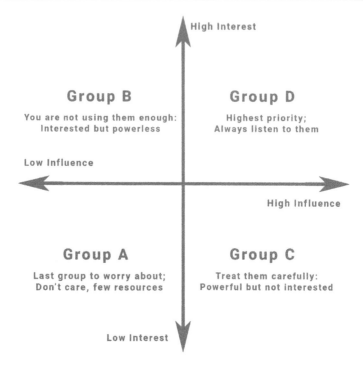

High Interest

Group B
You are not using them enough;
Interested but powerless

Group D
Highest priority;
Always listen to them

Low Influence

High Influence

Group A
Last group to worry about;
Don't care, few resources

Group C
Treat them carefully:
Powerful but not interested

Low Interest

FIGURE 5.1 A Cartesian graph showing where each group is located based on its interest and influence.

Source: Author.

One of your most important stakeholders is the players: if they hate everything you are doing with a game, even if you have tons of investment from other stakeholders, it will be a financial disaster, as there won't be anyone to play it—we'll get into the details in a second.

How do you use this tool? There are two possible ways:

First, take a Cartesian plane, put on the Y-axis the "influence"—the power each stakeholder has—and on the X-axis how much interest they have. Now, taking a look at Figure 5.1, let's analyse each outcome:

The second way to analyse a project's stakeholders is with a table, where on the first column you put every stakeholder of the game, and on the first row, you put five parameters, that are: influence—the power we talked about earlier—interest—a number between one and ten—objective—what they want from the project—resources—the amount of money/time/people the stakeholder can invest in the game—and dependence—who does this stakeholder depend on?

Let's create an example of a hypothetical studio with medium scope and budget to analyse some of its stakeholders in the next table:

	INFLUENCE	INTEREST	OBJECTIVE	RESOURCES	DEPENDENCY
CEO	10	7	Money	Infinite	Publisher
Publisher	8	7	Money and Quality	Very limited	Development Team
Creative Director	8	10	Quality	High	Player
Design Team	7	9	Money and Quality	Medium	Creative Director
Art Team	7	9	Money and Quality	Medium	CD + Art Director
Animation Team	7	9	Money and Quality	Medium	CD + Animation Director
Programming Team	7	9	Money and Quality	Medium	Technical Director
Customer	0	10	Quality	Non-existent	None

The person with the most influence is the CEO, meaning they can make whatever decision they want, as they also have infinite resources—which are never really infinite, but you get the idea; however, they depend on the publisher: they need to follow the publisher's instructions.

The publisher depends on the development team—this meaning the design team, the art team, and so on—which depend on the creative director and specific directors. This already shows us one possible problem: the creative director has a tremendous amount of power over the project. Is this a good or a bad thing? Neither, it depends on how much you trust this director: if you know they are someone trustworthy, it's a good thing, as they will take care of most decisions and problems by themselves; if you don't really trust them, however, this could lead to a crash of the project caused by one single person.

All these pieces of information are useful to understand who is making your ship steer in which direction: the CEO of the company has the most influence but isn't that interested, because their goal is the money; when facing the publisher—who wants quality, other than money—they may try to take two very different directions.

The creative director depends on the player—who has no influence—therefore, the creative director needs to be the voice of the players while being only interested in the quality: this is a problem too, as no one has infinite time and money, so they could keep the game under development forever—this is why you need a CEO, who takes control when the ship is steering toward a waterfall but can't see it as the whole team is fixing some holes in the hull.

The player, who has no influence and the highest interest, is a bit of a wild card: they have no resources in the production—except with early access/KickStarter games, MMOs, live games, and similar, where they actually have influence over the game—but they are the ones who needs to be satisfied with the result, and that is why they need a spokesperson.

This was, of course, a theoretical example; if you wish to use this tool on your team, you need to understand all the components of each element. You can go further into detail by analysing each person working on the project—for example, instead of having "Design Team", you would have "Name One", "Name Two", and so on—assigning to each one a numerical score, with the only catch that the sum of all the scores must be 100. I, however, highly suggest not to use this tool so "zoomed in", as it could create a sense of competition among your co-workers—someone would want to have more influence than the others.

Whatever type of analysis you conduct, note that you should keep it updated: dependencies, as well as interests and everything else, can change over time, so be on the lookout!

Also remember that there are countless different objectives: money, quality, reputation, social impact, experimental product, and many more: none of these is, of course, more important than the other; the important thing is that everybody on the boat is looking at the same objective.

BOX 5.1   THE TASK FOR THE STAKEHOLDER TOOL, DIFFERENT FROM OTHER TASKS IN THE BOOK BECAUSE IT IS NOT A SHORT-TERM ACTIVITY

STAKEHOLDERS TASK

For the Stakeholders, you don't have a short-term task; what I ask you to do, instead, is to, as soon as you get into a team, create either a Cartesian graph or a table as shown before, compiling them with the stakeholders you can spot and their interest, thinking about the possible problems that might emerge.

For this task, as you can tell, there won't be any confrontation with me, so I highly suggest you do this with someone, then compare your points of view to spot things the other person has missed.

SWOT ANALYSIS

The SWOT analysis comes from the marketing/business fields, as it consists in taking a project, a team, or a company and analysing four key elements: strengths (What does this project do well? What is your biggest pride?) weaknesses (What can you improve? What do people dislike about the project) opportunities (What actions can the project take to grow? What are you not taking enough advantage of?), and threats (What could harm you? What other games would the audience purchase instead of yours?).

How can we use it in game design? First of all, it's an analysis tool, therefore it's always good to have it in our tool belt; second, it allows your team to be on the same page while using the different points of view to identify the SWOTs of your game: it allows the perceived value—and possible problems—of the project to arise.

To use this tool, you need to take each one of the four macro groups, and analyse how your game is doing; let's say that, after a SWOT analysis, you find out your game has a lot of opportunities; you might think it's a great thing, but it's not necessarily that way. It could mean that your game has limiting time constraints that depend more on said opportunities than strengths: your game will sell only if it comes out in the time slice when said elements are trending, therefore you either need a project easy to make—even though nothing is ever really *easy*—or really good producers who can ship the game on time.

What if the game has, instead, many threats? This would mean that it might not have enough strengths, that the market is too saturated, or that it's too similar to the other games in that market chunk.

Too many weaknesses? The design is most likely flawed; the game won't work and it will fail.

No opportunities or threats? You are in an unexplored chunk of the market, meaning either a possible success or a niche too small for your game.

There are tons of these possibilities, and, if you combine them, there are tons more. No, you don't need to hypothesise every single possible outcome—again, we only have limited resources—but what you can do is, after discussing it with your team, think of what combinations apply the most to your game and decide if they represent a possible threat to the project; note that no combination is *good* or *bad*; they are just a lens to see your game with a more critical eye, allowing you to modify and fix the route before your ship crashes on an iceberg or lands on the wrong shore.

PERCEPTUAL MAPPING

This tool comes from the idea of taking two pairs of values—one the opposite of the other—and putting them on a Cartesian plane: for instance, cheap and expensive, realistic and fantasy; you can of course take elements from the Big Five or the quantic foundry model too, as well as any other model.

These values, however, shouldn't be random; they should come from the analysis of your competitors or the market you are trying to fit in: you can—and should—make multiple maps, each one testing different aspects of the market.

Let's say you are designing a racing game: first you analyse n competitors; then you identify common elements for the graph—realistic, simulative, multiplayer—with their opposites; now you create n Cartesian planes—depending on how in-depth you want to go, as always—with said elements—realistic/cartoon and simulative/arcade. Now you need to place each competitor in the plane, and beware that the position in the quadrant matters—if in the arcade simulative quadrant a game is near the centre, it's less arcade and realistic than a game on the edge.

What do you see now?

First, you see the market: where is it saturated? Where does it have a hole? Neither of those two means that you *must* do or not do a certain game; they are just guidelines: if there is a hole in the market, maybe it's because no one ever thought of that—which, let me tell you, is almost impossible—or maybe it's a market with low interest/a bad resulting combination—say, splatter and educative—but remember that this is just a tool; don't let it stop your he*art*.

Second, you see when your product is in a niche: once you design your game, you can gather the unique selling points of your competitors and create a perceptual map with it. Let's take, once again, a racing game: one of your competitors has damages to vehicles, the other has weapons, one other has transformations that allow you to go underwater or in the sky—where are you located? Maybe you do have weapons but also a feature to sabotage other players' vehicles before the race: none of your competitors has it, so you just found a unique selling point—or USP for short. Your game now fills a hole in the market where no other game is present or, on the opposite, you are in a cluster with too many games so you need to change your design. The more maps you create, the more accurate your analysis will be—but, as always, the more time and resources it will require.

PROBLEM VS NEED

There will always be unexpected events during the production, some of which, if not treated right, will become a source of stress: maybe you didn't understand its true cause—thus you didn't use the 9 Whys technique—or maybe you mistook a problem for a need, or vice versa.

A problem is an event that rises in an already existing structure, which doesn't need a substantial change to said structure to be fixed but only a patch—you need to understand the source of the problem and then act on that. A problem is like having a headache: it comes from yourself, and once you know it's there, you either relax for a while or take a medicine to make it go away; there are, however, different types of headaches, and the same medicine might not work for all of them: you need to understand what type it is, what caused it, and how to prevent it from coming back.

A need is, instead, an event that can't be solved by adding something but that rather needs the creation of a special structure to be satisfied—you may need to rethink the previous structure from the foundations. This is like a broken bone: you can't just pretend it's not there—it wouldn't let you do your normal activities—and you can't put a Band-Aid on top of it—it would have no effect; you need a plaster cast to keep the bones in place, as they take their time to heal—therefore, you need a new structure.

One of the most common mistakes you can do early in your career—and later too, if you don't learn from them—is mistaking a problem for a need and a need for a problem: while it may seem that you fixed the issue at first, you will soon see that the patch you put on isn't going to last: it's like fixing a hole in a water pipe with some tape; while it works for a bit, eventually it will fall off.

Let me tell you about what happened in *Tom Clancy's The Division*: at the start of the game, you need to go through a door to receive a mission from an NPC; some players found out that, since the collisions between players were active, they could block the door to prevent other players from entering—these were, of course, trolls, who liked to ruin other players' experiences. At first, the team thought this was a problem, so they made bigger doors: it worked for a bit, until players started standing in a row to cover the whole bigger door, and, again, block the way for other players.

The solution, as they then discovered, was to disable the physical interactions to rethink that tutorial area; why did all of this happen? The first was a decision made out of panic—Ubisoft has no fault, they had to think about a solution easy to implement in a short amount of time—but once you see the problem without said panic, you understand that it's a need: the players needed a safe space where they wouldn't be interrupted by other players as they went through their journey.

Said this way it looks pretty easy, but there is no mathematical way to tell if an issue is a problem or a need; there is, however, a question you can ask yourself—and your team—to have a hint about which one of the two your situation is in: "If we change the structure, does my problem get fixed? Or do we need a new structure?"

Think about having 1,000 instances to solve, instead of just one, for example "What happens if we have 1000 trolls blocking the doors?"; by doing so, you can use your—and your team's—critical and analytical eye to understand when you have a problem—and when you have a need—before trying to solve it.

Another way to understand if something is a problem or a need is understanding which of these categories it falls into:

Simple: can be solved by using already existing structures.
Complicated: it requires you to implement a structure already used in another game but more complicated from a design and/or technical point of view.
Complex: you have no way of knowing if the solution you thought of will work.
Chaotic: you are trying to fix a problem, but there is a problem prior to that preventing you from fixing it.

Usually, therefore not always, the first two are problems—they arise by themselves—while the last two are needs—there are elements arising from the inside, connected to other elements too in the last case.

SECTION THREE

Game Design Tools

Introduction to Game Design Tools

6

This chapter is the most important part of your journey, the one I'm sure you've been waiting for the most, the one where you will find the tools to be a professional game designer. Why *professional*? Because a book, a course, or a university can't make you a *good* designer—to become good, you need to practise—but it can, partially, teach you how to be ready for your next job or project. This is also the reason why this part, while being the core of the book, wasn't put as the first: the first chapter—the introduction—was meant to let you understand how important being a professional figure is, introducing you to the production of games rather than pure game design theory—this doesn't mean that is not important; it means that the theory is a part of the bigger picture. Later chapters talk about a key element of our job, the analysis: before every great design comes a great analysis—and not just in game design but in any development process; take a look at Figure 6.1—as, if you want to make a commercial game, you need to find and use the right data to both support it and guide it. For example, before you decide the key mapping for your game, you need a study on the dominant design to understand if that works for you, and, if it doesn't, you need the data to guide you into a new set of key binding.

So, to sum it up, the order of the chapters of this book follows the same steps of the production; while some names can be different, the content of each step is the same.

BOX 6.1 A DEFINITION OF DOMINANT DESIGN

Dominant design can be defined as the predominant answer set by other games in the market: when playing an FPS game you have never tried, you know that the key to jump is the spacebar; you didn't read any instruction or watch any tutorial, you just knew. Are you a genius? Not really, you took pressing the spacebar to jump for granted, since you are used to it. The designers of the said game asked themselves "how do we make the player jump?" and, by checking which key other similar games used, they found out spacebar was the most used one.

This is useful for two reasons: first, you set a coherence between multiple games, and second, you allow a smooth beginning for the players; they don't need to learn *your* keys, meaning that as they start playing the game, they feel like they already know how to do something—thus they are more likely to play it.

DOI: 10.1201/9781003229438-9

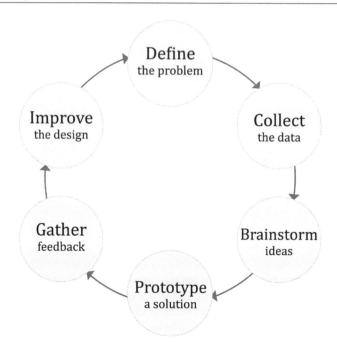

FIGURE 6.1   A picture showing the process of designing a new product or service, used in many fields other than game design.

Source: Author.

Now, what if you skipped the previous chapters to jump right into this one? I mean, after all this book should be about game design, that's what we are all here for. On the other hand, though, I'm sure you would never skip two whole chapters; that would be rude, right? Let's say, for a second, you *did* skip a chapter—again, we both know you would never do that—well, my best advice, both as a designer and as a colleague, would be to go back and read whatever you missed: if you trust me enough to purchase this book to let me teach you game design, you should trust me enough to follow the order I had in mind, so close this chapter and go read the ones you missed.

Now that *everybody*—I'm not looking at you—has read the first two chapters, we can proceed with one of the first things I teach my students, right on the first few days of lectures.

DEMOLISHING THE CREATIVITY MYTH

Being *a* Creative

In this world, there is a small group of people who are blessed with creativity, who don't need to rack their brains to come up with great ideas; all the other people, the ones not in this group, will never be on their level, no matter how hard they work.

Right? Wrong.

There is no magical group of creative people; we are all on the same boat: sure, some people see the world in a more creative way than others do, but this does not mean that anything you have read in the previous phrase is true; it's not the creativity you have when you were born that makes you a great designer—or, in general, a great creative person—it's the one that you develop and practice over time, the experiences you live: no one is born creative, what makes us creative is the differences we face, the culture we live in, and everything that affects our life. Once you are exposed to something new, you start seeing things differently, like "unlocking" a new colour: the world is exactly the same; your vision is what changed. You can train yourself to have a broader view simply by living: read books, travel, meet new people, and do all the things that can affect your life; if it changes you as a person, it surely changes your point of view.

Sure, maybe some were better than others when they started—they have lived wider experiences—but remember that hard work always beats an advantage you have when you start: if you rely too much on that advantage, without feeding your skill as you should, you will eventually fall behind.

We—as game designers—however, are creative on cue; let me explain: being creative is not about having a great idea once every ten months, it's about having as many valid ideas as possible when you are asked to do so; note that I said *valid*, not *creative*: we need to have ideas that could work, not ones that completely change the world.

Let's face it, most of the things that could have been thought have already been thought, therefore it's hard for us to invent something; what we can do, however, is take one already existing thing and mix it with an already existing context but not the one they were intended to be in. Let's say I pitch a game where you play as a blender in space, you need to blend some objects scattered but you can't because there is no gravity, so you need to find a way to fix this. Is this *creative*? Not at all, I didn't create either a blender or the space; they already existed. Is it original, though? Maybe, as I've never seen such a game around, and maybe it is good for us—it means you have something to work on. Sure, it will need to be improved—for example, how do you move in space? How do you fit objects in the blender?—but it's already an idea.

Now, there is a difference between people who are creative for a hobby and people who are creative for a living, and that is the amount of output they generate and the goal of each created idea: a creative for hobby likes unique and strange ideas that work for a small group and only has ideas when they come to him. A "professional creative" doesn't wait for ideas; they seek them, and their goal isn't to obtain something new but something that solves the problem they were called for.

Does this mean that the most creative idea can't be the most valid one? Of course not; it can happen, but it most likely won't.

I know you might be a bit confused right now, so here's an example to break it down a bit: the smartphone is one of the most revolutionary ideas we had in the last decades—we can all agree on that—but it's not a creative idea: it's a clock, combined with a phone, combined with a calculator, combined with a computer, and so on. Not one of these elements is new or creative to solve problems, but their combination is valid—meaning, it works great.

From now on, I want you to think of creativity not as *creating* something new but as *combining* existing elements in a way no one did before.

Does this mean that if I take some random objects and put them together I'm a creative person? Yes and no: while you may obtain a valid option, combining objects without criteria is more like gambling than creating; to know which objects you should put together you need analysis and data: with the right research, you know in advance which of the thousands of possible combinations will not work and which, on the other hand, will be valid—and this is also why the analysis tools are located before this chapter.

There are now two types of readers: the first one, the one who doesn't feel creative at all, in despair thinking they will never be creative; the second one, the one who feels creative, thinking they are already good to go.

They are both wrong, and there is actually a third type of reader: the one who, no matter their actual level of creativity, wants to improve—and this leads me to my next point.

Creativity, like everything else in the human mind, can be trained and improved: while there aren't physical exercises that I know of, there are much more useful steps you can follow: go see new places, read new books, live as a different culture, do things you are too scared to do, ask yourself the 9 Whys for everything you don't understand; each one of these technologies will expand your creativity because it will change—even if just a bit—the way you see the world.

Another way to improve your creativity is by forcing you to come up with ideas: take a problem, give yourself one hour, and come up with 50 possible solutions for the said problem; the first times most of your ideas won't be valid, maybe you won't even have 50—and that's completely fine, it's part of the learning process—but, time after time, you will have more ideas and, most of all, more valid ones.

Being *the* Creative

Another common idea—a wrong idea—is that only the designing team can add creative value to a product: a programmer—during brainstorming or even just when talking to other team members—has an idea but doesn't pitch it to the team because he is not *the creative*; this is completely wrong: a good designer isn't just someone with good ideas; a good designer is someone who sees the creative value in everything—and everyone—around them.

While I was working on a game, the best idea actually came from a programmer: we listened, studied, and implemented his idea, and it became one of the core mechanics of the game. Of course, the design team still had to do its job: do the research, adapt the original idea to fit in with the game, and fix it when needed, but it's the exact same process it would have done with an idea coming from a game designer.

Before you go out asking the janitor, your neighbour, or a friend to find the perfect idea, however, you need to prepare yourself to also tell them it doesn't work: a designer needs to come up with 50 ideas, but they also need to listen to all the ideas around them and be able to understand which can work and which just won't—listen to anyone, but don't say *yes* to everyone.

Once you gather tons of possibilities, the design team needs to choose the best one for the game, no matter if it comes from the "creative team" or not—like parents with our babies, we need to do what's best for them, putting our ego aside.

This said, you have everything you need to know to face this part of your journey: it's probably going to be the hardest one, I'm not going to lie, but it sure is the one you came here for. If you ever get lost, don't worry, as you can always retrace your steps to the point where you got lost and try again from there.

Brainstorming Techniques

7

As you know, a good designer needs to have ideas when they're asked to, and while creativity sounds impossible to control, there are some techniques to help your team—the people in a creative role—come up with as many ideas as possible: not the best, just many, as you can then choose which ones to use and which ones to discard.

In every brainstorming you will have, there are five golden rules that need to be always respected:

1 The objective of the brainstorming needs to be crystal clear to everyone.
2 Everyone needs to feel free to say their ideas, without being judged or made fun of: there are no stupid, wrong, or brilliant ideas, even if your inner voice tells you otherwise. While it's hard to shut that voice up, you can't, for any reason, let it out. Always remember that the first phase is aimed at obtaining ideas, not having a working mental prototype right away.
3 The brainstorming needs to have the right amount of time: don't expect your team to generate 1,000 ideas in 10 minutes—that's just not going to happen.
4 The group needs to be as diversified as possible: the higher the diversity, the better; this includes—but is not limited to—diversity of gender, culture, roles, and anything that can broaden your point of view.
5 Your team needs some breaks: if the brainstorming session lasts three hours, people are going to be tired and have their minds killing them. Take a break when the members are starting to feel drained: let them go to the bathroom, have a smoke, scroll on their phones, or whatever they need to take their mind off the task for a moment. Note that, in these breaks, you can't work on something else: to work well, you need not to work for a moment.

LIMITATION

The limitation technique is one of the most common ones, but this doesn't mean it's any less valid than the other—if it's so used, it means it works. It is based on the concept that limits help us be more creative, thinking outside of the box or just from a different point of view: in this technique, in fact, you need to impose extreme limits on the problem you are trying to solve, limits that you would never put in the final game.

DOI: 10.1201/9781003229438-10

For example, in *Red Dead Redemption 2*, there are different types of ammo—each one has its bonuses—but the majority of players either didn't know about those variations or just didn't use them, as they felt those weren't so important or needed. Let's pretend we are still in the developing process of the game, and we see playtesters only use the basic ammo, what do we do?

First, during a brainstorming dedicated to this problem, we add extremely constraining limits that force the players into using the different types of bullets: you can only use one weapon, therefore you will eventually need to switch bullet types for different purposes or because you ran out of the basic ones; certain enemies don't take damage from certain bullets types; in specific areas of the map, only specific types of ammo are sold in the shops; and so on.

We can all agree that these limitations are too tight—they would ruin the experience for the players—but the second step consists in toning down said limits, to have a restraint that, while making the player follow our design, can actually increase the depth of the experience: certain shops sell discounted secondary ammo, some enemies take a lot more damage from a specific ammo type, guns have less basic bullets so that, to keep using your favourite weapon, you need to switch the ammo type.

Those are limitations that generate gameplay and aren't too much of a burden for the player: you can still only use the basic bullets, but, if you follow the game's golden path, you spend less money, deal more damage, and so on.

The strength of this technique is exactly this: creating impossible limitations to then find the sweet spot where the limitation isn't a problem but a feature of the game.

OPPOSITE DESIGN

This technique finds its core in the Yin and Yang theory: you take two opposite elements that have nothing to do with each other, merge them together, and see the outcome. First, you start with the problem: in this case, the problem is the lack of ideas for a new game, so you find the game that is the exact opposite of what you have so far—or what you wish your game to be like. Once you've done that, you mix the elements of each game and have a result that probably is something new.

This result isn't what your game should be like, as this is just a tool to find new elements that you couldn't think of before, also because, in most cases, the resulting combination is something that just doesn't work for most games.

One of the biggest innovations in the gaming industry was adding RPG elements in shooter games, which are opposite to each other; one day, someone decided to merge the RPG preparation phase into FPS games and completely changed the genre. This doesn't work only for FPS: *FIFA*, for example, went from focusing on the characters' skills to focusing on each in-game players' stats.

For example—note that this is a simplified version of the process, when doing it with your team you should go as in-depth as you need: say you want to design a game similar to *The Medium*.

The Medium game qualities are single-player, horror, realistic graphics, strong narrative, single-player split-screen.

Now, single-player split-screen doesn't have an opposite because it's a unique selling point, but the opposite of the rest would be: multiplayer, cosy/wholesome, create your own story, non-realistic graphics.

The first three games that come to my mind are *Animal Crossing*, *Stardew Valley*, and *The Sims*.

BOX 7.1   AN OVERVIEW OF GAME QUALITIES ACCORDING TO BRENDA ROMERO AND IAN SCHREIBER

Game Qualities, according to Brenda Romero and Ian Schreiber's framework, are the atomic elements that compose your game. Imagine you are telling your friends about a game you are working on: is it a first-person shooter or maybe a third-person shooter? PvP, PvE, or both? Is it multiplayer? And so on. Basically, any ground information your game relies on, from gameplay to graphics, from a technical to an artistic point of view. With a list of those elements, you need to let them picture an image of your game, without even seeing it—they will get some things wrong, but the core should be clear.

Now that we have three opposite games—you can, of course, find more, depending on your needs and resources—it's time to move to the second phase: the mixing; for this example, we are going to look at only one combination of games. Remember that the goal isn't to make a good game but rather to find new and unexplored ideas—as we've seen before, new ideas just mean a never-tested combination of already existing ideas.

What game would *The Medium* and *Animal Crossing* make together?

The core of this hypothetical game can be summarised in: build your own world, multiplayer, and a *Doki Doki Literature Club*-like narrative;

The game would be divided into two phases:

In the first one, single-player, you get inside people's minds, in a horror setting and mood: you need to help the real them, shown in a realistic graphic, escape the feeling and fears that torment them to gather resources.

In the second phase, multiplayer, you use the resources to make your mind as scary as possible, so that other players don't want to spend time there, in a cartoonish and cute graphic.

Would this game be good? Probably not, but it makes interesting ideas arise: a positive and light narrative from outside that gets scary the more you dive into it; Two different styles combined to highlight the negative parts; collecting resources by navigating others' minds. Are all of these options valid? It depends on the problem you wanted to solve, but, while your team had no ideas before, now it has some elements to consider just by mixing two games—think of how many and strange combinations you can get with more games and more detailed combinations. If we mixed *The Medium* with *Stardew Valley*, we would have gotten completely different ideas—maybe better, maybe worse, but we surely wouldn't have had these ones.

Now, I don't want you to think that smashing two elements together will make you change videogames forever, just like that: these opposite elements need to be fitted together perfectly, by removing a bit of the first, changing something in the second, re-thinking the outcome, and so on. Just like games, new genres aren't born perfect: they come from an idea, which is then tested, fixed, and changed countless times before becoming the perfect fit that you experience as a player.

WORST IDEA

Similarly to the limitation technique, the worst idea is based less on pure creativity and more on submitting as many solutions as possible; in this case, however, the goal isn't to find the right solution but the worst one—not just a *bad* solution: the *worst*.

First of all, what am I even talking about? Yes, this is a real technique, and it really works in the right situation: if you can't come up with good ideas, let the bad ones out, trying to get worse with any new solution your team thinks of. The players don't notice when they get hit in our new FPS? Let's play an extremely loud noise in their ears! What's worse than that? Create a device that pinches the players when they get shot; even worse, every time they get hit, $1 is taken from their bank accounts—imagine paying $1 for each bullet you take in an FPS game; it would be the most expensive game ever, but you would have a strong reason to get good at it.

Now that all the terrible ideas are on the table, take a look at each one asking your team "What happens if we remove the terrible part?" and see what you are left with: hurting a player is terrible, but what if the controller vibrates with each bullet you take? The solution is very different, but the original concept is still to physically communicate to the player the incoming damage.

This technique works really well when your team is frustrated or tired, as suggesting terrible ideas can be liberating and hilarious; it also works with new entries in the team who don't feel comfortable sharing their opinion—remember that everyone can have the idea you need, so try to help them speak up.

DIFFUSE MODE

Let's start this method with a premise: this isn't an actual method; the diffuse mode is a mental state that we live while half asleep—but that can be reached in different ways too—which doesn't let the mind be limited by your usual constraints, allowing ideas to flow with more freedom—it's like removing certain filters your mind sets on its own. Limits aren't bad, don't get me wrong, they help us save a lot of time—when coming from our gut feeling—but they can be too tight as if the mind is scared of erring or creating something nonsense—these are the ones removed while in diffuse mode: errors or nonsense ideas don't exist.

This "technique" is often used by artists, and there are many ways to access the diffuse mode: Salvador Dalí, to let his ideas come out of his mind, used to grab two marbles in the palm of his hand, sit on a chair, and try to sleep. When he fell asleep, the hand's muscles would release, the marbles would fall to the ground, and the outcoming noise would wake him up: at this moment, his mind was still half asleep, allowing him, according to him, to have more creative and free ideas.

Now, this doesn't mean you have to replicate the exact same process every time you need a solution, as there are easier ways to enter this state: taking a shower, the moment after a workout, and generally anything that includes a physical exercise also work; in these moments, our brain is relaxed—it's either doing something automatic or it was focusing on the muscles moments before—and it enters the diffuse state.

The first time you will probably fail—especially if you think precisely about what you are doing, so don't have high hopes about it—because our brain works in three modes:

Zombie mode: when we do something automatically, our brain isn't thinking about the actions, allowing it to save calories or to let us think about something else.

Focus mode: this happens when doing something that requires our active attention, either because it's something new or because it presents a danger—walking in a foreign city, cutting with a sharp knife, solving a mathematical problem. In this mode, we are more aware of everything, and we have more control, but it makes us tired after some time—our brain is working nonstop.

Diffused mode: while asleep or while being altered by specific substances that change one's perception of their surroundings, our brain thinks in this mode, where no limits—either about the world or ourselves—exist, no common rules or prejudice blocking your mind. This can be considered a "creative" state because rules don't apply, so your brain isn't afraid of thinking outside of the box.

Ideally, when facing a problem you can't solve, you should enter the diffuse mode to see the situation differently and come up with an idea you would have never thought of in focus mode—and neither in zombie mode, as this can only give you ideas you already had.

My best advice is to try as many possible techniques as you can think of and then stick to the one that suits you the most—there is also room for improvement, as you can "train" your brain to enter this state after a specific event, like showering.

Once you are in this mode, you can go back to the problem you were facing with a different point of view, not limited to what *should* be done but rather thinking about what *can* be done.

Also remember that sometimes, when facing a hard problem, taking a break from it and coming again with a fresh mind can let you have different ideas: if you think about it for eight hours straight, you are limiting yourself to what you can think of in that environment, but if you go take a walk, watch a movie or play something, you are exposing your mind to different inputs—as we've said, being creative is all about combining things that you would never think about.

BREAK THE THEME

This technique allows you to find new ideas by changing what defines something as we perceive it—it's easier than it sounds. Let me explain: first, you need to understand what pillars a concept is composed of—for example, a restaurant: a restaurant is a physical place where you pay to eat, there is either a menu or a buffet, there is a cook in the kitchen, and so on. "How many of these pillars do I need?" you ask. As always, the more the better, but be careful with the time it takes.

Once you have your pillars—the defining elements of the concept—you need to break some of them—you can choose randomly or select a subgroup—so, let's say our restaurant wouldn't have a cook and you don't pay to eat, but you would still have a menu, and it would still be a physical place. Now, we just create some holes in the structure of our concept, so we need to fix them with ideas; these, however, can just be the opposite of what we took out: if there is no cook, the customers cook for themselves; you don't pay to eat, but you pay for the bills and the raw material you use.

A typical dinner in this restaurant would be something like the following: you enter, sit at a table, choose a dish from the menu, the waiter takes you to the kitchen, you cook your meal, go back to your table and eat it, pay for the gas/electricity/food you used, and leave! We just created a new business model, something similar to laundry, but for food. Would it make us rich? Probably not, but certain aspects—maybe the "cook your meal" part—can work, and, most of all, we just discovered a new way of seeing something old.

The goal isn't creating something perfect—the answer isn't this strange restaurant—the goal is finding new pillars that have nothing to do with the original structure, and to create those pillars you need to break some of the old ones—otherwise there just wouldn't be space.

ACTING BRAINSTORMING

Differently from the previous methods where you need a solution for a specific problem, this is more based on pure creativity: each person picks a famous character—real or fictional—that is known by the other people in the brainstorming and that is well known by the person picking it.

Once everyone has their character, you need to check that no two people picked the same character and, if that happens, either one person or both people change character.

Before starting with the brainstorming, the team has a few minutes of chit-chatting, both to enter the diffuse mode and to overcome the shyness coming from acting—just like real actors on stage for the first time: and just like actors, everyone needs to behave—*act*—as their character, until they forget they are not actually that character. When the team is comfortable—meaning they don't need to stop and think about their answers to fit the character, but they come naturally—the brainstorming can start.

The brainstorming phase itself is exactly like any other brainstorming, meaning you discuss a problem and suggest the solutions that come to your mind—it doesn't matter if the solutions are impossible or nonsense; you'll take care of that later. Let's say I'm Batman; my first suggestion—since I'm rich—is to hire 1,000 people to do the job for us. Is it realistic? Not at all, but it's an idea we wouldn't have thought of otherwise.

As you reach a number of ideas that satisfy the team, everyone has to "leave" the character and go back to being themselves—it's extremely important to have a break to let people stop acting, or they will keep seeing the ideas as their character.

Now, your team is back to being itself, and you have some nonsense and impossible ideas, and that's great: one suggestion at a time, you take out the impossible part of the idea, and what you are left can actually be useful; Batman's "hire 1,000 people" idea doesn't work, but what about hiring a consultant? Maybe that works for us.

Why does this work, though? Because when you become someone else, you also change your point of view: Batman thinks in a physical and monetary way, Albert Einstein would think about the physics behind the game, and so on.

As always, the more ideas the team has during the acting phase—and the more diverse the characters are—the more possibilities of finding good ground to start from there are but the more time it will take to analyse each idea.

TRIZ

This specific technique needs a short introduction: the TRIZ, also known as TRIP (translated from Russian as *theory of inventive problem solving*) is a problem-solving, analysis, and forecasting tool invented by the Soviet inventor Genrich Altshuller in 1946. At the time, people couldn't search for a solution online when having a problem with a machine; they needed to have the necessary knowledge of both physics and the machine itself to understand what the cause of the problem was and how to fix it; as you can imagine, this process would require a tremendous amount of time even for a technician.

To improve the needed time and knowledge of this process, Altshuller and his team did research on problem formulation, problem-solving, failure/system analysis, and patterns of systemic evolution, and this research produced three main results:

First, problems and solutions are repeated across industries and sciences—they might have different names, but the theory behind the cause is the same.

Second, patterns of technical evolution are repeated across industries and sciences as well.

Third, the innovation used scientific effects outside the field in which they were developed.

Basically, every problem and solution coming from a field happens in many other fields; therefore, if you gain enough data, you can create a macro matrix containing every problem and every solution—put in a simple way. Researchers found out that every virtually possible problem could be traced back to the combination of two of 40 inventive principles: for example, a problem showing loss of time (number 25) and productivity (number 39) can be caused by stability of the object (number 13), loss of substance (number 23), or durability of moving object (number 15); this doesn't mean that your problem is exactly one of those three—this isn't a magic eight ball—but the physical cause of the said problem is the evolution of a situation created by one of the results.

Now, what does a 50-year-old Russian matrix have to do with game design? It actually has two purposes:

First, you can literally use the original TRIZ, because every design problem can be generalised as an engineering problem. Once you have the engineering solution, you use it as a starting point for you to understand its game design translation to obtain the cause of your problem—for example, "Ease of operation" (number 33) can be considered as the affordance of a mechanic. Of course, some numbers won't apply directly, but, again, this is just a tool to think of possible causes you weren't aware of. This way of using the TRIZ is great if you are brainstorming by yourself, as it is mostly based on physical aspects that need to be combined; this is one of the strengths of the TRIZ, as it's the only technique in this book—and one of the few out there—that works perfectly to brainstorm alone.

The second way of using the TRIZ, for group brainstorming, is by replacing the TRIZ itself with a game pattern and using the exact same thought process. A list of game patterns can be found on *gdp3*:[1] this site, created by Staffan Björk, is a wiki—meaning it's constantly updated—used to identify and list every gameplay element found in a game—just like the TRIZ but specifically for games.

Let's say we are designing a multiplayer game; we can look at the multiplayer game page[2] and see how different gameplay elements are combined: multiplayer and late arriving players need summary updates meaning downtime for other players, multiplayer and AI games simulate other players allowing a player to play alone, and so on.

The idea is either to "scan" for other games, find one similar to yours and see how they solved a problem you are facing or to see each problem as a pattern and use this wiki to find the relationships with other patterns Again, this doesn't give you the solution; it gives you a starting point for you and your team to come up with a fix you wouldn't have thought of before.

This, among all the techniques, is one of the hardest to learn because of its mechanic component, but it's just as valid as the other ones; last, just because it *is* mechanic— it impartially is—it's not any less creative: creativity is the ability to combine two or more elements you normally would not think of together, and the TRIZ allows you to do exactly that.

NOTES

1 *GDP3*: http://virt10.itu.chalmers.se/index.php/Main_Page
2 *Multiplayer Games*: http://virt10.itu.chalmers.se/index.php/Multiplayer_Games

Praxeology

8

When talking about game design, it's hard to find a definition—as we've seen in the previous chapters; for me, it's the architect of choices: a game is a right balance among freedom, agency, limits set by the enforcer (take a look at the enforcer box to understand what it is), and much more. This subject borrows elements from many other subjects: sociology lets us understand how groups of people make their choices; psychology studies the human mind—thus the players' mind—partially setting our behaviour, and there are plenty more that we'll talk about. game design, however, isn't any of these topics, as it has a different objective: our goal is to generate emotions for our players—after all, you play a game to feel something specific, that being immersion in a story or adrenaline through explosions. We are like leeches, sucking knowledge from other fields that are working for their own goals—we don't share the goals, only the knowledge—and we don't care if a theory comes from psychology or sociology; as long as it works for us we'll just borrow it and apply it to the design of our game. I know it sounds bad to put it this way, but it really isn't: we rely on existing and more expert people in their field rather than creating every theory from scratch, and, if we didn't, it would take ages to make a single game, as we would have to formulate a theory, test it, and fix it multiple times for one single element we want in our game—why would you reinvent the wheel if it already exists?

Think of how a cook sees an oven: it's a tool you set with the right values, where you put in the right elements, and your outcome is the desired recipe; sure, an oven is a tool with thousands of years of evolution—from bonfires to the stone one, from gas to electric—with an amazing story and engineering, but is any of this useful to a person who wants to bake a cake? Not at all: if you had to learn everything about ovens before using them no one would bake anymore, for a cook it's just a tool to get the desired outcome.

The same goes for us game designers: sure, we need to understand the fundamentals of a theory to properly apply it, but if we spent our time studying its story and the details of why it works, we wouldn't have time to design games—you wouldn't go to a restaurant to learn the story of pans, you go there to eat.

BOX 8.1   A DEFINITION OF THE ENFORCER AND THE ROLE IT PLAYS IN GAMES

The enforcer is anything—or anyone—who imposes the game rules and makes sure they are followed: in a board game, let's say, *Monopoly*, the enforcer is the person who stops you from stealing money from the bank. In a digital game, the enforcer is

DOI: 10.1201/9781003229438-11

the game itself: if a rule says "you can't drive cars in this part of the map", you won't be able to drive cars in that part of the map. It's not like the police stopping you from doing something illegal; it's more like a physical rule, not allowing certain actions to happen. An example is the no-PVP areas in MMORPG games: if the game tells you that you can't deal damage to other players in a certain location, you just won't be able to—even if you cast an attack, it will deal no damage.

This part focuses on the role of a game designer, how to gather data correctly, and the techniques to apply in the design phase: after the brainstorming, you have a concept—either for a game or a solution—therefore an idea, but this idea still needs to be defined—we need to find its identity—with the design techniques. For the way I see it, it's like a tabletop zen garden: you can create whatever drawing you want on the sand; the result is already there somewhere, but you need to bring it out by moving the sand in the right way; just as a zen garden, if you are not satisfied by the result, you can shake it to bring the sand back to its original state, with the knowledge of what worked and what didn't in the previous tries.

Some of these techniques are more suitable for defining the initial concept, others for specific problems, finding weak links in your design, for narrative purposes, and so on. As always, they need to be applied at the right time—remember: the right tool for the right job—and you don't need to learn them all perfectly: my advice is to learn how they work, test them, and see which one you work better with. One day you may come across a problem that requires a specific technique, so you'll grab this book and read more carefully how it works.

BOX 8.2   A DISCLAIMER ABOUT ETHICS AND MISUSE OF DESIGN TECHNIQUES BEFORE ENTERING THE TOPIC

The design techniques are usually based on psychological manipulation and are therefore in a grey area ethically speaking: they touch certain buttons in our mind connected to chemical reactions in the brain or primal instincts we can't control. They can be used with good intentions—our case, to deliver the best possible experience—or shady intentions. It's just like a knife: it can be used to cut a cake, save someone's life, or kill; the knife itself has no guilt, it's all about how it is used.

Since this book has the highest respect for you and your understanding, I will cover all those techniques, and it will be up to you how to use them; I can only hope you use them wisely.

I found out about praxeology one random night at 2 AM, one of those nights where you browse through the recommended videos on YouTube and end up in the rabbit hole: I had no idea what the video was about at first, but the more I watched it, the more I felt like it was talking about game design. Sure, it had a different name and was invented way before videogames, but the theory supporting it was extremely similar to what game design is built on; they just were applying it to the wrong environment: it couldn't work in reality, but it works perfectly in videogames—I'll get to that in a second.

The word *praxeology* comes from Greek's *praxis*—meaning deed, or intention—and *logia*—study of—therefore, praxeology is the study of humans' intention. The word was first coined by Clemens Timpler, but it had a different meaning back then, as today's conception of praxeology comes from Alfred V. Espinas, French philosopher and sociologist: praxeology is the study of deliberated human actions, meaning it focuses on purposeful actions rather than reflexive and unintentional ones.

Praxeology took a bit of a weird path: it comes from a sociologist; it's widely used in economic theories—especially thanks to Ludwig von Mises, Austrian economist and historian—and, now, it's used in game design. Even the conception of this topic depends on who you ask: Arnold Kaufman, a French engineer, saw praxeology as a framework used to understand humans' choices, Collins saw it as the deductive study of human actions, while, for us, it's a tool to better understand and manipulate players—don't worry, I'm not trying to give you a historical lecture, I just want you to see how wide its uses are.

Now, praxeology is an extremely vast topic: it's composed by the disclose theory—focused on human actions—and the economic side; I'm not going to cover this last part, not because it's not important but because it's a lot closer to Game Economy Design than this book is, and it could be a whole other book by itself. Instead, I am going to cover the discourse theory, since it can be applied to any game and any design; before we dive into that, however, I need to open a small parenthesis: praxeology, when applied to game design, is an extremely powerful resource, but before you think about using it in "real life"—meaning outside the design world—just know that it doesn't work, the same way videogame rules don't work in life—you can try to double-jump as much as you want; it's just not going to happen, *sadly*.

Now that you know some background information about praxeology, let's take a look at when you should use it: the situations that make the most out of this tool are the development of a concept—after the brainstorming phase to understand how said the concept should work—or at the end of a production cycle—when you need to analyse a product from a behavioural point of view—since, if your design isn't working, there is a behavioural problem: for example, if your players don't feel motivated enough to act toward the goal you planned, they are going to drop the game; before panicking and throwing all your design in the garbage, just know that it happens, and praxeology may be just the right tool for you.

Praxeology divides human behaviour into a series of axioms—this being truths that guide the human mind; since each axiom plays an important role, be sure to read it as many times as needed, or, if you are more interested, I encourage you to read articles, watch videos, and find material about it—you might just discover something I missed.

FIRST AXIOM

The first praxeology axiom states the following: *human action is purposeful behaviour.*

The human action can be divided into two parts: reactive actions and purposeful actions:

> Reactive actions are instinctive; we generally don't think about the action before doing it, we just do it—for example taking your hand off of something hot,

sneezing, breathing, our heartbeat, and so on. This part is not covered by prax-eology, not because it doesn't exist but because those are actions we have little to no control over—you don't try to make clouds disappear when it's rainy, you just take an umbrella.

What about *purposeful* actions? Those are our actions taken for preferences, desires, or objectives we want to achieve, and there are four subtypes of them: inactivity—the act of not doing something is an action by itself—choosing—thinking about an action is an action—acting—doing something toward an objective—and, last, complaining—just as with inactivity and choosing, it's an action you choose to do. If you ask yourself "what am I doing?" and the answer falls in one of these four categories, you are performing a purposeful action—even if in a subconscious way.

This is extremely helpful to game design because each action performed by the player belongs to the gameplay, and gameplay can be divided into three types:

Active gameplay: the player looks for gameplay situations, like in a walking simu-lator where nothing happens if the player doesn't progress.
Planned gameplay: this is self-explanatory and is especially seen in games like Sid Meier's *Civilization* saga, or the *Mario + Rabbids* one.

Reactive gameplay: events happen, and the gameplay mostly comes from how you react to said happenings, such as in action games.

BOX 8.3   A CLARIFICATION ABOUT REACTIVE AND PURPOSEFUL ACTIONS IN SITUATIONS WHERE THEY MIGHT LOOK THE SAME

You may be thinking "you said I shouldn't care about reactive actions, so I can ignore reactive gameplay", but reactive gameplay isn't really *reactive*; let me explain with three questions:

When playing an FPS game, how can you dodge enemies' bullets? You crouch, right.
The first time you played/saw an FPS game, did you think about crouching to dodge? No, because you didn't know you could do it, so it would have made no sense to you.
So, when playing an FPS game, why do you crouch to dodge? Because the purpose of dodging is to stay alive: you performed this action so many times that you don't even need to think about it—you just do it, *as if* it was a reaction—but, every single time, you did it with a purpose.

This means that reactive gameplay isn't reactive for praxeology, it's just a really fast—almost subconscious—purposeful action that you choose to do and, as such, we can manipulate it too.

Since every action is part of the gameplay, it can be seen as a series of choices made by the player: from small and easy ones—like the colour of their hat—to harder and more impactful ones—would you save your companion dog or your strongest weapon you spent hundreds of hours to get? In game design, this is called *agency*, meaning the balance between the perceived freedom of choices a player has while playing a game and the control a player has over said choices—knowing what choice the player is making, the reason for that choice, and the consequences; as designers, we are constantly juggling to maintain the right balance between not giving enough choices and giving too many: if the players have too few choices, they won't feel in control—it will feel more like watching a movie than playing a game—but if they have too many choices, they will be overwhelmed—this is called the paradox of choice: the more you have, the harder it is to choose.

Seeing the game world through the first axiom allows us to see agency from a new perspective: since reactive actions aren't really reactive—as, even if you don't realise it, every action you take in a game was once learned and is now part of your thought process—we have the power to control each one of the four types of action the players face: not acting, choosing how to act, acting itself, and complaining, giving us a new lens to see the interactions between the game and the players.

This axiom is also useful to understand how we are making the players learn to do what we want them to do but making it feel like it's their choice and, most of all, not making it a reactive one.

Reactive actions should be pretty clear by now, but what do I mean by "making it feel like it's their choice"? If I ask you to choose between $10,000 and literally nothing, it's obvious which one you are going to pick; I'm not saying you didn't have a choice, but the best decision to take was so obvious that you probably didn't feel like it was a real choice—your brain decided in a reactive way; money is better than nothing—and this, in a game, removes agency: every time your players aren't making a purposeful decision, they are losing immersion from the game, meaning a lower likeableness of their experience.

This, of course, works on the opposite way too: if you give the players a choice for which they don't have enough information—these are called *blind choices*—they will choose randomly or base the decision on the wrong elements: if they get it right the will feel lucky—not *good*, lucky—while if they fail, they will be mad at the game, because how could have they known?

I'm not saying you should never use blind choices, for example, gambling is all about not having certainty on the outcome—and it's part of one of the next axioms in this chapter—but be careful, know your design, and know your players.

To sum it up, the first axiom allows us to control players' choices, create reactive-like ones, and manipulate the perceived freedom of the users using agency: by adjusting the quantity and the depth of the choices we give, we can create tighter or more free gameplay scenarios, changing the outcome of players' experiences.

SECOND AXIOM

Humans act to remove a personally perceived uneasiness, in order to reach a state of higher subjective pleasantness.

The second axiom can sound a bit technical, but it means that people act because they feel they are in a condition of uneasiness—discomfort, greed, desire for more of something, and so on—and they want to be in a state where such uneasiness is either absent or reduced. To do so, they need to be able to picture a situation in which they feel better: for example, Buddhist philosophy claims that the source of negative feelings is desire because when we want something more, we don't settle for what we have, and we will always want more—meaning we will always feel an uneasiness—so, once we remove desire from our lives, we can live happy and free.

This is very important, because, while the first axiom had a more in-depth point of view about choices, the second axiom states that human actions, to be triggered, need three components:

First, an uneasiness: something bothering the person enough for them to wish it wasn't there if it's a burden or making them want it more if it's a desire; this makes them willing to perform actions they wouldn't normally do—or they wouldn't be motivated enough to do—to reach their goal: removing a pain, gaining more money, and so on. If you don't perceive any uneasiness, there is no point in acting, because you are in a state of happiness and you don't wish for something to change.

Second, the power to think of a better situation: people need to picture what it would be like without that uneasiness, otherwise said problem would become part of their routine and they would eventually get used to it, thinking "it's useless for me to try, it's just impossible". If you can't picture a state without uneasiness, you have no reason to act: if you can't think about how life would be without a problem, you will never try to solve it—it becomes part of your life.

Third, self-efficiency: a psychological concept stating that an individual needs to feel like they have the skills needed to perform an action, otherwise it's pointless for them to even try. If you don't see how your actions can solve a problem, you won't act, because, from your point of view, it would be pointless. This is one of the reasons why games are dropped: players face a problem they feel is too big or not clear enough, so they just stop playing—it's like if someone asked you to solve a Rubik's cube while blindfolded: sure someone can do it, but the average person doesn't have enough clues, especially if it's their first time, so you just quit.

Note that the self-efficiency theory can be used in the opposite way too: in Metroidvania games, you often see an object—for example, a collectible—before you can actually reach it, as you need a skill you don't have yet: this creates the uneasiness in the players, and it's up to your design how deep this uneasiness should be. You can either show an item to create the uneasiness and then give players the tools to solve it—this motivates them in the short term—or you can show the item but wait to give them the tools, to create a deeper uneasiness—this leads players to backtrack as soon as they obtain the required skill.

Both cases require a careful balance: if you don't wait enough time to give them the tool, they won't perceive the uneasiness, but if you wait too long they might forget about the item or be frustrated by not having the tool when they need it.

This is the best way of using the second axiom: you create the uneasiness, make it clear how to solve it but make also clear that the player lacks one of the elements needed, in order to motivate them to obtain the tool and finally solve the problem. Some games, though, use this wrongly, creating uneasiness and either not making clear how to solve it or not letting the players know they need something they don't have yet, frustrating those who will try multiple times thinking they are doing something wrong.

To better understand how this applies to game design, let's take the drowning person effect: as designers, we can throw a person in a river, meaning we create a problem, to then ask said person to save themselves—and they will be happy to do so because it's part of the game. Most games use this technique by presenting an uneasiness that you wish wasn't there: the game essentially creates a problem, gives you a motivation to solve it, and then makes you act toward it.

An uneasiness can also concern desires, like in RPG games, where when you are offered a quest of which you can immediately see the reward: let's say the reward is the *legendary assassin demonic sword of the death* level 50, and the sword you have now is just the *mythical killer cursed sword* level 40—don't look them up, I know they sound cool but they are completely made up—the game just created the uneasiness, as the first thing you think is "I would be so cool and powerful with that new sword, compared to that mine is a mop"; this is desire-generated uneasiness—the first part of this axiom—and, since you can see the reward, you are already picturing a state where you have the sword and the uneasiness is gone—the second part of the axiom—but, to reach that goal, you need to act toward it by completing the quest—the third part of the axiom.

Problems, however, are not only gameplay-related, as sometimes they are about the narrative of the game: in *Fallout 4*—spoiler ahead—there is a narrative segment where you are locked inside a cry chamber; some enemies arrive and kidnap your son. After this event, the main narrative objective becomes saving your son. Since you lost your son—and, *theoretically*, you now want him back—you will work toward a state where you save him; if you didn't care about your own son, there either wasn't enough self-efficiency, so you thought you just couldn't save him, or the uneasiness wasn't motivating enough to create in you the desire to save him: this is a narrative design mistake, meaning the game failed to make you bond enough with your in-game family during the dedicated game-play session in the beginning—either that or you just really didn't like him.

The second axiom is one of the most powerful ones when used correctly but also one of the hardest to master, as you need a well-balanced uneasiness and a solution clear enough to be understood but not clear enough to be solved without putting any effort in. You also need the players to feel the right amount of self-efficiency: too low and they will feel powerless, not even trying once—too high and they will attempt something they can't do tens of times, leading to them feeling bad about themselves, blaming the game or even dropping it—it's like going to the gym: if I ask you to bench 1Kg, you will feel no challenge and your muscles won't grow, but if I ask you to bench 100Kg, you'll just think it's impossible and quit instantly.

THIRD AXIOM

The third axiom states that *human action is always rational*; in this case, "rational" means that it makes sense to the person performing the action—they are doing it to remove an uneasiness—even if it makes no sense to anyone else because we don't perceive that uneasiness the same way they do.

There are two elements we consider internally when thinking about whether something makes sense or not: feasibility and statistical rationality.

Feasibility is *your* perception of being able to achieve a goal: it is personal and can't be taught or imposed by others; let's say you are 55 years old, and you decide you want to win a gold medal in the high jump: is it feasible? Not really, because humans usually reach their peak performance between the ages of 20 and 25, even if you train every day for 5 years, your body's capabilities at 60 are much lower than an athlete's in his/her/their 20s who trained since they were a child.

To understand if an action is feasible to you, you should ask yourself "is my goal feasible at all?" If yes, "is my action plan too?", getting more in the details with every question.

As game designers, however, this part doesn't really concern us since players don't have *freedom* when in our games but *agency*: if a player wants to jump off a cliff, and we don't want them to, we are going to place barriers or invisible walls to block them—remember, if the game doesn't want something to happen, the enforcer won't let it happen—and since we are the architect of our worlds, players are limited to what we allow them.

It's clear by now that designers have the power to manipulate the player into doing whatever action they want them to do, but the third axiom of praxeology tells us that we can make players perform only the actions they think are reasonable: if I ask you to follow a recipe for a cake but instead of sugar I ask you to put chilli peppers in, you are probably going to stop because it makes no senses to you. The same goes for players: when they are asked to perform actions that don't make sense to them, they lose agency and feel obligated to do so—if it's not perceived as *their* choice, they either feel forced or drop the game.

How do we create actions that have sense, you ask? We can use multiple nudges—manipulation techniques covered later in this book—or guidance techniques: tutorials, level design clues, narrative concepts, and so on; these tools allow us to implant an idea in the players' minds and let them think it was theirs.

I know it sounds evil, but look at it this way: we get the actions that we wanted, and they feel smart for thinking about that action—it's a win-win scenario for me.

The second element the third axiom is based on is statistical rationality: from a statistical point of view, how many times did similar actions—to the one you are performing now—lead you to the desired result?

This, on the contrary of feasibility, isn't personal: it can be based on actions you saw, stories you heard, books you read, and so on—basically, any source of knowledge is counted for statistical rationality—meaning you can use NPCs to show an action, alert the player, or make them learn a combo: the *Uncharted* series often uses NPCs to show paths, while in the first *Half-Life* an enemy is used to show how other enemies attack, so the player knows how to recognise and avoid them. Both a new path and new enemies are changes, announced to the players by the use of NPCs, so that the players create first feasibility and statistical rationality structure in their head—this is often called *mental model* by other frameworks, once again showing how praxeology manages to include so many aspects of the game design theory.

When performing a new action, therefore developing their statistical rationality for this action, people need to be in a focused state to avoid mistakes, so it must be clear to them they are going to face something they've never done. Most of the time, however, we keep our brain in *zombie mode*, because it consumes less energy, for example, if you need to pour a glass of water, you don't really think about it, you just pour it because you are used to that action.

What if, while in zombie mode, we perform a new action? Like pouring a glass of water while walking down the stairs: chances are we are going to panic and mess both actions up, tripping down the stairs and pouring the water all over.

This is where feasibility and statistical rationality meet: when doing something new, you need to be focused on the task and supported in the new action—you could take a step down the stairs, pour some water, take another step, pour more water, and so on—or you will encounter anxiety, panic, or failure.

It works the same way for videogames, since, according to the 13 gameplay principles, before facing a change that requires actions different from the ones in the previous state, the change needs to be announced—the bigger the change, the bigger the announcement must be—because praxeology tells us that any change refers to the players' statistical rationality: if they don't understand that a change occurred, they will apply the same actions they used until that point, but, since the situation isn't the same, the action will fail and they won't understand why. If you correctly announce the change, however, they will formulate new statistical rationality for the new actions they will try, and they won't be frustrated from failing a couple of times, because they perceive it as something new that they still need to master—toddlers are excited to learn how to walk, not frustrated, because it opens up a world of possibilities, and the same should happen with your players.

What if I don't add any change to my game? You could of course do that, but know that the lack of changes creates habits in the players: once they find a combo, a gun, or a vehicle they are comfortable with, they are going to always use that same element over and over again, even if it's less efficient than others, bringing repetitive gameplay and possible blocks—for example, they always use a water pistol, but the new enemies are immune to water damage. Most of the time, players are not going to like a change—that's human nature; we are a lazy species—because they need to learn something new and change the way they behave in your game, so it's up to you to make it look like a good thing, for example with new rewards and features they will like. To do so, as always, you need to know your players—even better than you know yourself.

You can, however, include this *lazy factor* as part of your game: in the *God of War* series, players can complete the game by using the combo *square, square, triangle*, an easy-to-learn sequence that always works, even with the most powerful enemies, creating a layer players can always rely on: whether they panic or don't feel like actively thinking of a good combo, they can always use this three keys to avoid failing—their statistical rationality states that it has 100% success rate. This has, of course, its downside, because if players aren't encouraged to use different combos, they will feel like the game is too easy or repetitive, but, if used in the right way, it creates a safety net for the players to fall on without resulting in frustration or even them dropping the game.

FOURTH AXIOM

According to the fourth axiom, *humans choose based on a scale of values: these values are subject to perception and thoughts and change constantly.*

Choosing based on a scale of values means that each one of us has a series of values—moral, ethic, social, work-related, and economic—that drive our choices; this is an already-existing theory, present in many structures such as Jamie Cleghorn's B2B elements of value[1] or the pyramid of needs, which essentially states that humans divide everything according to certain values: the most fundamentals are basic needs, meaning elements you couldn't survive without—such as water, food, safety—followed by psychological needs, concerning one's connections and well-being—like friends, relationships, prestige—and, last, there are the self-fulfilment needs, the ones we seek in our lives to reach a better version of yourself—achieving one's full potential, expressing our creative values. The lower you are in the pyramid, the more crucial those elements are, but the higher you go, the higher the satisfaction coming from your achievements is—landing your dream job is more satisfying than eating, but it's not as crucial to survival.

Praxeology recognises these scales of values and the fact that it's subjective, as one's values are different from someone else's values—if you value money above everything else, you have no problem taking a bribe, while if ethics was your most important value, you could never accept it.

This subjective element comes from one's perception and thoughts: our idea of what's right and what's wrong depends on what we see, hear, and understand, as each piece of information is processed by our brain, which then evaluates the situation and tells us what to think about it: it's like an extremely complex scale, with tons of plates to put information on, that then evaluates the combination of all those elements based on what we value the most. It usually tells us if something is right or wrong for us in the background, while other times—for more important decisions—we need to take a look at each one of the plates and maybe check that our scale of values still represents us.

Let's say you are a cashier at a local store and you see someone stealing some bread and a bottle of water; you'd stop that person because stealing is wrong; what if this person was homeless, and stole to bring food to his starving child? Some of you would still see it as wrong, but they would let it slide, while others would stop that person anyway. While legally there is a definition of right and wrong, as a human being there isn't; it would be up to your morals—and scale of values—to see it as ethical or not—this is one of those cases where you need to enter your mental scale and manually look at the plates you value the most.

What if, in the same scenario, instead of stealing water and bread the man stole a bottle of Chardonnay and some Wagyu meat because his child is picky? You would see this as unacceptable because, the more valuable the item he's stealing, the less ethical it is; as always, we're not here to discuss ethics, I just want you to focus on the different feelings that similar scenarios generate.

Another important element in your mental scale is the target of action—you wouldn't give $5 to a stranger, but you would give it to a friend—because, being the creator of our game's universe, we can manipulate the players into making choices they would see as unethical for them to help a character they really care about. Despite what you may think, players love to make choices—if, of course, they are meaningful to them—because choices in videogames are often in a grey area, where there is no right or wrong, but it's all up to the person's ethic: humans like to use it, but, in life, we often can't do it without facing important consequences, while in games players are the judges of the world and don't need to follow anyone's law except for the designers'—remember that if the enforcer doesn't want them to do something, they just won't be able to do it.

Note that, however, one's ethics in real life don't apply to videogames, because they offer a safe system: if they make a bad decision and mess up, they can always reload the game from a previous save or start a new run, while in reality they wouldn't kill someone to see what happens. This is good for us, as we can modify players' scale with design techniques such as framing—I'll talk about framing later in the book—meaning that if your character's class is *thief*, you are more prone to steal from others—because it's part of who you are—or if a city is owned by an evil empire, you won't feel guilty for destroying it and eliminating the evil NPCs.

These techniques also allow us to trick the player into feeling guilty using plot twists: maybe you spent 90% of the game killing evil NPCs, just to find out they were never evil, or we can use them to build a stronger power fantasy: they really were evil NPCs, and you saved the world by eliminating all of them.

Of course, each player will have their definition of *evil* while playing, for example, when I play Western RPG games, I feel like the hero, so if anyone disrespects me, I either rob them or kill them: I am the hero so they need to be respectful—but it only works like this in those videogames.

As I've said, we can manipulate players' perceptions during the game, with narrative or mechanical progression, and this is the last point of the fourth axiom: values constantly change over time; a player's needs at the beginning of the game are completely different from what they will need at the end, and, during the playthrough, their priorities will change over and over again: they may need a weapon to fight a boss when they start, then armour, then grinding currency, then back to the weapon, and so on. It can also be a narrative variation: in *Bioshock Infinite*, the main character first needs to rescue a girl, but—**spoilers ahead**—ends up sacrificing himself to break a constantly repeating cycle: if done right, these narrative variations help to create a lasting and meaningful experience, but the new needs must be perceived by the player as their own, or they will feel like the game is forcing them into the gameplay.

FIFTH AXIOM

This axiom states that *human actions require time.*

It may sound obvious—of course, an action takes time—but, if you stop to think about what time is, you realise that time is a construct that we—as humans—created to manage our lives, our actions, our jobs, and so on, therefore it's not *real*.

The first part of the axiom tells us that we designers control players' time, and, since actions require time, players will evaluate the time they spend in the game based on those actions: understanding the difference between the action we make and the time that passes is extremely interesting because, as designers, we have full control over the players' time—note that we're not talking about the day-night cycle but about *pacing*—all the game design theories regarding pacing are related to timing: you can't have always-increasing pacing; you need to change the required actions and the outcoming gameplay, otherwise players will get tired.

For example, when I was playing *Evoland 2*—and note that I played and really liked the first *Evoland*—I quit it almost immediately because I was presented with a puzzle in which I had to move certain blocks to open a way for my character, three times in a row: the first time was to introduce the mechanic, the second was the actual puzzle, but the third one was just a harder version of the second. This is a design flaw because repeating the same action as before, just with a higher difficulty, is a waste of time: if the designers would have introduced a small combat moment between the second and the third puzzle, it would have changed the pace while working as a brief pause from repeating the same actions.

I know I can sound too strict, but this was a design mistake: players need to feel engaged by the pace, not dragged by it—imagine the pace like a river you are swimming in: you want to feel its flow and follow its water, but if the flow is too strong you will feel like you are drowning. This is the reason why most commercial games intertwine different activities: one moment you are fighting, the next one you are exploring, then back to fighting, and so on; this example shows how, with this new lens, designers must assign the right pace to each mechanic, and even the best mechanic in the world would be perceived negatively if paced wrong.

The second part of the axiom divides time into three categories: past, present, and future time:

The past is seen as the uneasiness and the motivation from the Third axiom, and it's the reason why players are acting in the present, what is motivating us and driving our actions.

The present is the action itself: our second-to-second gameplay, composed of the visceral emotions, because those are the emotions we feel *right now*, which don't require time to be processed and leave no time to be elaborated—as soon as one is gone, another one is coming right away.

The future is an imaginative and resolutive state where complex emotions are found: *Fiero*, satisfaction, sorrow, and so on because the future is based on the anticipation we created until we reach that moment: when you are working hard to beat a boss, you are projecting the state of having killed the boss from the future, and the more you picture this state, the bigger the anticipation becomes—it's like waiting for your favourite dish at a restaurant: you think about it while you are driving, you start to picture the smell in your nose when you sit at the table, and you think about the taste when waiting for it to arrive.

As we've seen in the previous axioms, we thrive on desires, and the fifth axiom recognises this too: the future is composed of the satisfaction of reaching an objective, the creation of a new desire for our brain to focus on; these three categories are a perfect description of the core loop of a game, just seen under a different lens.

The last part of the fifth axiom tells us that time is a limited resource and that it's more precious than any other resource; you now know that one's values change constantly, and this axiom states that the best way to change one's perception is with time: the closer an action—and its rewards—are to the players, the more it's perceived as easy, but longer and more complex actions will be seen as hard and less motivating, so we need to have a reward that is perceived as more worthwhile then the time they spent to obtain it—if a friend suggests a TV show for its amazing ending but it has 500 episodes, you may not be willing to spend that much time for an ending, because you feel like you could make better use of your own time, but if every season finale had a great ending too, you would enjoy watching it more, as every 20 episodes you would watch a great moment you would remember, like a shorter-term reward.

SIXTH AXIOM

Human actions have a degree of uncertainty: even the most basic actions aren't 100% certain and therefore can fail.

While it can sound obvious, this is where a lot of designs go wrong: the designers create a problem, give players the tools to solve them, and take for granted that they will succeed, but what happens if they fail? The most common example for this situation is the *Souls* saga: they transformed death—a failure—into part of the gameplay, since once you die you leave your *souls* in that spot, players now have a reason to go back to that part and either go back to use said souls or try again in the task that they failed before—in this process, they also get new souls from the respawned enemies, meaning a form of learning for the players.

Every designer needs to remember that players' actions aren't certain—dynamics are very hard to predict—and we can never be sure that they will do what we want them to do, therefore a good designer is someone who transforms a failure into a gameplay element, not someone who avoids any possible failure for the players.

This axiom divides human uncertainty into three categories, these being gambling, speculation, and engineering:

Gambling: the user knows the frequency of something happening but has no control over it; as the name says, this is like a typical casino situation, or, applied to videogames, loot boxes, and critical strikes, as you know how rare something is but can't do anything to increase your chances of getting it. Gambling is completely controlled by the designers.

Speculation: with their mental skills, the user can speculate on the odds of something happening but without full certainty. This is like stock market speculation: you can apply your knowledge of the stock market and the principle of economics to predict if a curve will go up or down, but you can't be 100% sure about it. Speculation can be divided into skill-based speculation and number-based speculation:

An example of .skill-based speculation is parrying: the players know they can deal more damage by performing a perry; they know they need to get the timing right—making this a classical high-risk high-reward situation—but they can't be sure it's going to happen every single time—even if they fail once every 1,000 attacks, there are always factors that can lead to them failing.

Number-based speculation, instead, can be seen in deck games: by increasing or decreasing the number of certain cards in the deck, players can increase the chance of getting a specific card. An example of this situation is in *Magic: The Gathering*, where players can use *fetch land* cards to draw a land from a specific basic land type: considering a 26 lands card deck, if the player has 14 true land cards and 10 fetch land cards, their chances of getting land cards are almost half—because for every fetch land card, they also get a true land card—meaning they are speculating the drawing more of these cards to avoid them later in the game. Speculation is controlled by the players: they are using the designers' rules to find strategies and ways of improving the odds in their favour.

Last, engineering: with a series of specific actions and tools the user can change the source of uncertainty to obtain full certainty over an element; one of the most used tools in videogames is RNG values, used to reduce the skill gap between players, create *wow* moments, increase the *black-box* complexity—having a random element makes it harder to understand how a game works in the background—and to balance the game—having elements that reduce the success rate of certain strategies, therefore reducing the speculation. Take the critical chance of a *build* in *Monster Hunter Rise*: the gambling is the critical strikes—since you have an $n\%$ chance to deal critical damage, you know the chance but can't control it—with engineering, however, you can create a build with 100% critical chance, transforming the gambling—something not certain—into engineering—something you make sure happens.

In real life this can be seen in assembly lines: where once we had people assembling pieces together—meaning they could make mistakes every once in a while—we now have machines that, if properly working, have an extremely low chance of failure for that task: we created a system that lowered that risk, making it almost non-existent—of course, in real life there is no 0% risk chance, but in-game there is, and that's the goal of engineering. This last part, as you just read, belongs to both worlds: it belongs to the players with the game progression, but it also belongs to the designers for the mechanics they created, which work as a life jacket.

The sixth axiom, differently from other design theories that focus on what RNG can do, looks at each random element as something that belongs to different worlds—the players', the designers', and a common one—meaning that designers need to acknowledge the existence of gambling, speculation, and engineering techniques, and they need to decide what should be allowed and what should not be allowed in their worlds: remember that if something isn't enforced, players will see it as fair for them to do, so it's important to choose what you are willing to let your players do even if it wasn't designed, and even if you don't like it as long as it doesn't ruin the core of the experience—if you prohibit everything, it will be more like a jail than a game.

SEVENTH AXIOM

The seventh axiom talks about humans' scale of value, similar to the fourth axiom, but it states that *another critical element for the humans' scale of value*—other than time—*is the marginal utility.*

This means that the ability of a resource to remove an uneasiness depends on how many times, in a short amount of time, said resource has been used to solve a problem: if I'm thirsty and I drink a glass of water, I will enjoy it a lot, if I drink another glass I will probably still enjoy it but less than the previous one, but from the third glass on, drinking will become unpleasant, because my need for water has been satisfied. The ability to solve an uneasiness depends on the uneasiness, not the resource: if something isn't satisfying your players, giving more of the same thing will only make things worse; you need to change the resource.

This tells us something that many videogames get wrong: they always give the same rewards, just in a higher quantity. As I'm writing this book, I'm playing *Assassin's Creed:*

Valhalla and it has this exact problem: the player can level up until level 400,=; I'm currently at level 170 and I already have the build I wanted, therefore getting more Ability Points when I level up is completely useless to me. The fact that I reached my ideal build completely changed how I played the game: before, I used to do a lot of side quests to improve the build, but since I got it levelling up is pointless to me, therefore I'm not motivated to complete quests that only offer experience points as a reward—and this is probably why I'm going to drop the game. This is, of course, a huge problem, but how could it happen? Most likely, the designers thought that everything should be linked to experience, so experience should always be a reward; instead, players should have different rewards for different actions, and at a different pace: sometimes you obtain experience, sometimes money, and so on. This axiom tells us that having a single reward brings marginal utility—just think about when you cook something you really like and you have some leftovers: the first meal was great, but eating the leftovers is already less satisfying, so imagine how it would feel to eat them every day: rewards are players' food; be careful what you feed them on.

The second part of the axiom focuses on the law of diminishing utility, stating that every progressive obtainment of a resource is perceived as less worthy than the previous one, especially if received in a short period of time: 1,000 gold coins the first time are super cool, but the second time they already begin to lose value; each reward is considered a *reward* because it satisfies the need generated from an uneasiness, meaning that once you get it a part of that uneasiness is gone.

This leads to a *disutility*: the resource you get as the reward has a perceived value so low that it becomes a burden; it frustrates you that you got that resource instead of any other possible reward; this can be applied to anything, from bosses to achievements, meaning that—and I can't stress how important this part is—everything needs to follow a pace: not just the gameplay, but rewards too must have a non-sequential progression for each currency, or they will quickly lose their gap to the players or they fall into disutility.

BOX 8.4   AN EXAMPLE OF A SPECIFIC USE OF THE SEVENTH AXIOM

I found that this axiom works really well with needs-driven AI, for example, an NPC in a village: he has a set of needs that drive his behaviour, sometimes making him drink a glass of water, other times making him talk to other NPCs, go for a walk, and so on. With a scale of values, this NPC would act differently depending on what their highest priority is at the moment, instead of scripting a linear path that you would see them follow hundreds of times. Picture a whole town of NPCs with this system, each NPC with a different set of values: they would walk around, go eat at different times, talk to each other, and potentially generate unscripted dynamics—an NPC could get mad because another NPC goes to her house to talk at 3 AM, or another could go eat at a diner and starve there because the chef's value for work is so low that he doesn't care anymore.

EIGHTH AXIOM

This is the last axiom covered in this book; note that there are other ones strictly related to the economic side of praxeology, but they are a more in-depth topic I suggest you take a look at if you're interested.

The eighth axiom tells us that *humans produce, and, in order to do so, three elements are necessary: land, labour, and time.*

First, the land: the structure that generates the primary resources needed in a production process.

Second, the labour: the sequence of actions and decisions that transform the original resource into the desired outcome or, in case the outcome is the resource itself, that allow a person to gather it.

Third, the time: the amount of time needed by labour to transform or gather said resource.

This is one of the most suiting definitions of gameplay I've ever seen; take a look at each element from a game design point of view:

The land becomes the problems and the rules of a game, therefore it is the game itself.

The labour becomes the objective derived from a perceived uneasiness, thus the gameplay alone.

The time becomes the game's pace, coming from the correlation of land and labour: the game, combined with the actions a player makes, generates the experience the players live.

This lens makes you look at gameplay not as something that just exists but rather as the outcome of the interaction between the player—the actions—and the game—the world in which said actions take place; this axiom is more academic than the previous ones and it's a bit more abstract, but it's an amazing lens you can use to analyse a game.

PRAXEOLOGY FRAMEWORK

Taking a look at Figure 8.1, the framework starts in the top left corner with an uneasiness, either perceived or imposed by the game, that gets added to the scale of values of the players, which contains all the other uneasiness. The user evaluates each element of the scale, also considering the required time for each action and the outcoming reward—as seen in the previous axioms—and, once an uneasiness is picked as the most important to get rid of, they wait for the right condition to act.

The condition to act requires the production of the land—meaning that the structure the players are using must allow them to solve the uneasiness or it will be pointless to act—and the evaluation of the degree of uncertainty: those two elements are combined with the third axiom, to let players decide if the conditions to act combined with their actions would solve the uneasiness; if the answer is no, the players go back to the scale of

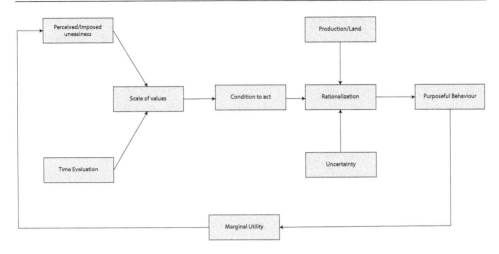

FIGURE 8.1   A scheme of the praxeology framework.

Source: Author.

values to pick another uneasiness—note that this process creates frustration because players failed while trying to solve a problem—while, if the answer is yes, they move to the purposeful behaviour section.

Purposeful behaviour is essentially the labour: the players generate gameplay and obtain a result, which gets measured with the marginal utility, where players ask themselves how many times they got that reward, how worthy it is perceived as being, and if it satisfies their uneasiness or not. These rewards change the perceived uneasiness, bringing players back to the first step where they pick another uneasiness to start the circle over again.

Analysing a game's gameplay, from a second-to-second to a month-to-month side, allows you to choose where and when to control your players but, most of all, it lets you see where mistakes are made: have I generated the right uneasiness? Do I know my players' scale of values? Did I use the pacing correctly to manipulate the scale of values? Does my structure support the player as it should?

There are countless questions you can—and should—ask yourself while designing a game, and praxeology's strength is its versatility: it can spot from the smallest mistake in your second-to-second gameplay to a huge hole in your design, just by looking at the players' needs during their journey in your game.

Understanding and learning all these axioms is an excellent design lens, and this set of lenses is soon to become one of the strongest tools in your tool bag, either to design your game or to analyse someone else's.

NOTE

1   The Marketing Journal, *"The Elements of Value"—An Interview with Jamie Cleghorn*: www.marketingjournal.org/the-elements-of-value-an-interview-with-jamie-cleghorn/

Self-Determination Theory

9

The self-determination theory is a macro theory of human motivation that focuses on one's innate desires that motivate people into doing whatever they do; it's a *macro* theory because, unlike praxeology—which is a set of axioms coming from the same field (economy)—the SDT was born from the merging of various theories coming from different fields: it includes studies such as cognitive evaluation, organicity, basic needs, goal theory, and many more.

EXTRINSIC AND INTRINSIC MOTIVATION

The main aspect of this theory you need to remember is that the SDT focuses on intrinsic motivations, but what are those?

We can divide motivations into two types, extrinsic and intrinsic; while it's true that this technique only covers the intrinsic ones, it's important to understand both of them.

Belonging to extrinsic motivations are all those actions you perform not for the action itself but just for the reward: "I don't like playing football, but I love to win", or "I don't like baking cakes, but I love eating them". There are countless possible motivations, from the feeling of winning a match to one of the most common, money: tons of people hate their jobs, but they keep doing it for the pay check, which then allows them to purchase things they actually like—don't get me wrong, there is nothing wrong with that as long as it works for them, and no motivation should be frowned upon.

This type of motivation is perfect when you want someone to perform a series of actions in a precise way because extrinsically motivated people put little to no creativity in their actions; it's also useful to generate routines, grounds for habit loops—which I'll cover later on—and it also works great as an incentive—you don't care about doing something? I'll give you a reward you will like, so the craving brings you to perform that action.

Intrinsic motivations, on the contrary, include everything a person does for the pleasure of performing the action itself, getting rid of uneasiness, or fulfilling one's true calling; these are the actions you truly enjoy, not just like, *enjoy*: going for a run not to lose weight but for the feeling of the wind in your hair and the fresh air rushing into your lungs, working on your project to see your dream slowly building up, baking a cake to set your mind free from that day's worries.

Intrinsic motivation is best used in creative jobs, in developing people's mastery, it sticks more—an intrinsically motivated person will perform an action for as long as

DOI: 10.1201/9781003229438-12

they feel motivated—and in social interactions—group projects and anything requiring collaboration.

I know that intrinsic motivation sounds way more meaningful than the extrinsic one, but don't get misled: as I said before, no motivation is superior to another; they are both positive—as they lead us to work more—and they both have their pros and cons, which are different for everyone—I might love working to gain more money, while a monk would see no point into working to gain physical possession.

Let's take a deeper look at some pros and cons of both motivations type, starting with the extrinsic one:

First, each one of us has an internal value, a "price" we must receive to be willing to perform any action—note that *price* doesn't necessarily mean money; it can also be a moral outcome like helping make the world a better place. The extrinsic value that motivates you need to be higher than your inner value—or you will feel like the time and energy you are investing in action just isn't worth it—and the reward, the extrinsic value, grow in time: the more time you perform an action for, the more you feel like you deserve, both because you get better at doing that and because repetitive actions tend to bore humans. This is also connected to the marginal utility principle you read in praxeology: the same resource loses perceived value over time, just like money loses value due to inflation, the same way after some years in a workplace you get offered a raise even if your responsibilities didn't change.

Second, extrinsic motivation is great for starting something off, but it has a terrible stickiness: the idea of the reward feels great, and it gives you the energy to start a new task right away, but after some time your mind lowers the perceived value of the said reward, as it gets compared to the cost—time, resources, energy—of working toward that goal. This is extremely common in gyms: many people start going to a gym with the picture of themselves in better shape, healthier, and more disciplined, but, after a few weeks, they realise that the result they imagined doesn't come from just spending time there, but from constantly putting effort into lifting weights, following the right diet, dedicating time even when they'd rather relax on the couch and eat junk food: if their motivation was just the final result, they are more likely to quit—however, if the motivation comes from the process itself, the stickiness of that motivation allows them to reach their goal.

Third, this type of motivation leads people to show off: they are more likely to show the perks coming from the process they're going through, bragging about how much money they make, how nice their office is, and so on; note that showing off isn't necessarily bad, others could even find motivation from one's pride, but it creates a dangerous territory where toxicity can arise, so keep in mind that the more your product externally motivates your audience, the more likely negative behaviours might be generated.

Now, about intrinsic motivation:

First, the passion: passion is an extremely important factor that can make people work extremely hard for years; it can't be created or manipulated, and it can survive the toughest of the storms, but if it dries out, the motivation dies with it—it's like gas in a car, allowing you to go as fast as you can imagine, in sunny days and snowstorms, but if it runs out, it doesn't matter how cool or fast your car is, it just won't move.

Second, intrinsic motivation requires constant constructive feedback: to generate motivation, you need a system that provides people with feedback that allows them to grow, both in their task and as a person. The best example for this scenario is coaches in any sport: they give athletes feedback to generate experience and keep their motivation high, telling them what they are doing right and whatnot, what can be improved, what has improved since the previous training, and so on. It's crucial that the feedback is constructive: it doesn't matter if it's positive or negative, but it needs to be candid, showing a person an impartial point of view to guide them in their journey—a sailor can't see their way out during a storm, but someone on the land can.

Third and last, it's crucial to be relevant: a person needs to feel like their job is contributing to the bigger picture; they need to know that they aren't just another gear in the machine; one of the things that removes most motivation out of someone is receiving irrelevant tasks just to "fill the day". This doesn't mean being *important*; they don't need to be the head of the project, but, even if they are the new entry of the team, their work must have a real value.

Once again, there is no motivation objectively better than the other; they need to be used in the most suitable scenario; as you recall, though, the self-determination theory focuses on the intrinsic motivations, allowing you to understand and maximise the elements that increase or maintain this type of motivation. What are those elements, you are asking? We call them *needs*, and they are the following three:

First, humans are inherently proactive with their potential and mastering their inner forces (such as drives and emotions), meaning that, as humans, we *want* to do what we like, and we are driven by our inner passions and motivations.

Second, humans have an inherent tendency toward growth development and integrated functioning: we want to get good at whatever we do, we want to grow, and we want to bring the skills we learned in a field into another context to learn it even better.

Third, optimal development and actions are inherent in humans, but they don't happen automatically: growth doesn't happen by itself; we need a context and characteristics that allow us to gain an interior growth, otherwise our situation will stay still; it's Newton's first law, the law of inertia: if a body is at rest or moving at a constant speed in a straight line, it will remain at rest or keep moving in a straight line at constant speed unless acted upon by a force—if the context doesn't provide new elements for us to encounter and grow, we will keep doing the same thing in the same way forever.

According to the self-determination theory, these three statements are axioms—just like the ones from praxeology, meaning we just take them as true—and we need to satisfy them with certain characteristics to generate intrinsic motivation, while if an activity doesn't satisfy them we might lose said motivation.

How do we satisfy them, then? Again, since we are talking about human beings, we can identify three macro-areas that compose our every action—we are zooming out to better spot common behaviours, similar to how we zoomed out to identify trends in our target audience in the previous chapters; those three areas are competence, autonomy, and relatedness.

COMPETENCE

Competence is the process that brings a person to increase their mastery of a particular skill they are learning, essentially what allows you to become good at doing something; this is based on the second axiom, stating that people tend—and need—to be good at something, and it tells us that the system where the action they perform takes place must allow them to obtain competence.

In videogames, there are multiple systems that make players gain competence: I'm going to cover the most important ones that every designer should know, but note that you can spot other ones yourself during your journey.

The first is the feedback: this is the most important of all and needs to be constructive feedback; it doesn't matter if it's positive or negative—as you remember from the coach example—the important part is that it tells people where they made a mistake and how to improve. A person that receives this type of feedback feels motivated because instead of getting punished they are shown how to improve and do better the next time around, developing the skill they are trying to learn. This is where a lot of videogames make a mistake: they may give players *juice* feedback—meaning cool effects, pleasant to look at, and with a high *cool factor*, which is always positive but not enough by itself—but they lack the constructive side, not telling players how to improve, leading to the loss of perceived competence by the players—meaning a loss of intrinsic motivation, because, as you recall, we want to be good at what we do. Imagine you are baking a cake for the first time in your life, following a recipe you have found online: you are beating your eggs, adding some sugar in the bowl, and everything looks good, so you keep following the recipe and eventually put the cake in the oven; after some time for the cake to rest, you cut a slice, looking amazing and with a great smell filling the kitchen, a friend takes a bite and . . . "it's extremely lumpy", they say. You followed the recipe step by step, so what happened? Your friend gave you feedback, but it lacks in constructive value, because, while you know the overall result, you have no idea of what you did wrong; another friend takes a bite, and they tell you that you didn't beat your eggs enough, so it didn't mix well with the baking powder and it created all the lumps. What's the difference between the two feedbacks? One was about the result and nothing more, while the other was about the process that led to that result: always focus on the process that led to the mistake, not the mistake itself, or the person you are talking to may not know what caused it.

While feedback is, hands down, the most important of these competence-increasing systems, there are many more:

Exaggeration: exaggerating the outcome of a challenge—like telling a kid they did an amazing job performing an extremely simple task—makes a person feel good about their skills and their progress in the learning curve of a process; this is a very risky technique because if the target understands that you are exaggerating their perceived skill, they will feel fooled, but, especially in the early stages of an experience, it can be helpful to boost one's motivation. In videogames, you can create easier challenges after introducing a new mechanic or use levelling to make players feel stronger than their enemies.

Progression: Any progression technique that shows players their progress in a measurable way provides them with a sense of competence; there are tons of ways to show their progression: bars, levels, badges, leader boards, and so on; as always each one has its upsides and downsides, therefore you need to pick the ones that suit your players' needs the most—for example, a leader board in a single-player game, comparing their scores with NPCs' scores, is perceived as less motivating than the same leader board in a multiplayer game with real people competing for the higher score.

Mastery: as you've seen in the second need, players need to both grow and become good at what they do, so it's important to create complex elements that give players a chance to create mastery, from a boss they will fight tens of times before defeating it—in this case the mastery is in the learning of the boss' movesets, timings, windows for attacks and so on—to specific challenges that develop players' skills vertically—for example, mastering a movement combo to reach specific spots in the map. Note that mastery is also created at lower levels, such as with resultant actions: initially, players learn the operative actions of your game, but once they master them, they will move to resultant ones to get a higher mastery of your game—if they can smoothly move in your level, it will feel like a perfectly timed dance, with steps and pauses. A good example for this type of mastery is *Super Mario Odyssey*: the way a player moves in the first three hours of the game and the way they move in the last three hours of the game is completely different because Mario has tons of resultant actions that the player will experience during the game and, just like a dance, the more they play, the more their movements will flow flawlessly. You can see this change by looking at any blind walkthrough online; the first and the last hour of the video will look like two completely different people, and even the same level played at different times will be navigated differently, also providing a high level of satisfaction.

Last, innovation: still referencing the second need, humans want to integrate different functions, meaning we want to apply a skill we learned in a different context from the one we learned it in; that level of integration of different environments and skills provides a sense of mastery in what we do, because not only we got good at something, but we also used that knowledge to solve a problem in another field. This is, of course, harder to its biggest strengths, where the skills and tools the players learned, for example, to fight enemies can also be used to, let's say, explore certain areas of the world.

In videogames, designers can also create elements of *fake* mastery, meaning that they generate mastery in the players with an illusion, thus not really making the player grow in that gameplay segment. This is important because they keep the players motivated even where the learning curve would be flat and players would lose interest, but, just as the exaggeration tool, they need to be used carefully, because if players notice this trick, they will feel tricked, if not treated as not good enough for the *real* game. These tools are:

Dynamic Difficulty Adjustment, or *DDA*: when the player is struggling in a certain gameplay segment, designers make the game easier, for example by lowering NPCs' difficulty without telling the player, adjusting the challenge to their skill level.

Forgiveness Mechanics: the player isn't as good as they think, so designers use mechanics that make it look like the player succeeded, even if they would have lost—20 bullets are going to hit the player, but they can only take 19 before dying, so one of those bullets, let's say, *missed* the player.

Guidance Techniques: there are many ways we can guide players into following a path, performing a certain action, and so on, and these come from both Game and Level Design, depending on what you want players to do; for example, there is an item on a desk that only half the players notice, so in the next version of the game, the lamp on the desk that casually points toward the object flickers a bit when players get close.

RNG—Random Number Generators: as you've read in the praxeology section of this chapter, players can use speculation, gambling, and engineering to overcome a challenge they didn't have a high enough skill for; for example, while playing any of the *Souls* series, I always completed the game by levelling like crazy: where the average player defeated a boss at level 40, I ground until level 80—I didn't win by getting better, I won by getting statistically stronger.

Grading Systems: designers communicate to the players their results with a grade, for example going from D to SSS, but the system is designed in a way that even the worst grade sounds cool, like in *Devil May Cry 4* where D stands for *Deadly!*, C for *Carnage!* and so on—it's true, D is the lowest rank, but doesn't "deadly" sound cool?

Last, Progression Systems: players get a promotion, like a badge or a new title, but nothing really changes in the game; if players can't tell the difference between real progress and a fake, awarding them with a title will make them feel better about their skills—"Sure, I have a 0.0001 KDA ratio, but the game gave me the *deadliest hitman* award; I must be great".

AUTONOMY

This is what, in game design, is called *agency*; as I'm sure you remember, agency is the feeling of being in control of our choices and not feeling like they are blind or meaningless:

if you know agency, you know autonomy—in fact, autonomy is part of the freedom of choice, and it too has to keep in mind the paradox of choice. Everything that makes a choice perceived as valuable generates autonomy, therefore feeling of control, and the feeling of control generates intrinsic motivation; this is bonded to the first of the needs: humans are proactive, and they want to master their inner strengths, *their* choices over which they have control.

RELATEDNESS

Relatedness is the feeling of being connected to something, thinking that it applies to you too; it is divided into three types: relatedness with a story, relatedness with people, and simulated relatedness.

Relatedness with a story: this happens when a product/experience creates a narrative element you feel connected with; the story has always been a huge element of motivation even outside game design: from your favourite book to the newest big Hollywood movie you just saw, they all create a bond with you that makes you stick with the product until the end—I bet that, even right now, you are thinking about your favourite story and how the way you related to it made you live the experience as if you were the protagonist.

It doesn't matter if a story is *good* or *bad*; it always has certain related elements that will make certain people stick with it. What people, you ask? It's very simple, their target audience: knowing your audience allows you to create a story that feels relatable to those who experience it. It might be something as simple as being a kid—we've all been kids, therefore we can all relate to that to an extent—or something more specific, like bungee jumping—not a lot of people normally do bungee jumping in their lives, so the relating audience will be smaller, but your story can be more specific because of how distinct that experience is.

Of course, having a great story, other than just a relatable one, is a huge plus for your game: narratology is a whole separate subject too long to be discussed in this book—it would be a whole book by itself; I may even write it in the future—so, for the time being, I suggest you take a look at other already-existing books and materials, as there are many techniques to write relatable and compelling stories.

Simulated with people: no man is an island; being able to relate to others means interacting with them: playing, competing, being part of a group, and any element that involves other players generate relatedness, with, of course, all the outcoming risks—toxicity, bullying, hate toward a specific group of people, and so on. You can create this type of relatedness in single-player games too, with the use of meta-game elements like Discord/Reddit servers and Twitter hashtags, and this is why the role of Community Manager has grown a lot in the past years—games like *Undertale* and *Pokémon* are examples of entire subcultures of people, coming together to talk about the game, share artworks, theories, and much more.

Simulated relatedness: this type of relatedness is achieved with companion NPCs, romance elements, pets, or with more complex systems like the *Nemesis System* in *Middle-Earth: Shadow of Mordor*, or *Shadow of War*: the system creates NPCs that interact in a complex way with the player to create the feeling of relatedness—they aren't just NPCs, they are *your* NPCs, helping you the first second and betraying you the next one. When I was playing *Middle-Earth: Shadow of War*, I had this orc that I played alongside for more than ten hours, and then, out of the blue, he betrayed me, telling me I was weak and useless, so he killed me: that moment had a huge emotional impact on me, to the point that my main goal became getting my revenge and killing that orc, meaning that the emotion the game created was so strong that it generated a feeling of relatedness that changed my perception of the game—it wasn't about the game anymore, it was about revenge.

Competence, autonomy, and relatedness are all important in their own way, and it's up to you to choose the ones that suit your games the most; each one of these three elements can be present to a certain degree in your game: of course, the more the better, but, as always, designing systems takes time, and you can't have 100% of each one of the three. There are games that only have one of them, others that have two, and others that have a bit of all three, but the important part is that the more you try to understand how your mechanics satisfy these elements, the bigger the players' motivation will be. A game with none of those elements isn't necessarily bad; remember that the self-determination theory is a guide that we use to ask ourselves if we have enough mechanics to generate the kind of motivation that we want our players to feel. The opposite is also true: if your game is extremely motivating but there isn't something specific to like, once the game is over players will have no reason to come back. For example, I used to play a group game with an incipit my group and I thought was really cool, so we played it until the end, but, once it was finished, we never touched it again, because the concept was extremely motivating; playing with my friends was motivating, but no one liked the game itself; this means that the self-determination theory is not a game's pleasantness, it only is a game's *motivation*— it's like a cake that you love to bake but you don't like at all to eat.

Habit Loop and Operant Conditioning

10

The theories you are about to read are based on the assumption that humans are a habitual species: we tend to have habits in videogames, at work, in our personal lives, and so on, because habits are extremely helpful when performing recurrent tasks: they come from evolution, as we've learned to reduce the cognitive workload on our brain by putting it in *zombie mode*. Now that you know the fundamental statement for these tools, you may dive into the frameworks themselves.

HABIT LOOP

In order to be created, a habit needs two elements: first, it must be repeatable, otherwise it's only a one-time task that, no matter how pleasant it is, won't become a habit. Second, it has to be composed of the following three steps: a trigger—an event that signals us into the routine—a routine—the action itself—and a reward—a positive element that closes the loop. If any of these three steps is missing in the initial phase of setting up a habit, it won't be created (Figure 10.1).

The habit loop works for all living creatures: the same way it's used to train animals, it's used to reward babies when they perform an action considered "good"; to show an example of the power of habit loops, think about when someone is cooking dinner and calls you by telling you "dinner is ready": this phrase is the trigger that makes you sit at the table and start eating—the action—to then feel full and not hungry anymore—the reward, or, in the case that you are eating a food you really like, tasting that food is the reward.

From the second you heard "dinner is ready", your mouth started to salivate, and your body prepared to receive food, but what if, after the trigger, there was nothing to eat? You would suddenly feel the emptiness in your stomach, and you would crave food, all of this from a simple "dinner is ready": this is the power of habit loops, generating a physical and emotional response with only the use of a trigger—if, of course, the loop successfully happened enough times before.

Generating a response with a trigger has a huge manipulative power, so how can we use this in game design? You can, as always, manipulate players into unethical actions, use

DOI: 10.1201/9781003229438-13

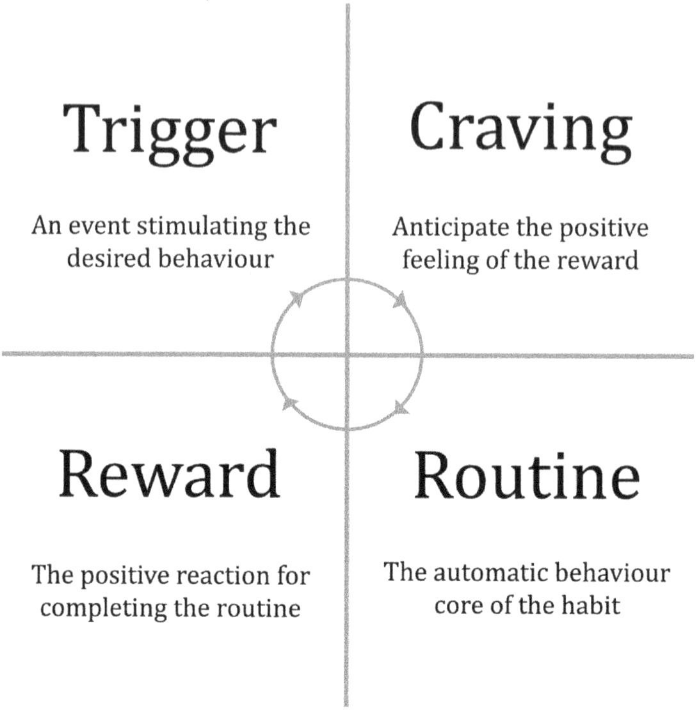

Trigger | Craving

An event stimulating the
desired behaviour

Anticipate the positive
feeling of the reward

Reward | Routine

The positive reaction for
completing the routine

The automatic behaviour
core of the habit

FIGURE 10.1 The visual representation of a habit loop, composed of trigger, craving, routine, and reward.

Source: Author.

it to teach new mechanics, create emotional responses, or even create a physical response that happens so fast that it looks like a reactive action, like dodging an attack.

A successful habit loop is created slowly over time, meaning that if you try to execute it while still teaching it to the players—who shouldn't know that they are being manipulated—you could make them notice the manipulation and break their immersion, but, once the loop is correctly created, it can be used to deliver the desired experiences to the players. You can also break the loop by providing a negative element instead of the reward, like *The Last Of Us 2* does with a workbench—an element perceived as positive and safe from enemies—where enemies ambush the player, creating an impactful *wow* moment but breaking the trust players have in the designers—that's why I usually do it near the end of an experience.

There are three main alterations to the classical habit loop you can use once it has been learned:

Uncertain Reward: you can change the reward from *certain* to *possible* or from *fixed* to *random*, creating a layer of gambling: sometimes players get the reward, other times they don't, sometimes it's something they like, other times it's something with no value; this strongly increases the emotional impact of the loop, but it also generates a proper addiction.

Craving Addiction: once the players get the reward, keep them from performing the loop again for a certain amount of time; this creates the desire for an action that can't be executed, having players in a state of desire for the loop that increases the pleasure of performing it the next time.

Sunk Cost: execute the trigger, but ask the players to pay a price—time or a currency—to let them execute the routine and obtain the reward; a player who already received the trigger will be far more likely to pay than a player who has to pay before hearing the trigger: their brain will trick them into thinking that, since they hear the trigger, they are already in the loop, anticipating the feeling of getting the reward at a subconscious level.

All of these three versions of the Habit Loop can be used to teach players something, generate strong emotions, and, with the use of random rewards, craving addition, and sunk cost, can be used for more complex behaviours; these techniques can be dangerous if used unethically, so be careful—as always, this book isn't about teaching morals; what to do with these tools is up to you.

OPERANT CONDITIONING

This technique is most commonly known as the *Skinner box*, a famous experiment with a mouse as a subject created by the psychologist Burrhus Frederic Skinner, and it's a type of associative learning process for reinforcement and punishment. It's a powerful design tool that is, unfortunately, unknown to most designers: to be precise, they *know* about the Skinner box and its theory, but they don't know how to apply it properly to game design—which is a shame, because this tool is perfect for teaching and correcting players' behaviours: teaching and correcting are two of the most important pillars in our field, because players are introduced to a world with rules different from the real world and different from the ones in other games, therefore it's our duty to create a smooth transition between worlds, especially to provide them with the best possible level of immersion. A good design isn't a world that teaches everything perfectly from the beginning—as you know, dynamics can't be predicted, so you never know how players juggle all the rules in your game—instead, a good design is a world that teaches most of the rules but then corrects the unwanted behaviours that arise—you are like a school, and the players are the children: of course they won't behave perfectly; they are in a brand new world to them, so it's up to you to direct them in the right way—and keep in mind that if a behaviour is unwanted it's not because we're evil, it's all in the players' best interest.

The operant conditioning is a system of punishments and reinforcements applied to the player, depending on if their behaviour is respectively wrong or right.

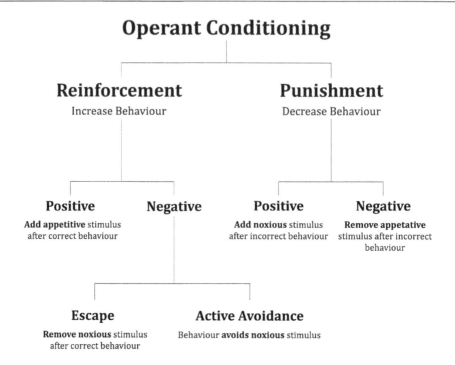

FIGURE 10.2   A scheme showing the branches of the operant conditioning theory.

Source: Author.

Starting from the punishments—aka the right side of Figure 10.2—the operant conditioning uses said punishments to reduce a behaviour that we—as designers—don't want to take place; there are two ways we can do this:

First, adding noxious stimuli after the behaviour happens: this is called positive punishment, because we *add* something perceived as negative to correct the behaviour—for example, getting yelled at by your boss, as the yellings are perceived negatively.

Second, removing an appetitive stimulus following the behaviour: this is called negative punishment, because we *remove* something perceived as positive to correct the behaviour—for example, having your pay check reduced after bad performances at work, as your boss is subtracting something you perceive as positive.

Before going any further, I want to make one thing clear: punishing the player is an extremely powerful tool, but it's just as dangerous. The right side of Figure 10.2 should always be used with the highest possible care: players perceive any type of punishment very strongly, and their experience will be influenced by those punishments, therefore you should either use mild ones or only do that when they are adopting a really severe behaviour—just like you wouldn't yell at a child for dropping a pencil; you don't want to traumatise them.

That said, also note that you can include multiple negative punishments at the same time, if you think they are needed for your game.

Now, moving to the left side: if a player does something you want them to do, and you want them to do it more often, there are two types of reinforcement you can use:

Positive reinforcement: you reward the player with something perceived as good when they act in the way you wanted, meaning you add an appetitive stimulus following the correct behaviour—like giving a cash bonus to the top salesman of the month or complimenting someone who did a great job.

Negative reinforcement: this is particularly interesting because the players are rewarded *indirectly* for adopting the right behaviour, and it's divided into two separate techniques.

First, active avoidance: it's a cool way to say "fear"; the player adopts the right behaviour because they are scared of what happens if they don't—I'm scared of missing my train, so I get to the station ten minutes early.

Second, escape: the reward for the correct behaviour is the removal of a negative stimulus. This is very useful in videogames, while in the real world it can be extremely dangerous—your boss stands next to you for hours to check that you don't make mistakes, and the reward isn't a bonus or something more but the boss leaving you alone, therefore the removal of the anxiety given by their presence.

This was the theory behind the operant conditioning, but how do you actually apply it? It's pretty easy: you should use this technique to generate or correct behaviours; let me explain. Create a scheme just like Figure 10.2, and instead of the "Operant Conditioning" title, describe the desired behaviour (meaning the dynamic)—for example, in a hypothetical FPS game, I want players to take their time to aim to the enemies' weak spots, like in *Horizon Zero Dawn*—and then, under each type of reinforcement and punishment, write a mechanic that leads the players to the desired behaviour: let's see what it would look like with the previously mentioned FPS game:

Positive reinforcement: the player deals critical damage when hitting a weak spot—the added appetitive stimulus is dealing more damage.

Negative reinforcement, active avoidance: the enemies have special attacks that deal more damage and are hard to dodge until one third of their weak spots are destroyed—the player is scared by the heavy attacks, therefore they follow our desired dynamic to avoid them.

Negative reinforcement, escape: when the player moves at high speed, their accuracy is reduced, and the crosshair moves a lot, while if they move slowly or stand still both accuracy and the crosshair are perfect—the player can remove the noxious stimulus by following our desired dynamic.

Before moving to the punishment side, note that you should test your game to see if these mechanics are enough to teach players the desired behaviours: if they are, there is no need for punishment—as said before, it's better not to use it if it's not needed—while if they are not, you can start designing it.

Positive punishment: the player loses health if they don't hit a weak spot—losing health is perceived as a noxious stimulus that is added to generate the desired behaviour.

Negative punishment: hitting a non-weak spot deals no damage to the enemies—removing the appetitive stimulus that is dealing damage reduces the appeal of performing this unwanted behaviour, therefore leading to the "correct" one.

Not all those ideas will be correct for our game—maybe they'll all be terrible—for tons of different reasons—one ruins the flow, another generates unwanted dynamics other than the one we wanted, and much more—but in just a few minutes, with this technique, you brainstormed five new mechanics that you *know* will support the game mechanic you want to be adopted by the players—"know" because, if the new mechanics respect the tool theory, psychology proved it will lead to a specific behaviour thanks to years of studies on actual living creatures. This allows you to teach players how to play your game after enough iterations: in the first round you may notice that some manipulations are too strong, others are too weak, and so on, but it's a starting point you would not be at without using the operant conditioning—and I can't stress this enough—all the mechanics are supporting your objective for the players.

BOX 10.1   THE TASK FOR THE OPERANT CONDITIONING FRAMEWORK, WHERE THE READER CHOOSES A GAME AND FIXES ONE OF ITS FLAWS USING THIS TOOL

OPERANT CONDITIONING TASK

Now that you know each type of reinforcement and punishment used in the operant conditioning, it's time for a task to make you design some mechanics yourself—it's been quite some pages since the last task since, as you can tell, the last parts you just read are very theoretical and very specific for different scenarios, meaning that comparing your results with mine would have given you no insights to follow.

For this task, pick a game of your choosing where you see a problematic dynamic, then design a solution using the operant conditioning, proposing a mechanic for each reinforcement and punishment.

Remember, they don't need to be *perfect* solutions for the problem—to do that, you would need tons of research and data about the game you are talking about—they just need to be valid and respect the operant condition framework.

As always, if you have problems performing the task or if you notice that a solution you proposed doesn't belong to the branch you put it in—for example, you designed an active avoidance mechanic for the escape field—go back to the part of the chapter you missed and spot where your mistake came from, or, if all the framework is foggy in your head, don't be afraid to read the chapter again—even Thomas Edison designed 3,000 bulbs before getting the one that we all know about, always remember that.

Game Design Patterns

11

Humans have always been pattern-recognising machines, meaning that our brains evolved to better see patterns and make the most out of them since we were cavemen: we saw the sky getting cloudy, so we knew rain was coming and we would seek shelter in a cave—we didn't know how clouds worked, but we understood the pattern, so patterns allowed us to make better decisions; despite many years passed since then, we still use pattern this way, and this is the cause of many of the nudges that you'll later read in this book.

In every existing field patterns are born: a series of actions takes place, and a specific outcome is more likely to happen; they don't have a perfect accuracy, but they still help us make up our minds about something—think about the stock trading market: patterns are crucial to understand how the market is going and, most of all, how it will behave next, and while they aren't always true, patterns are used by most traders out there because they provide a good starting point from which the trader can make a decision. Since it would be very hard to memorise every single pattern with its characteristics, pattern libraries are an important tool to understand, to then mix patterns and take advantage of the outcomes.

For game design, the founder of this pattern library is Staffan Bjork—professor at Gothenburg University and senior researcher at the Interactive Institute—who, before anyone else, tried to spot series of patterns in games—both board and digital; he first published the newly found pattern library in his book *Patterns In Game Design*,[1] to then release them publicly on a dedicated wiki[2]—from which came the name "Game Design Patterns" or "Patterns Design".

What does it mean to design trough patterns? It's a work of abstraction, where you look for a series of patterns you want—or that a competitor has—and you take note of their pros and cons, other than the details provided in the pattern description. This process gives you a superficial but interesting picture of the game mechanics that you may want to implement in your game, making the design process easier if used correctly and allowing you to zoom out a bit—this lets you spot potential flaws you would otherwise have missed.

It sounds tricky, so let's take a look at a pattern as an example:

Say I am designing a game where I'm not sure if I should put a Character Levels pattern; I open the wiki on its page,[3] read the description to see if it fits the game's current needs, and take a look at the listed examples—and *anti-examples*—to see which is more similar to the one I had in mind. Then I look at how the pattern is usually used, its consequences, and its relations with other patterns: in a short amount of time, I have a list of what the pattern does well, how the dominant design uses it, how it relates with other patterns I might have, and so

DOI: 10.1201/9781003229438-14

on. The goal is not to open a page and find a pattern perfectly designed for your game but rather to have a bigger picture of how that pattern would behave in your game: maybe it would have consequences that are against your high vision, or the way it's usually used doesn't fit your game, so you will need to use it in a new way, and so on.

Now, this is not how I would use it personally: I'm not really fond of game patterns, so it probably wouldn't be my go-to tool in this scenario; first, I see the patterns analysis as too superficial, and if taken out of context they lose what makes each pattern different, even with the same mechanics. Second, at the time I'm writing this book there are just over 600 patterns, which can sound like a lot but isn't at all: there are tens of thousands of game patterns out there, so even if those 600 are more than what you need, you would be missing many patterns that exist but aren't listed.

For both these reasons, on the occasions I do use this tool, I find it most effective when used as the TRIZ: it's great for brainstorming alone; I start reading various patterns and ask myself how each one may or may not solve the problem I'm having; in this case, the fact that the patterns are described in a generic way is helpful for thinking about a solution you wouldn't have thought of.

Another great way to use this tool is combining it with analysis: by analysing your game through a patterns lens, you can see how each mechanic can be linked to a pattern of belonging—for example, half of your mechanics belong to *combat*—and seeing how many mechanics are connected to a specific pattern is a quick way to understand the macro-systems of the game—50% of your mechanics belong to combat, therefore 50% of your resources will need to go there, but you notice that combat is less than a third of the game, so it's clear that there is a problem with the vision.

But why did I put it in the book then? Simple: I'm here to teach you about game design, not *Diego's view of game design*, meaning that it's my duty to provide you with all the tools I think a professional game designer should have based on the present and upcoming needs of the industry, even if I don't like them—just the same way you might hate my favourite tool.

NOTES

1 Bjork, S. and Holopainen, J. (2005), *Patterns in Game Design*. Hingham, MA: Charles River Media.
2 *Wikipedia*: http://virt10.itu.chalmers.se/index.php/Main_Page
3 Character Level, *Wikipedia*: http://virt10.itu.chalmers.se/index.php/Character_Levels

MDA Framework 12

The MDA is a framework developed by Robin Hunicke—game designer, producer, professor at University of California Santa Cruz, and co-founder of Funomena—Marc Leblanc—educator and game designer, who theorised the *8 Kinds of Fun*[1]—and Robert Zubek—game designer, writer, and co-founder of SomaSim—as part of the Game Design and Tuning Workshop at the Game Developers Conference, San Jose 2001–2004.

This is by far the most famous game design framework, both in the industry and at the academic level, and it should be known by everyone in this field: it's taught in every videogame course/university, and it's also one of the pillars from which many other frameworks were invented—MDTA+N, SSM, my own [(MDA)*N]P, just to name a few.

The same way there is no objective definition of "game"—since, as you have previously read, it's the reflection of a designer's soul—there is no framework suitable for every game and every task you might encounter: no framework is perfect, and this is why there are tons of them out there—I know it can sound scary to have so many tools in your bag, not really knowing which one to use and when, but it's one of the best parts of being a designer: we all see games in such different ways that we need to combine multiple tools to bring our vision to life; isn't it fascinating? We are creating brand new worlds and, as such, there are countless aspects we need to decide before letting our players in, therefore frameworks are tools that help us make the right decision with our players' best interest in mind.

Both as a designer and a researcher, I encountered, read, and used loads of frameworks, and each one of them is potentially positive and potentially negative at the same time—you could say they are Schrödinger's tools, with the key difference that you can tell whether one is going to work by learning how it works, saving a lot of time not having to test each one of them every time you need to make a decision—they all have certain strengths and certain weaknesses; they all work on certain games but not on others. The important part, when talking about frameworks, is understanding that not one of them is perfect, and it's up to you to find out which framework works best in each scenario—you may apply a framework made specifically for something on a totally different aspect of your game and discover that it works great there, too.

One of the goals of this book is also to give you a set of tools—mostly frameworks—used to solve specific problems you may encounter: Game Design Patterns are useful for brainstorming, the Self Determination Theory is great for a product's stickiness, and praxeology is the best to have an omni comprehensive vision of your product, but none of

DOI: 10.1201/9781003229438-15

them is the holy grail of frameworks—it just doesn't exist, but the same way a chef knows which knife to use on different foods, a designer knows which framework to use in different situations.

I know you are probably wondering "why dedicate so much attention to the MDA, if there are so many other frameworks?" and the answer is that the MDA, compared to other tools like the MTDA+N that focuses on the narrative of a game, is the most generic of all, meaning that it adapts to any kind of game, both board and digital. This is, however, its biggest weakness too: when a tool is generic, it won't spot and understand the details of a game, which can lead to a superficial understanding of the product—differently from, for example, the SSM, which focuses heavily on the Level Design of a game.

The MDA is often seen as a purely theoretical framework, when, in reality, it's a great practical tool: this chapter focuses, indeed, on its practical use, because the theoretical part can be found on the original documents explaining this framework—it would make no sense for me to copy and paste what you can find out there for free; I am still going to talk about it to explain how it works, or the practical part would mean nothing, but note that these are only the fundamentals of its theory; as always I suggest you take a deeper look into the free resources available online.

THEORY

The MDA framework states that a game is composed of three main components: mechanics, dynamics, and aesthetics.

Mechanics are the core pillars of the game, its rules, structure, and the technology used to create the game—including algorithms, engine, and game world: these are completely controlled by the designers.

Dynamics are essentially the behaviours, the actions that players perform coming from a game mechanic, the players' tactics, strategies, and way of playing the game: these can't be controlled by the designers, instead, they are generated by the players themselves and therefore can never be fully predicted—you might predict some more obvious ones, but most of the times players won't behave as you expected. They are how the player perceives the game is telling them to play, also in indirect ways such as how the space is used in a level; the presence of the player itself can generate a dynamic when related to the game world: an open world generates exploration because the space is mostly free and each area invites the player to reach it, often without the need of explicit clues—for instance, guiding lines are a perfect example of implicit communication with the player. Since these games offer so many spaces to explore, it's very common to give the player enough tools to do so: a car to move faster, a plane to get to the other side of a lake, a fast travel mechanic to skip most of the travelling aspect.

Aesthetics are the emotions that players feel through the dynamics: these belong to the players, aesthetics are *their* emotions, and it's the players' right to live them as they truly feel, meaning we have no power here. Aesthetics can be divided into eight aesthetics sub-categories:

Sensation (game as sense-pleasure): amazing visual and audio effects.

Fantasy (game as make-believe): imaginary world.

Narrative (game as drama): a compelling story the players can connect with.

Challenge (game as obstacle course): mastering and improving.

Fellowship (game as social framework): being part of a larger group, a community, often limited to multiplayer games.

Discovery (game as uncharted territory): exploring, testing the game's rules, answering *what if?* scenarios.

Expression (game as self-discovery): conveying yourself via in-game tools, such as avatar customisation, skins, character titles.

Submission (game as pastime): connection to the game itself.

According to the MDA, a game is created with mechanics—which we control—then by testing the dynamics—which we don't control, as they are generated by the combination of mechanics and agency—hoping to obtain the aesthetics we wanted.

Players, however, live this process in the exact opposite way: they live the aesthetics while testing the dynamics and rarely understand all the mechanics, rules, and technology behind them.

This framework is often underrated, especially in the initial relation between mechanics and dynamics, which is—in my opinion—the most brilliant part: it tells us that designers control the mechanics—including rewards, punishments, the whole game world, and so on—and each of these mechanics generates one *or more* dynamics: a single mechanic can make players behave in different ways, generating different emotions and potentially changing the experience players live completely—this is also why testing is so important: you expected a mechanic to generate a certain dynamic, while, upon testing, you find out another completely different dynamic takes place: you could have not known without letting players do what they do best, playing.

This view on the connection between mechanics and dynamics makes the MDA suitable for almost any game—more on that later—and even sports: for instance, soccer has tons of strategies like counterattacks, padlocks, and so on that weren't predicted when the sport was first invented; these strategies aren't defined by the mechanics, but, analysing said mechanics, they emerged from the players themselves—and they're all forms of dynamics. The role of the coach, in football, is essentially to define their team's dynamics and adapt them based on their opponent's dynamics—does this ring any bells? Exactly, this is what happens in esports too.

Another important element of this framework is that designers can influence and manipulate the players' behaviours creating mechanics that support the strategies we want to take place, but the more we move away from the mechanics, the less control we have: if you think of a game as a series of consequences, where players only live the aesthetics, it's easier to understand where our power ends. It doesn't matter what designers create; what matter is what reaches the players: if I create *A*, but they live *B*, it's not the players' fault for "not playing as they should have"—remember, never blame the players—it's my fault for not taking into account that a mechanic can transform into a completely different aesthetic, based on who is playing.

This player-centric view is crucial for a designer—and it's too often forgotten—because it give us a new way to look at both games and players and the way they interact with each other, the same way it tells us that the breaking point; while designing a game it's in the dynamics: they are the core of the game, the gameplay itself and how players react to it: if a game fails, it doesn't mean the mechanics were *bad* or poorly designed, they just weren't right for the dynamics the designers wanted—if you put gas in a diesel-engine car, you wouldn't blame the car for not working, right?

As I said earlier, no framework is perfect, therefore it's important to take a look at this framework's flaws:

One of the main ones is connected to the aesthetics sub-categories listed before: this taxonomy is too generic and not sufficiently useful to express all the emotions that the game can generate.

Another issue is that, since the MDA has a strongly mechanics- and dynamics-oriented point of view, games based on other elements—such as walking simulators, based on the narrative of the game—can't truly be represented with this framework.

Those critics, however, brought designers to develop new frameworks, more suitable for the scenarios where the MDA was failing: the same way narrative is a core component of the relatedness, working as an emotion multiplier, the combat system you use to fight a base enemy is also used to fight bosses, but the generated emotions are completely different, because there is a big emotional and narrative difference acting on your feelings—all of this to say that, while this framework is one of the most important, it's not perfect, so it won't always be your go-to tool, just keep that in mind.

Is this all there is to the MDA theory? Absolutely not, but, since it's an extremely well-known and valid technique, you can find a lot of material about it online and for free, meaning that I can dedicate more pages to the practical use of this framework—which is where people often lack—and explain how to use this as an actual tool and not just as a theoretical resource.

PRACTICE

Now that you know the theory behind the MDA framework, it's time to take a look at its practical uses:

The first way to use it is to analyse already-existing games: I suggest you to use a spreadsheet, divided into three main columns—Mechanics, Dynamics, and Aesthetics, as shown in Figure 12.1—and customising it based on your needs, for example adding another column for a narrative multiplier, creating a page for each level, or adapting the format to suit the game's characteristics.

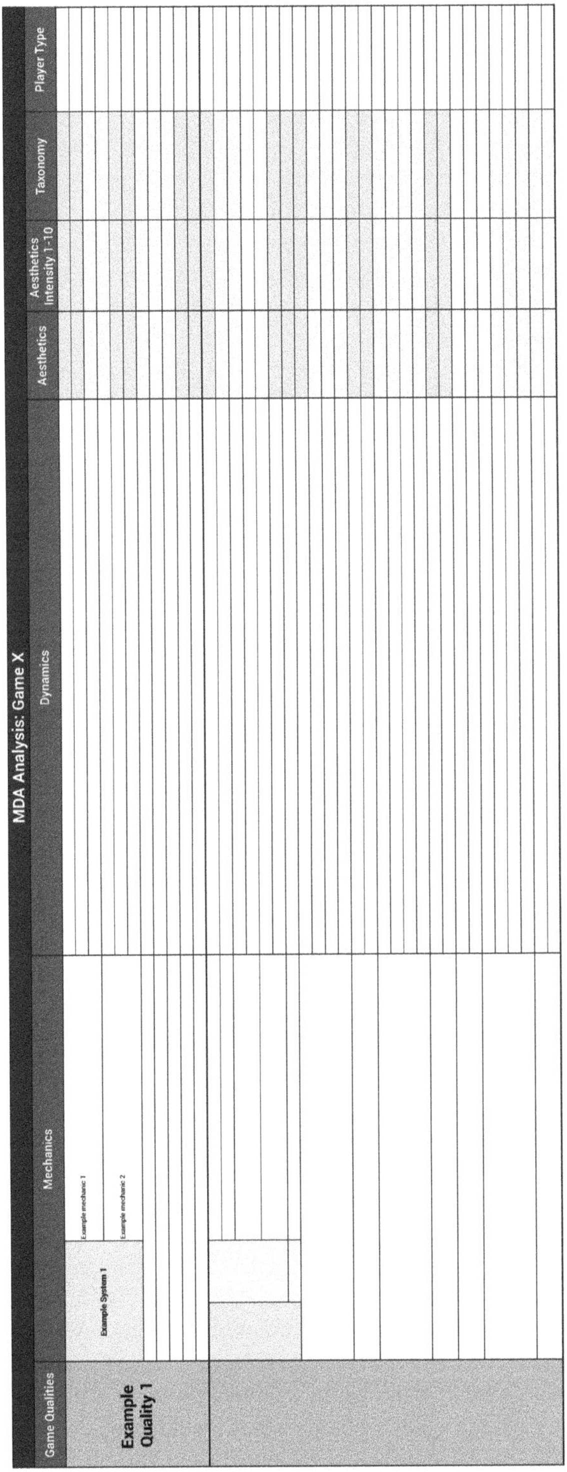

FIGURE 12.1 The most simple form of an empty MDA document using a spreadsheet.

Source: Author.

The first main column—Mechanics—is divided into systems and mechanics—systems can be divided into Brenda Romero's game qualities, Epics for those working in Agile Scrum, or any other taxonomy relevant to your analysis—starting from the biggest elements first, then zooming out to list every single mechanic in each system. Each system can contain multiple mechanics, and each mechanic must be written in a way that it describes the mechanic, the interaction and the agency that it provides the player with.

Each mechanic generates at least one dynamic: no mechanic can generate no dynamics, but any mechanic can generate multiple dynamics—think of a door: the mechanic is that it can be moved, the first two dynamics it creates is that it can be both pushed and pulled, and even if it has to be pushed, some people will try to pull it anyway, and as designers we need to acknowledge that.

On a practical level, dynamics are the strategies that players will adopt based on what and how a relative mechanic works: they can follow the expected behaviour designers had in mind—pushing a door that has to be pushed—or be unpredicted by the designers— pulling that same door; if a mechanic generates dynamics unpredicted by the designers, they need to choose: accept the existence of that dynamic but ignore it, accept it and modify the design to embrace the new dynamic, or modify the mechanic to get rid of it—as always, there are no right or wrong answers, it really depends on the situation.

For instance, in the game *Cats & Soup*,[2] the "cook cat" generates a soup every X seconds, each produced soup is located at the bottom of the screen, and soups can be sold to gain money, but only a limited number of soups are stored in the bottom section; what dynamics does the first mechanic generate? The players will keep the game open to sell soups to optimise their gains, and the players will keep opening the game every Y minutes to gain as much money as possible.

Each dynamic has one matching aesthetic, meaning the emotion the players will feel when performing the described dynamic; some emotions are very powerful—possibly because they come from long gameplay segments or because of a different narrative value—while others are quicker and less intense. This is the reason why you can associate a value—between 0 and N, based on your needs—to each aesthetic, indicating how intense that emotion was; for example, the joy coming from defeating a boss is very different from the joy you feel after defeating an enemy just like many others: they are both joy, but each one has a very different value perceived by the players.

There are many ways to differentiate aesthetics: the classical MDA framework uses the eight sub-categories covered before, but, as I said, it can be very limiting, and this is the reason why each designer can use the taxonomy they prefer or even mix multiple taxonomies together—types of fun by Lazzaro, gameplay emotions, Caillois' taxonomy, and so on. Choosing the right taxonomy for your game is crucial, as different ones will give you different information: if you use Bartle's Archetypes and the six main types of emotions, you will know what are the most common emotions for each player type and what archetype the game is for; if you use Lazzaro's types of fun you can see the main types of fun present in the game and which system each one belongs to; using an intensity value you see which dynamics generate the strongest emotion, which player type experiences those emotions the most, and much more.

Doing an MDA analysis for a whole game is an extremely long and time-consuming process, because you have to break down every single aspect of the game—like a scientist discovering atoms for the first time, how they connect to create objects and finding the differences between different atoms—then asking yourself what dynamics are generated by those atoms, what emotions come from the dynamics, and how powerful those emotions are. The results coming from such a long analysis, however, are priceless: you will then have the 50% science of that game, what the game is at its core, how it works and what it makes players feel, and this allows you to develop your design skills and critical eye, have a better understanding of the game itself and its competitors, see how the mechanics are divided across all the systems and how each system impacts the players' emotions; basically, it allows you to see through a game, like putting a mysterious device under an X-ray machine to understand all of its components.

Does this mean that to understand a specific aspect you need to break down every single inch of a game? Not at all: if you want to X-ray just a specific element of the game—say, the combat system of an RPG—you can focus on that part only, but remember that a complete analysis always provides the bigger picture—as always, it's up to you.

The second way to use this framework is to analyse the product you are developing right now—using the same spreadsheet format covered before—for two main reasons:

One, a complete MDA analysis of the game—in this case it has to be a full analysis—in a non-initial stage, for example during the alpha tests when you already have a playable build, tells you if the product is following the original vision: it's really easy to lose track of the initial vision when you see your game grow day after day, especially during the first projects you work on; therefore having a tool that tells you mathematically if your game changed, how deep each system is, what the generated aesthetics are, and so on allows you to have a scientific vision of what is happening in your game. If the MDA results show that your game has changed, you can either adapt your vision to the new circumstances or modify the game elements that are generating different dynamics and aesthetics compared to the ones you first had as a goal—it lets you compare what you wanted to be with what you really are now: if the game is different, it isn't necessarily *better* or *worse*, it just may need a different audience.

Two, a comparison between your ideal MDA—an MDA spreadsheet filled with the dynamics and aesthetics you wish your players to experience—and the actual MDA of a segment of the game shows you which dynamics you predicted right and which ones you missed, and the same goes for aesthetics and the intensity of the aesthetics. You can now use the tools covered before—such as Operant Conditioning and praxeology—to understand the causes of these differences, decide whether you want to keep them or change the design, and use those manipulation techniques to guide the players into your desired experience; for instance, if the players attack with a different strategy from the one you spent most time polishing—therefore perceiving a lower quality side of the game—you can add rewards and punishments following the Operant Conditioning to lead players into using the *super cool amazing killer* combo that has stronger intensity of emotions and is more fulfilling to experience.

To conclude this framework, now that you know how to *fix* your game with it, how do you use it to *design*? Well, the MDA is great into early designing phases to have a clear goal of the dynamics and aesthetics you want to achieve, but if you are designing a medium/

big game, I suggest you not write a whole MDA analysis yet: there would be too many guesses and uncertainties, so, in that case, it's better to analyse each system as you are developing it, so that after the first playtest you won't have a hundred holes in all the parts of the design, just some in a specific section—it's way easier to put out a matchstick than a whole wildfire.

Such analysis helps you prevent major flaws in your design before investing time and resources to implement it, and, as you've seen, if something lets you save time you should always have it in your tool bag; this is also a great tool both for veterans and new entries in the design field, as it trains you into seeing things from a player's eyes but as a designer.

NOTES

1   *8 Kinds of Fun* website: http://algorithmancy.8kindsoffun.com/
2   *Cats & Soup* IOS: https://apps.apple.com/ph/app/cats-soup/id1581431235
     Cats & Soup Android: https://play.google.com/store/apps/details?id=com.hidea.cat&hl=en&gl=US

Nudges

13

The Nudges theory comes from Richard Thaler and Cass R. Sunstein's book *Nudge*,[1] published in 2008; since its publication, this theory has expanded to basically every type of design, from product to event and to games too: since the first version of the theory, many new nudges have been found for specific fields as well, bringing under the term *nudge* other theories such as all the ones belonging to *Cognitive Biases*.

This theory shows that the brain isn't a perfectly operating machine; it's neither completely logical nor completely emotional, therefore there are some sorts of glitches that exploit those imperfect sides of the mind to guide people toward a choice; of course, it's not like a brainwash, it doesn't work 100% of the time, and, most of all, it's not easy to do: at least once in your lifetime, you knew someone was trying to manipulate you into a specific choice, and once you realise that, no trick in the world could have worked—as you have read before, the first step of manipulation is not knowing someone is manipulating you. Using nudges makes it really easy for players to notice the manipulation, but they are an extremely powerful tool that every designer should know and learn to use in the right situation, so that players don't notice it at all—because the experience coming from the manipulation is stronger than the feeling of being manipulated.

There are many different nudges, some similar to each other, some completely opposite, and, for them too, I could write a whole other book just about nudges, therefore in this book I'll cover the ones that are the most important, the pillars of the nudge theory, and the ones that are less used but that every designer should know; as always, I suggest you go read more about nudges online, or in other books, as there are hundreds of them: read as many as you can—so that when the right situation comes, you have the nudge which is just the right fit—but focus on really learning a few of them you are comfortable with, to master their use and improve your design skill—who knows, maybe one day there will be a role called *Nudge Designer*, who only specialises 100% on the nudges inside a game, meaning they can be all studied at their best—until then, though, focus on the quality rather than the quantity.

GOD/SUPERMAN COMPLEX

I want to start off with one of the easiest and most commonly used nudges for an easy introduction: the god complex; in real life, everybody has the desire to feel responsible for something no one else can do, just like a comic book hero: this creates the desire to save or help people in ways the average person couldn't handle, strongly motivating those affected by this complex. Motivation is always a good thing in our field, and that's why many games use a narrative excuse to create and feed this feeling: such games are called *Power Fantasies*, with the main character—the player—described as the only person who can accomplish a goal unreachable for anyone else; for example, in *Saints Row IV*, you are the president of the United States and the only one who can save the world from aliens invading the planet—that level of power is hard to beat, isn't it?

One of the most common ways to lean the player into this complex is retention with glorification: in *The Elder Scrolls V: Skyrim*, the player is constantly reminded of being the *Dragonborn*, the only one who can save the world, throughout the entire playthrough. This game also glorifies players from past games of the series: there are in-game books narrating the story of *Oblivion*—the previous *Elder Scrolls* game—and those who played it know that they are the person the books are talking about, glorifying them not only for what they are doing and what they will do but also for what they did—you are not just playing a game, you are playing in a whole universe that comes to life every time you launch a game of the saga.

This technique is very simple but very effective, so much so that many games still adopt it despite it being used for years; a quick way to increase its effect even more is with the *stigma effect*: give the player a positive visible stigma that already tells them they are different—a big scar, a unique mark, and so on. Long story short, if you want to increase the retention of your game, glorify the players, not only by making them feel special but also by giving them a tangible sign that differentiates them from all the other NPCs in the game.

FEAR OF MISSING OUT

This technique is one of the most used even outside of game design, so it's very likely that you already know what I'm talking about, maybe you just didn't know its name; the fear of missing out is the idea that humans fear missing an occasion, because when we think we could regret not taking the chance, we act in a very impulsive way and we become more motivated by the fear of regret than by the actual desire we have for the product itself; this can further be improved by a scarcity in resources or time—those are different sides of the same nudge.

It is often used in marketing campaigns to lead people into impulsive purchases: do the phrases "Only until Sunday!" or "Just 100 products left!" ring any bells? Exactly, you've seen this countless times and not only in videogames.

There are three ways this is applied in our field:

First, to sell the game itself, for example with limited editions, pre-orders with bonus content, and so on.
Second, for in-game monetisation, like "the *super amazing cool bundle* at 4.99$ instead of 12.99$ just for today!"
Third, as part of the actual gameplay, such as with daily rewards for logging onto the game to bring players back every day or with daily quests that rewards players with premium items—items they would normally have to purchase

with a real money-related currency—to make players play a bit to complete the quest—which is usually randomly generated—hoping they would get caught in the loop and keep playing; in this case, the theory is used to generate extrinsic motivation via the reward—for those of you who remember the types of motivation covered earlier in the book.

This technique is also used with narrative excuses: "you only have three (in-game) days to reach that city" or with events-related quests/game modes, like *Overwatch*'s *Junkenstein revenge*, a Halloween game mode only available for around three weeks every year.

Before you start to use this tool in every aspect of your game, note that, while limiting a resource increases its value and generates motivation—as you recall from praxeology—the constant fear of missing something the players want is stressful for them, so each time you use it you also increase the neuroticism level of your game.

FRAMING

Framing is the concept of using nudges through syntax: one of the most common framing techniques is positive/negative framing, where you frame a sentence in a different way to change people's perception on the topic, even if it means the same thing as the original sentence"

If I ask a group of people "are you willing to retire keeping 70% of your current pay check?" most of them will agree, but if I ask the same group "are you willing to retire losing 30% of your current pay check?" most of them will decline the offer, even if the result is the exact same.

For the first question, I asked about *keeping* something, which the brain perceives as positive, while for the second version, I used *losing*, which is of course seen badly: no one likes to lose or give up something they have, especially when they feel like they have earned it—you earned your pay check, your work position, your office, and so on. This technique is often used in the medical field too, where doctors are trained to frame their sentences positively: "this operation has a 90% success rate" sounds way better than "there is a 10% chance you will die".

A famous example of framing happened with *World Of Wordcraft*, where, to stop people from spending too many consecutive hours on the game, *Blizzard Entertainment*—the developing company of the game—inserted a system that made players earn 50% of the normal EXP if they played more than a certain amount of hours in a row; many players got angry—because of the negative framing of the system—so the design team flipped the idea: if enough time passed from a player's last session to the current one, for some hours they would gain 200% of the normal EXP, calling this mechanic *Rested Experience*. Players loved it because they would get more points, but the effect was the same as the previous system's: in both cases they had to stop playing the game for some hours in order to optimise their EXP gains, but, with a positive framing, players perceived it as a reward instead of a punishment.

Another type of framing is accusatory questions: a question implying that the target committed the action they are accused of, therefore any answer that doesn't begin with *"it's not true that I . . ."* frames the person; this is really effective, because once the accusation is in the question, the person answering will focus on providing an explanation, rather than analysing the question—this is why it's commonly used among teachers, police officers, and parents that want someone to "slip" and admit their actions.

On a totally unrelated note, why didn't you do all the tasks I gave you?

You see, if you did all the tasks, your first reaction will be "How dare you?!", because you know the question implies something wrong, but if you didn't do all of them, you wouldn't even think about how I would know that, you would just think about a valid explanation to answer with—by the way, I'm sure you didn't fall for that question since you didn't skip any of the tasks, because you know that they are made for you to improve your skills, and transform the theoretical knowledge into practical knowledge . . . *right?*

Framing can also be applied with names—let me tell you an example, and see if this too rings any bells:

> The smallest cup size you can find in the menu of a coffeehouse chain is called the *Tall*, meaning that, while it is the smallest one, you won't perceive you are buying something small per se: having it named *Tall* makes customers see it as positive, as for years fast food chains divided their drinks in *small*, *medium*, and *big*—and *tall* sounds a lot more like *big* than *short*, don't you agree?
>
> The same can be done in videogames, as mentioned before for the *Devil May Cry* saga, where the lowest of the scores still stands for *Destruction*, making it look cool in the eye of a new player—imagine playing a game for the first time: you get a D score, where D stands for *"Damn, that was bad"*; it wouldn't be really motivating.
>
> Why is name-framing so important? Well, calling something *mana, energy, rage* or anything else has a huge perceived difference, even if it is mechanically the same thing—if in a wholesome game about unicorns the main resource was called *deadly rage*, it would be way less used than if it was called *kindness*. Always think carefully about the name of your mechanics based on the context they are in and on how you want the players to perceive them—in our field, a name is way more than the name itself: it is also its meaning, the emotions it generates, its affordance, and much more.

The last type of framing I want to cover is labelling: it consist in describing someone with the characteristics needed for the desired act—it sounds harder than what it is, trust me; if you wanted someone to lend you $20, you would frame the sentence with a note on how selfless that person is: "you are always so generous, can I borrow $20?" Of course, it needs to be done in a more elaborate way than this, but you get the idea. The reason why this works—if done correctly—is that you first create a superman complex inside the person's mind, you describe them as you need them to be, and, since our brain doesn't like to contradict others, they will be more inclined to accept your request—this is done tons of times in games to make players accept the quests, and most of the times it is very obvious too.

APOPHENIA

Humans are pattern-recognising machines that try to understand what is going on around them to spot potential patterns, even where there is no pattern. Apophenia is exactly that, trying to find a meaning where none exists. Sometime we choose to do that, while others it happen on a deeper level: finding what look like patterns to us give us a sense of comfort, as it leads us to believe that we can predict what is going to happen next—it can be scary to live without any clue about the future, so we sometimes make our own clues up.

In games, however, apophenia is usually used the other way around: players don't use the elements they find to spot clues about the future, but rather to understand the past, therefore in a purposeful way; games with a lore-narrative or a narrative-iceberg structure are for a big part based on this technique: instead of having a defined plot—a clear narrative sequence—they leave cryptic clues around the game world, to see what players will come up with because of the human desire to find a meaning, to fill the gaps. This creates a sense of community among players, who will be motivated to share their theories and compare them with one another, trying to find the "real" one, when even the designers may not have the "real" answer.

Many narrative RPG games—such as Bleak Spirit, as well as some D&D campaigns—are based on creating a world with random clues, to then ask the players to discover the story; it's not a hard technique to apply and it can be strongly motivating, but it needs a world where what happened is more important than what is happening and will happen next.

Note that apophenia works as the ground for many other nudges that designers can use. These aren't strictly part of apophenia itself, otherwise it would be very difficult to separate one from the other, so I decided to cover their "parent" nudge, so that if you like this type of manipulation, you can explore it more by yourself. For reference, some of these techniques are Gambler's Fallacy, Pareidolia, Tinkerbell Effect, and Anchoring.

IKEA EFFECT

The Ikea effect is very famous and present all around the world in multiple fields, from toys to food, from furniture to, of course, videogames; it's based on the concept that the satisfaction coming from a product is increased if the user put some type of effort into the making of the product itself—sure a chair is cool, but playing a role in making that chair possible is ten times cooler, because without you it would just be a pile of boards and screws.

Does it mean people have to build the product from scratch? Not at all, even a small effort can generate this effect, and even if the user had to follow a step-by-step guide no satisfaction is taken away from them—sometimes, following the step-by-step is part of the experience: think about Lego sets with thousands of pieces, where part of the enjoyment comes from placing every single piece into the right spot.

In games, both video and board ones, this effect is used in many ways: quick times events where you don't just look at a cutscene but you earn it by pressing the right key at the right time or creating a build for your character in an RPG—it's not just a build you bought, you made it yourself, one piece at the time—and again with the customisation of bases, vehicles, ships, and so on—it's *your* ship, with the sails you wanted and played to get.

PRINCIPLE OF LEAST EFFORT

The Marginal Utility concept covered earlier in this book comes exactly from this principle: humans are lazy creatures, they want to do the easiest possible thing, even if it's less satisfying than doing harder tasks; they will keep doing something until it leads to negative events—like feeling bloated after too many glasses of water—or the outcome's perceived value is close to zero.

In games, this is done with friction mechanics, which gradually make a task less efficient to bring players to stop performing it—they don't directly stop the players, who can keep doing it as long as they want, they just make the task perceived as a waste of time compared to other possible activities.

A common example can be found in grinding mechanics in RPGs: killing enemies in an area always gives you the same amount of resources, but, as you level up, that amount of resources won't be as worthy of your time, as you will now need ten times what you needed before to progress. If you want your players to stop doing something after a certain point of the game without enforcing it, introduce friction mechanics that will make them realise how that same action is not as profitable it as it was before.

ENDOWED PROGRESS

As you should know by now, humans are lazy, so, when you give them a task, their first thought will most likely be "*oh no*"; the bigger the task is, the bigger their *oh no* moment will be. There is, however, a catch: since we all are lazy, we love progress, because it brings us closer to our goal—progress is a very powerful source of motivation—but you know what we like more than progress? Starting ahead, especially when we didn't know we had to do something and we're already 20% through—I'll get to that in a second.

This technique is used a lot by businesses to retain customers: you go to a coffeehouse, buy something, and they give you a punch card stating that every five coffees you get one for free; your mind thinks "Well, five coffees are a lot considering that I don't even know if I'll come back to this place again", but then the trick happens: they punch one of the five slots right in front of you. Suddenly you made progress; you are already 20% through, and four coffees left don't seem so impossible to get, especially considering how easy it was to get the first one. Other than that, if you have to choose between this coffee place and another where you have no punch card, you will prefer the first one, because they reward you for your money and your fidelity to them—in reality, most of them won't care at all, but you don't really mind that, because that punched card made you feel like they did care.

In games, this is used primarily for EXP points: you just levelled up, but the extra EXP you had from the last level didn't go to waste; on the contrary, you already have some points toward the next level, making it feel easier to get there rather than starting again from zero points.

Another common usage is having a quest asking you to find, say, four keys scattered around the game world, but you already have one: it doesn't matter that it will take you hours to find the other three, because you are almost halfway there already.

While this technique works great, it can't be used too many times, or the players will soon figure it out and, as always, feel tricked and manipulated.

SURVIVORSHIP BIAS

The most famous example of Survivorship Bias comes from World War II: the American Army decided to reinforce the areas of their planes with the most hits, thinking it would have led to fewer planes destroyed by the Germans; Abraham Wald—a member of the *Statistical Research Group* (SRG)—however, studied that the army only accounted for the survived planes, meaning that the ones that didn't survive were hit in the areas with less damage—damages in that area would have made the plane crash and not return to the base.

This bias is very common among people who *create* something, whether it's a game, a tech invention, or a service; it's the tendency to look at successful stories to follow them as role models, especially their workflow and strategy, thinking "If *person X* could do it, I can do it too", without looking at all the other key factors that played a major role into the outcome we all see today. People often choose as examples those who started with nothing and ended up building an empire, thinking that by applying the same exact business strategy, they will have just as much success as their models; there is, however, a major flaw in this thought process: they are not the person they look up to, meaning that they don't have the same opportunities, the same decision-making skills, and they are not in the same historical period—it's easy to talk about the wheel now that it already exists.

This bias tells us that looking only at someone's successes will probably make you fail, because they are the only ones who can replicate their wins, but looking at their mistakes is where you can learn the most because anyone can commit their same mistakes. This is even more true for game designers: you all know you have certain *must-dos* during the production that are the pillars of the game—they remind you what the original vision was and what you want the game to look like—but people often forget about all the *must-nots* that tell you what you decided to avoid, because it would lead to failure—they are like pillars you don't want to use because they would break, making your whole building fall down.

It's easy to define what a genre of game is made of, but it's hard to say what it's not, meaning that if you don't understand the limits of your game, you won't be able to make the most out of how far it goes, and it will feel like any other game of that genre—or worse, it won't truly belong in any genre. Games can theoretically be anything, therefore it's easier to design where they end rather than going further until the production time runs out—it's a shame to know that your game won't go any farther than the line you trace, but if you try to go in all the directions you won't go far in any of them.

This bias can also be applied combined with the Authority Effect—stating that humans are used to following a hierarchy, and if none is present they tend to create one to either lead it or follow it; using these two together creates the meta of a game: players see pro players/content creators use a certain strategy/build, they often succeed due to their pro-level—or they only show the winning matches for better content—making players perceive that strategy/build as the strongest one and leading them to use it as well; this also works because people often look up to pro players/content creators, perceiving them as on a higher step in the hierarchy compared to themselves, further sustaining players following the current trends.

As a designer, you need to acknowledge this event even if you don't like it, because it could happen to your very own game, and you will either have to deal with it as a burden or use it to your advantage.

We also can use these scenarios to create an NPC with a high position on the hierarchy and with winning strategies, so that players can copy them for a higher chance of success in their run—especially when introducing new mechanics, having practical demonstrations increases their statistical rationality, as mentioned in praxeology.

MERE OWNERSHIP EFFECT

According to our brains, something we own has more value than the exact same thing owned by someone else or being brand new, both as an intrinsic value—mine is better, cooler—and as an extrinsic value—it's worth more money; this effect is very noticeable with kids, as they can create a strong emotional bond with an item they will not want to let go of—when your phone breaks as an adult you are more concerned about its cost than anything, but when your favourite toy breaks as a kid you basically go through the five stages of grief.

This can be brought to game design to manipulate players in many ways: you can give an item to the player, have them use it for a while to let them become attached, then take it away to generate craving and motivation, making them complete quests to get it back; or you can lend an item to a player for some hours, then make them pay money to have it back, even with a limited-time discount to further lean them into the purchase—a combination of Mere Ownership effect, craving, and Fear of Missing Out.

If you really want to have an impact on the player, however, you can have an NPC take an item away from them—something they like and they are attached to, like their most used weapon—and destroy it forever, to generate rage and hate against the NPC, framing them as their enemy.

SUNK COST

According to this nudge—called both Sunk Cost and Sunken Cost—our mind tries to convince us to perform an activity we don't like if we invested resources into it—mainly time and money, the two main resources you can invest in games—and the more resources have been put into that activity, the stronger this effect will be—it sounds a lot like a paradox, but bear with me; say you bought the ticket for a movie but you later found out it's terrible: do you stay home ignoring the money spent on the ticket, or do you go anyway because you already paid?

While the second option sounds like the best way to damage control your losses— "even if I won't like the movie, at least the money will not be completely wasted"—it's the one that will make you spend even more money and time: not only you will spend two hours for the movie itself, you will also have to drive to the theatre, pay for the gas and maybe even some popcorn; your mind sees the resources you already invested as more valuable than the one you will have to invest next, while staying at home—or doing something else—would have saved you more money and more time.

In videogames, the main way this technique is used is monetisation: many games create mechanics that extend the perceived length of the game—"you ran out of energy for today, come back tomorrow!"—for a couple of weeks, to then offer you a DLC at a discounted price, $10 instead of $15. Your brain will think "I've been playing this game for two weeks now, I could spend $10 dollars on it", because the time invested so far justifies—according to your mind—what you have yet to invest.

If you think about the actual playtime, however, your thought becomes "I spent two hours on this game over the last two weeks, was it worth $5/hour?", and your answer is more likely to change—escaping the framing that the game tries to sell you gives you a clearer idea of how you really feel about the game—demonstrating how nudges can be combined for a deeper and less obvious manipulation.

Another use for this nudge is increasing the emotional outcome of the game by asking players to invest resources in the action they are performing: in games like the ones from the *Fire Emblem* series, you invest resources into characters that you can lose forever, therefore increasing the emotion value of each action that could lead to the death of one of your characters—just like your movie ticket, you don't want something you invested in go to waste.

Picture a boss you can fight unlimited times with no negative consequences if you lose, and now think about the same boss, but each time you want to fight it you have to pay 1,000 *gold coins*—let's say those are a lot of coins; your behaviour toward the fight will be completely different in the second scenario: you won't be able to just suicide if the fight started badly, and you will also have a lot more pressure on your every move, because every mistake could cost you all that gold—it's like baking a cake for a party, but it's your first time baking and there are just enough ingredients for one attempt: every move you make feels like defusing a bomb.

EGO PREFERENCE

Similarly to the Mere Ownership Effect, the Ego Preference states that humans like things with our name on it more; you've seen this on many different occasions, from soda companies producing cans with names on people to coffeehouses writing your name on the cup—sometimes twisting it on purpose to add a layer of humour.

In games, this is done by letting players name their character, pet, weapons, and so on; for example, in GDR games, I always call my weapons the *Widowmaker*, because it adds a lot of value for me: it's not just a weapon, it's *the Widowmaker*, something I've used in tons of different games—almost as if it changed shape depending on the game, always being with me throughout every adventure.

To push this effect even more, thanks to the creation of both the metaverse and subscription services, the line between "reality" and "games" is getting thinner and thinner: if the game knows your name, it could create an NPC named after you, having them gain more and more relevance during the run and making you bond with them; then, in the final battle, the NPC sacrifices themself to save you, meaning that the game is exploiting your bond to the character to generate stronger emotions, or maybe the main villain kills them, so that you now want your revenge—they didn't just kill *GenericPersonNumber53*, they killed what could have been you. Many games already use certain user's data to provide custom gameplay moments, but, as more data is being gathered on the users, that information could be used to create an experience truly unique based on who is playing the game: it can be scary if done in an unethical way, but it can be great if done right—and, as always, I'm not here to tell you what you can or cannot do.

DIDEROT EFFECT

This nudge is based on two concepts:

>   The first one is that *goods* purchased by consumers will align with their sense of identity and, as a result, will complement one another.
>   The second one is that the introduction of a new possession that deviates from the consumer's current *complementary goods* can result in a process of spiral consumption.

Taking a look at the first statement, people buy things they identify themselves with—thus an extension of the concept of taste; for example, I love *Pokémon*, so I have a lot of *Pokémon*-themed t-shirts, while a fan of metal music may have tons of t-shirts from metal bands they like, and a cosplayer goes to an event cosplaying as a character they identify with: we buy and use products that represent parts of our identity for many different reasons, from a sense of belonging to the pride of being that character or liking that band or that game.

Now, onto the second part: first off, a *complementary good* is something whose appeal increases with the value of its component, just like a console gets part of its value from the exclusive games it has or how well games are optimised specifically for that console; this is the *status quo*, what you currently own and are used to. But what happens if a new possession is introduced? You obtain a new good that you like so much that every other related item needs to be changed to fit in with this new one, completely disrupting that previous status quo—this is the moment you realise how much you don't fit in your own world anymore and how much you've changed.

Maybe you always loved the colour blue since you were a kid, so, the same way you had all blue toys as a child, you now have an artic blue couch, a denim blue kitchen, stone blue walls, and so on; everything is great, until one day you find this amazing red carpet: you just love it, but as you place it in your living room, it doesn't go with anything in your whole house, so you start changing everything—new brown couch, light grey walls, white kitchen—not only to make it fit with the carpet but also to respects your *current* sense of identity. For me, our identity isn't an art piece that we create once and put on a shelf to be admired forever; it's more like a marble block that we never really stop working on: every once in a while we choose to sculpt it, other times the events we live do that for us, but if we forget to check on it for too long, it ends up just not being us, leading to a spiral of changes as big as the amount of time we forgot about our block for.

How do we use these elements in games, you ask? By introducing visive or mechanical elements aimed to generate a spiral of change in the players, with a double effect: first, creating a will to change in an arbitrary way to increase the variety of the player's experience; second, increasing the length of the game, as changing, say, one's build often requires resources—time and currencies—making the game tens or hundreds of hours longer, especially if those new elements that inspire change are added constantly with updates.

The best way to make the most of this effect is by introducing elements with a very strong in-game value that are also very specific: armours and weapons with very different appearances, visual effects or mechanics that don't mix together or that increase a single type of ability, inducing players into following that new build by changing their skills, gears, and so on. You need, of course, to allow players to find these items at the right pace, because if they get new elements by the second they will just wait to find the ones they like without needing any change, and the whole nudge loses its power.

Diablo III, for example, has *Legendary Gems*, an item that makes a specific build much more powerful, with the twist that said build almost never aligns with the one you are using: you play as a necromancer that deals 1,000 DMG/minute by blowing corpses up, and you find a Legendary Gem that makes you deal 2,500 DMG/minute with a Golem build; it's a lot more damage, so you may seriously consider switching your whole build—which requires you to find new gear, therefore more time—starting the spiral that will go on until you find a new and more powerful gem, bringing you back to the top of that spiral all over again.

DROWNING PERSON EFFECT

You may recall that I've mentioned this effect before in the book, but, since it's one of the pillars of how game design works, it's important to take a deeper look into it.

Imagine if you had a rescue company paid to get drowning people out of the sea: you would spend a ton of money to have lifeguards on shores and boats and helicopters constantly roaming around the sea to spot people in need of help; it would be a crazy expense, right? It would be way easier to get some people, throw them in the sea, rescue them, and ask for money, but they wouldn't be very happy about it.

The best strategy would be to throw them in the sea when they are distracted to then sell them a life jacket and let them swim back to shore; it would be wrong, sure, but they all would pay a lot for that jacket.

This is exactly how games work: we designers throw a player into a problematic situation; we give them the game tools—meaning the life jacket—and let them get out of the problem themselves, with the main difference that while in real life people would hate you—or actually, sue you—in games players are happy to experience all of this—they aren't just *playing* a game, they are living it.

In games, we have the incredible power to generate any type of problem we can think of, to then have players willingly work toward solving it while enjoying the time they are spending; if the problems and solutions are fair—meaning that we give them all the information they need to get out of that situation and the problem is at their level of skill—they will want more problems, more tools, more *gameplay.*

As you can tell, this nudge is more suitable for the design of a game rather than the gameplay itself, and, if it still sounds bad as a technique, just remember that from the moment the players open your game, they sign an implicit pact with you saying that they will agree to your rules and work on the problems you throw them into, as long as you respect their effort and time—and, most of all, use those to make them live the best possible experience you can create.

This concludes the part dedicated to nudges, but it doesn't mean those are all of them: as I said in the beginning, there are tons of nudges you can find and use—it's an extremely wild land with tools scattered all around—so be sure to look for more nudges everywhere, from dedicated books to the world around you—some will be easy to spot, while others may be hiding under a rock or behind a tree.

Also be sure to test them as much as you can to find the right balance between using them and not letting players notice the manipulation; as always, you can learn a lot of theoretical knowledge from books, but only by trying you will gain the concrete experience to improve your design skills.

NOTE

1 Thaler, R. H. and Sunstein, C. R. (2008), *Nudge: Improving Decisions about Health, Wealth, and Happiness.* New York: Yale University Press.

Behavioural Game Design

14

Behavioural game design is a branch of the "real-world design" used to create the structures, conditions, and things that direct people toward a specific set of behaviours, especially when there is the need to guide large amounts of people at the same time as, for example, urban planning: drivers have to behave in a certain way, as well as pedestrians in a different way to avoid accidents, therefore the same rules are explained to everyone to assure that they all behave in the right way—and when they don't, they get punished with a ticket or jail time, depending on the severity of their actions. Any field where people need to be guided falls under the wing of behavioural design, with different facets depending on the specific field.

This is especially interesting for game design, as it is the same as behavioural design, with the only difference that one is applied to the real world and the other to virtual ones; the two worlds have certain common aspects that allow us, designers, to use behavioural design tools in Game Design—therefore generating what is called behavioural game design—to help us manipulate players toward certain types of behaviours.

I won't cover the urbanistic or architectural sides of this design technique as they belong to Level Design rather than game design, but note that many Level Design rules come from a combination of concepts from the book *De Architectura* by Marco Vitruvio Pollione[1]—as mentioned in the *Book Introduction* chapter—and rules from real-life modern urbanistic and architecture.

Note that behavioural game design isn't a replacement for game design, because, just as with praxeology, it doesn't work perfectly in the real world, therefore they are complementary tools that can and should be alternated to gain a different point of view of the same problem, useful to find the best possible solution for each circumstance.

Behavioural game design studies the diagnosis and design steps of the design process; each one of the frameworks used is based on asking yourself a series of questions to understand if your design is missing something needed to guide the player into the behaviour, and the main tools covered in this book are the following:

Diagnosis tools: drive theory and theory of planned behaviour.
Design tools: B=MAP model and COM-B model.

DOI: 10.1201/9781003229438-17

DIAGNOSIS TOOLS

Drive Theory

The drive theory is mainly used in the process of identifying a problem and its solutions, meaning that it's great to recognise the elements composing a problematic situation in a game, to then reach possible solutions, just like many brainstorming techniques you have read in the previous chapters—I'm sure you didn't forget them, did you?

The drive theory divides the causes of behaviour into three categories: *ME*, *WE*, and *OVERSEE*; let's take a look at each one of them:

ME is the user—as you can tell, this theory takes the point of view of the user, to better make you (the designer) put yourself in their shoes; this is what the user likes, thinks, does, and everything that could affect their behaviour. As I mentioned earlier, there are certain questions you need to ask yourself to understand the user and affect said behaviour:

Who is the target audience? This can be answered by looking at their *personas*, fictional characters based on the data that you can use to represent your audience.

What does the target audience feel? These are the aesthetics and dynamics, thus coming from an MDA analysis of said audience.

What does the target audience want? These are their needs, their expectations from the game that you need to provide to them, to assure them the best possible experience.

What is the target audience driven by? This is the motivation that drives your players' action toward the game; this will most likely change during the game, meaning that you always need to know what the best drive is for each part of your product—for example, they are driven by the narrative at first, then by the mechanics, then again by the story, and so on.

What does the target audience plan to do? This is their intent, what they want to do in your game at any given time; if their intent is allowed by the enforcer, you need to make sure they can achieve it, while if it's not allowed, you need to make it clear that they could never accomplish what they have in mind.

What does the target audience think they can do? This is their self-efficiency, which you may recall from the second axiom of praxeology: your player must perceive their desired action as possible, or they will never attempt to do it even if they have all the needed tools.

Why is the target audience not acting? This means that there may be things not allowing the players to perform the desired behaviour, for example, they want to kill a boss with their new short-ranged sword, but he is flying 50 metres up in the sky.

Last, what ways does the target audience think? These are the cognitive biases that can stop a player from following a behaviour, because they have a prior misconception carried in the game; for example, in the first *Unicorn Murderer* game there was no double-jump, so in the new *Unicorn Murderer II: last horn standing* they don't even try to double-jump, failing multiple platforming sessions in a row.

If you don't have the answer to some of these questions, or if the answers are vague and generic, you need to find answers that can drive the player's behaviour toward your desired one, meaning that you—and your team—need to use one of the tools covered in this book to find the best answer for your players depending on what the source of the problem is.

Now onto the second category; *WE* are the other people, groups of friends, family, other players, and so on; this part analyses the social factor of behaviour, to understand how social pressure can change the player's actions. The questions for the *WE* are the following:

Do other people do it? This is a combination of social influence from other people and the authority effect, as if others do it the player will feel justified to do it too—imagine you are having a business dinner at a fancy restaurant, the food looks amazing so you want to take a picture, but you don't want to be rude so you hesitate, until your boss takes one themself and you now feel like you can take it too.

Do other people expect the user to do it? This comes from the set of laws, social norms, and trends currently standing; for example, in Japan, it's considered extremely rude to talk on the phone while on a train, so if you find yourself in that situation you won't pick it up because you would feel the pressure of going against everyone on that train. In games, while laws are enforced and therefore can't be broken, social norms are often purposely ignored by players who want to *troll* or disrespect others, like *tea-bagging* your opponent, or spamming *LOL* in chat.

Can the user brag about their behaviour with other people? This is better known as *virtue signalling*, meaning that a user adopts a positive behaviour only to brag about it with people, for example donating money to a charity just for the positive image people will have of you and not for the charity itself; note that, of course, not all positive behaviours fall under this label, but creating specific situations leading to this behaviours can be a powerful design tool if the status given by this action is a source of motivations for players.

The last category, *OVERSEE*, is the environment in which the behaviour takes place, and its questions are:

Where are the people? This is the context of the environment, meaning the technology.

What stops people? This tells you whether structural barriers—the enforcer—are set to forbid a behaviour.

What rules people? These are the rules and laws of the game, again coming from the enforcer.

What messages do people see? This focuses on finding the lack of communication about the behaviour to the player, not letting them understand what you expect them to do or what the goal of the behaviour is.

What are some different alternative behaviours? These are emergent behaviours that you didn't design or expect but that are performed by the player instead of the desired behaviour because they are more efficient or more aligned with their ideal experience.

The goal of this tool is to find the weaknesses of a designed behaviour by noticing the question with a vague or missing answer, to then think about a new one and make the action more appealing and suitable for the player. It can be hard to spot all the problems from far away, so this tool lets you zoom in on every aspect that comprises a behaviour according to this theory—you wouldn't use a bucket to throw water out of a sinking ship, it would only delay its sinking; instead you would carefully inspect each part of the hull one at a time to see all the holes letting the water in, allowing you to plug them one by one and stay afloat.

Theory of Planned Behaviour

The theory of planned behaviour is another tool that describes how people decide whether to follow a behaviour or not; As shown in Figure 14.1, it's composed of three main elements: Attitude, Subjective Norms, and Perceived Behavioural Control.

Let's start off with attitude: attitude is what a person thinks and feels about the behaviour you want them to follow—this tells you if they think it's cool, boring, scary, and so on; In order to obtain a positive attitude, the desired behaviour must answer positively to one of the following questions:

Is it beneficial? Meaning it gives the person a positive reward.

Is it enjoyable? Indicating whether the person finds pleasure in that activity.

As you may have noticed, those two elements have very different types of motivation: the first one is extrinsic—the person is motivated by the reward, no matter the activity—while the second is intrinsic—the person is motivated by the activity, no matter the reward. If your behaviour doesn't have any of those, the player won't stick to the behaviour—or they may never try it at all—while, if you manage to achieve both, you created a more engaging behaviour that is more likely to be followed.

Moving on to subjective norms, these are the support or discouragement given by friends, family, and NPCs. Just like attitude, they are composed of two elements:

Social: what do other people think about the behaviour? As well as the social norms that make the person consider whether the behaviour is frowned upon—similarly to the WE section of the drive theory, "Should I answer the phone on the train?"

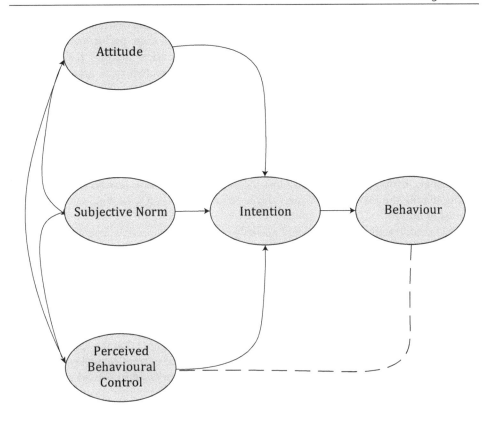

FIGURE 14.1   A scheme representing the theory of planned behaviour without repetition.

Source: Author.

> Meta: is there proven information that states which behaviour—or which actions belonging to the same behaviour—will provide the best outcome or will be easier to perform?—*meta builds* in MOBA games, *meta* strategies, and so on.

The last element is the perceived behavioural control, which is the combination of a player's efficiency and all the possible barriers (note that, while the theory calls this element *barriers*, I will reference it as *accessibility*, for an easier understanding of the framework) that prevent them from following the behaviour correctly, slowing them down, or increasing its difficulty—while it may sound good to then increase the challenge, it has to be done carefully: humans want to do things in the easiest possible way, and if the motivation isn't strong enough, a tough challenge will be seen not as an opportunity but rather as a burden.

As you can see from Figure 14.1, they are all related to one another, because they—together—generate one's intention, meaning their thought process leading to the decision of whether to perform a behaviour or not—they are like flour, sugar, and butter for a white cake: they all are needed, and if you try to bake it without one of them, you will probably get a random mess.

If the player's intention is high enough they will perform the desired behaviour, and their perceived behavioural control will change based on their performance—maybe it was harder than what they expected, or maybe it was easier, and they'll keep this in mind in the future. While this technique, just like the drive theory, is great to analyse how people decide whether to follow a behaviour or not, it really shines when used to compare choices from the same in-game context: will players pick the heavy sword or the katana? Do they prefer melee weapons or guns? It's important to find the answers to these questions while in the production phase of the game, as if the players' choices don't align with your expected gameplay, you still have time to understand what led to those choices and "tweak" them in your desired direction—if you reached this point of the book, I imagine you already lost the negative perception around the concept of "manipulating the players", so there is no need for me to say it's all done with their best interest in mind.

To transform all this theoretical knowledge into a design process, you need to assign a value to each one of the elements composing the three pillars of the theory of planned behaviour: attitude—*beneficial* and *enjoyable*—subjective norms—*social* and *meta*—and perceived behavioural control—*player's efficiency* and *accessibility*.

These values can go from and to any two numbers depending on how accurate you want your results to be—going from 0 to +100 is more accurate than going from 0 to +3, but it's a lot harder to tell the difference between each unit; the data can either be collected from your audience with surveys or from the team itself, but note that the team will more likely answer with their vision in mind, thus not based on the current gameplay itself—not because they aren't good designers but because it's hard to be objective when you have your head in your game seven days a week.

Here's an example: in an RPG game you are evaluating the *heavy sword*, and the following are the results of the survey given to the player, on a scale from 0 to 10:

Beneficial: 3, it's not a very powerful weapon; enjoyable: 8, the sword looks great and the moveset feels very empowering.

Social: 0, everyone tells you it's a terrible sword; Meta: *N/A*, doesn't exist in the development.

Player's efficiency: 8, it's very easy and intuitive to use; accessibility: 3, you need to complete 50 side-quests to obtain it (if the element was called *barriers*, a low value would have been perceived as an easy task, while for the processing of the data higher values means positive experiences).

Once you have all the values, you add the two of the same category together and calculate the weighted average depending on the game's characteristics: in a multiplayer game, the meta is more important than the attitude; in a single-player one the norms can often be ignored completely, and so on.

After you get this average value, you can compare it to other elements' values to see which ones are off, indicating a more probable choice by the players: if the *heavy sword* has a total score of 3, while the *God's Toothpick* has an 8.5, most of them will easily choose the second one—and not just because of the name.

While this sounds like a tool for balancing the game, it allows you to do much more: you can make certain choices very obvious and others really hard, even influencing the pace of the game or the stress level of the player—if you ask the player to kill one of their two favourite NPCs, making them make another tough decision right after might be the moment they just close the game and never open it again.

Since this theory is useful to guide players toward a specific behaviour, it's very important to let them know when they completed an action, and I mean *really* let them know: fireworks after killing a boss, an amazing VFX when they swing their sword, an explosion sound upon shooting a red barrel. Giving players as much feedback as possible is crucial for both their understanding and their enjoyment of an action, as shooting a rocket and seeing a gigantic mushroom-shaped explosion feels way better than seeing the enemy hit disappear; in videogames, as you may recall, this is called *juice*, and it's the art of increasing an action's enjoyment through the feedback of the action itself—it may sound complicated, but it's really just making cool things feel even cooler.

DESIGN TOOLS

COM-B

The COM-B is the first design tool of behavioural game design, and it divides the process of performing an action into three categories: capability, opportunity, and motivation—the B stands, of course, for behaviour; each one has a checklist of questions you need to answer to find the users' perception of the action and identify possible flaws.

First off you have capability: this requires the player to have the physical and mental skills needed to act as intended. The physical capabilities aren't just one's reflexes, but also body parts or functions such as fingers, sight, hearing, and so forth; those may sound obvious, but remember that part of the design is accessibility: it varies from colourblind filters and resizable UIs to support for specific peripherals.

This doesn't mean that it's all about accessibility; one's capabilities are very important for them to play a game as intended by the designers, but it's important to keep games as accessible as possible or, if you design a game with willingly very restricted accessibility, just know that many people won't be able to play it—and, to be fair, it could get your studio a bad reputation.

Then there are the psychological/mental skills: can the user play if they have never touched a game of this genre, or do they need an in-depth tutorial? Can they bluff if the situation requires them to, or will they panic and make their teammate lose? There are countless questions you can ask yourself to spot all the mental skills needed by your users and, just as for physical impediments, you can decide to adapt your design to include them or make it clear that the game is not suitable for them—if you call the game *Lie*, those terrible at bluffing will immediately know that they may not win even once.

The checklist of questions you should ask yourself is the following:

CAPABILITY CHECKLIST	
PSYCHOLOGICAL	PHYSICAL
Does the TA understand the benefits? Does the TA understand what will happen if they do? Does the TA understand what will happen if they don't? Does the TA find it easy to do? Does the TA need to pay attention to do the action? Does the TA remember to act? Does the TA feel in control? Does the TA understand what is required? Does the TA have the mental skills needed? Does the TA have the concentration to follow through?	Does the TA have the physical skills needed? Does the TA have dexterity and ease of movement? Does the TA have the ability to overcome physical limitations?

Once you know your player has all the required capability, you need to make sure they have the right opportunity: do they have the chance to act? Are there any elements that block the player from doing so?

There are two types of opportunities: physical and social:

Physical opportunities are the presence of *something* that tells the player what to do and when to do it, and in game design this is composed of *guidance* and *anticipation*, communicating the action they need to perform, how they are supposed to do it, and when to act.

Social opportunities are the presence of rules or groups that either sustain or try to stop a behaviour: while an action is not forbidden by the enforcer, those groups act as an authority to limit it as much as possible, for countless possible reasons—there could be a rule inside a guild not to talk with rival guilds' members, getting kicked out by the guild owner if they find out, or there might just be a group of trolls that block the door leading to a quest.

This is the opportunity checklist:

OPPORTUNITY CHECKLIST	
SOCIAL	PHYSICAL
Does the TA have the social support required? Does other TA help or hinder the behaviour? Does another TA do it differently? Does another TA remind them to do it?	Does TA have the physical skills needed? Does TA have dexterity and ease of movement? Does TA have the ability to overcome physical limitations?

Now, the player has the capability to act, they have the opportunity to act, so what do they need? Well, the same thing stopping you—at least I suppose—from going for a ten kilometres run right now: motivation.

As you recall, there are reflexive responses, like habits and reflexes, that are hard to change and control, and just like praxeology, COM-B doesn't take those into account; what it focuses on instead are the purposeful ones: what elements from the self-determination theory could motivate the player? What intrinsically? What extrinsically?

As before, here is the motivation checklist:

MOTIVATION CHECKLIST	
REFLECTIVE	*AUTOMATIC*
Does the TA think the benefits outweigh the costs?	Does the TA have an emotional response?
Does the TA feel they want to do it?	Does the TA feel good about doing/not doing it?
Does the TA care about the consequences?	Does the TA feel bad about doing/not doing it?
Does the TA have other goals that may stop them?	Does the TA do it repeatedly? Can they start to form a habit?
Does the TA have enough incentives?	Does the TA need a way to avoid actions?
Does the TA see the behaviour as everyday?	
Does the TA know how to do it?	
Does the TA have a plan to achieve it?	

As I mentioned before, the COM-B technique is based on asking yourself questions, to then solve problems through the answers you find: if a question has no answer, you need to create something new in the design, while if it's a negative answer—players don't have the opportunity to act, or they have a negative perception of the action—you need to identify the source of the problem and fix that part of the design, to at least bring players to a neutral attitude toward the behaviour and then increase it to a positive one by letting them understand the advantages of following your design.

BMAP

The second design tool coming from behavioural game design is the BMAP: behaviour = motivation + ability + prompt; it's also called FBM (Fogg behavioural model) and BMAT (with triggers instead of prompt).

This framework places the ability and motivation factors of a person toward a behaviour on a Cartesian plane, respectively on the X and Y axis, to identify its curve and visualise where that person is located on the plane with a dot—this is very important for later, keep that dot in mind—showing whether they will be able to achieve the action or not (Figure 14.2).

To correctly represent the behaviour's curve on the plane, you first need to understand what each element is composed of.

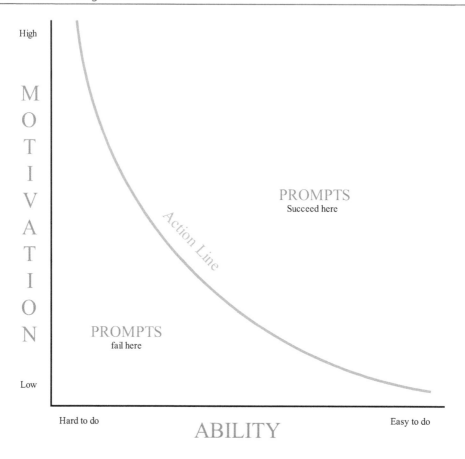

FIGURE 14.2 A Cartesian plane showing an example of a behaviour's curve found using the BMAP framework.

Source: Author.

Starting with Motivation, it is divided into three categories, each of which can be the source of the motivation experienced by the player:

Physical level (sensation): according to BMAP, humans seek pleasure and avoid pain, making this the only motivation type with an immediate effect.

Emotional level (hope/fear): humans are motivated by either the hope for the reward or the fear of the punishment.

Social level (acceptance/rejection): humans are driven by the social acceptance of an action and the resulting status.

Once the player is motivated, they, of course, need to be able to complete the desired action, which is why ability divides behaviour into six points that define if the person can act or not:

Time: is there the physical time to perform the action? Could the player make better use of their time?

Resources: does the player have the resources to complete the behaviour?

Physical effort: is performing the action too physically tiring?

Mental bandwidth: is performing the action too mentally tiring?

Social deviance: does the player have to go against any rule? Note that people rarely go against the present norms—which is fine with game rules controlled by us, but community norms are harder to control.

Habit: is the action part of the player's habits? If not, it will be harder to make it so.

You can calculate the level of ability by using the answers to these questions, with an average, weighted average, or anything that suits your situation, to get the value of how hard the action is for the player.

Now that you have the motivation and the ability level of the behaviour, you need to place them onto the Cartesian plane—it's easier if you use the same scale on both axes, *i.e.* from 0 to 10—and see the resulting curve: this allows you to decide which type of prompt you should use depending on the values of motivation and ability (Figure 14.3).

FIGURE 14.3   An example of a behaviour's curve, with values showing which type of prompt to use for this specific scenario.

Source: Author.

Based on the combination of motivation and ability, there are three types of prompt you can use:

Spark: the person doesn't have enough motivation, but the behaviour is easy to do; this is the act of informing the player of the rewards of the action or even increasing the reward itself just for the player—Would you delete your game world for $50? "No". What about $100? "Deal". By better explaining the reward to the player or by increasing it if the previous one isn't enough, you can get them to perform the desired action if what they are lacking is motivation.

Facilitator: the action is too hard, but they are motivated; in this case, you add something to ease the difficulty of the behaviour to make them perceive they can accomplish the action, *i.e.* using DDA (Dynamic Difficulty Adjustment) to make the game easier or giving them power-ups to get back on track while they are still motivated—for example the *Bullet Bill* power-up in the *Mario Kart* saga, letting players gain easy ground when in the last few positions. In this case, the player *wants* to keep playing; they just don't have enough skill—it's like using a mixer when you can't beat the eggs while making a cake.

Last, signal: the player has a medium level of both motivation and ability, neither high nor low; in this case, you need to tell the player to act at that moment, getting rid of any hesitation, for instance with the UI of a quick time event: "you can do it, just press X *now!*"—A great example of this prompt is the *press triangle to throw counter* in the *Batman: Arkham* series, always letting the player know what to do and reminding them of the presence of that action.

Just using the respective prompt for each situation, however, isn't enough to make the player act, and this is where the BMAP gets even more powerful: do you remember the dot I mentioned before, meaning where the player is located on the chart? *You do?* Great! Their vertical distance from the curve tells you how strong the prompt needs to be: the further above it they are, the lighter and less invasive the prompt can be, while the further down, the stronger and more invasive the required prompt is: if they are very motivated and the action is easy to perform, a simple pop-up notification may be enough, while if the action is harder but they have no motivation you may promise them a huge reward.

What about the combinations I didn't mention, like extremely low motivation and a very hard action? These are the "crucial cases", where even the strongest of the prompts alone won't be enough to get the player to perform the behaviour: in these situations, you need to combine the prompts with other design techniques such as nudges or operant conditioning to—hopefully—rescue the player from that pit. It won't always be possible, therefore you might need to fix your design to make it more accessible, but the decision is up to you: if there is one player every 100,000 that falls in this pit you may choose to ignore them and lose 0.001% of your audience with little consequences, while if half of your audience is in that area, ignoring them probably isn't the best decision from a commercial point of view.

For this tool, too, there are sets of questions to identify the levels of motivation and ability, as well as the needed prompt to achieve the desired behaviour; note that prompts aren't mutually exclusive, but having multiple of them at the same time could be overwhelming, so use them carefully.

These are the questions needed for this tool, let's call it the **BMAP** Checklist:

MOTIVATION	ABILITY	PROMPT
Is the TA motivated by something visceral and automatic? I.e. pain? Is the TA motivated by fear or hope? Are people TA for a desire to belong? Is the TA motivated by avoiding rejection by peers?	Does the TA have the time? Does the TA feel like they have the time? Does the TA have the resources to act? Does the TA feel it's worth it? Does the TA know others also do it?	Does the TA need a motivation boost? Does the TA need it to be easier? Does the TA need an in-context cue?

NOTE

1 Pollione, M. V. (15 b.c.), *De architectura*. s.l.: s.n.

Emotional Game Design

15

Let's start with a clarification: the word "emotional" is improper, as it implies that all the other types of design aren't *emotional*, which is of course a false statement; the correct titles for this design category would either be *Decisional-Ethical Game Design* or *Adult-Emotion Game Design*, but they don't sound nearly as fascinating as *Emotional Game Design*: I'll keep using the most known form, but keep in mind that *emotional* is referring to a specific set/depth of emotions.

These can be everyday emotions studied at a deeper level or more adult ones—such as melancholy, sadness, mourning—which I'm not saying kids don't experience, but only as adults do we truly understand the weight they have; the fact that those emotions are more profound than most of the ones we live on a daily basis doesn't make a "non-Emotional-Game-Design based" game any worse or less worthy, it just means that using this field of game design lets one explore a deeper side of one's self. By pushing specific buttons, you can reach a level of the player that wouldn't be reachable with ordinary game design techniques, therefore it's, of course, harder to design this way; well, *harder* isn't the right word, as the perceived difficulty is very subjective, so I'd say it's *more delicate*: if you don't know what you are doing it's like defusing a bomb with a chainsaw, but if you know your players you'll be given the proper tools—it's still a bomb you have to be careful with, but now it's a lot easier to avoid mistakes.

As with every other type of design you've seen so far, remember that this isn't a standalone tool: it only works if you combine it with the others you may need depending on your situation.

Before talking about the emotional game design frameworks, I need to make one thing clear: a designer has to be empathetic at all times, even for the most random of the games, because part of our job is to understand the players not just as the audience but as people: what are they feeling right now? What do they want? What will they do next?

The more sensitive an issue is, however, the more empathy the designer must have and the deeper this empathy needs to be, across the whole team, to create moments of true connection between the team and the players: during the development of *Hellblade: Senua's Sacrifice*, the design team worked with many psychologists, psychiatrists, and people suffering from mental disorders to increase and deepen their understanding and sensibility toward such sensitive topics.

A common misconception is that, similar to creativity, empathy is something you are born with and can't develop, which is false: it can be trained and discovered; while it's neither an easy nor a quick task, it's completely possible if you set your mind to it,

DOI: 10.1201/9781003229438-18

and this is why the first tools for this game design branch are aimed at developing your empathy.

WHITE WRITING

For this technique, you need to place a notebook—it needs to be physical and not digital, so no notes on your phone, tablet, or computer—and a pen next to your bed, and, as your alarm goes off, you need to write from one to three pages of *things* and add the date somewhere visible.

What *things* should you write about? Whatever crosses your mind at that moment: something you dreamt of, your worries for the upcoming day, your emotions, anything as long as it's true. Once you have written one, two, or three pages, close the notebook and go on with your day without reading what you wrote; let me repeat, you can't read anything you wrote in the notebook, not even if you know you misspelt a world, wrote something that didn't make sense, or wanted to erase something. Now repeat this "write and ignore" process for one month.

After one month of notes, keep writing your everyday pages as you just did, but now you have to read the pages you wrote that same day of the previous month: for example on April 26th you will write your thoughts without reading them and then read what you wrote on March 26th the next day; April 27th, you will write for that day and read the pages from march 27th, and so on for another month.

This needs to be done for at least one month of writing, therefore two months of total duration—you can only read the pages you wrote one month before, even if you stop writing.

This technique has two goals:

First, it trains you to think, write, and express yourself without any boundary: you don't care about spelling the words right, the syntax of your sentences, not saying something for many different reasons, and so on—partially because it's part of the task, partially because you are barely awake so all the filters your mind puts on haven't been loaded yet, which is a good thing. *Whitepapering*—aka using this technique—lets you express your thoughts without any filter or correction, also thanks to the fact that no one except you will read that notebook.

Second, analysing your whitepaper shows you recurring topics from any kind—psychological, artistic, work-related ones, and so on; those can change over time: one may be present for a week, another for the whole month, but it doesn't make the first one any less valuable; performing this task for multiple months, however, may lead you to topics recurring for multiple months in a row, indicating a key trait of your personality and empathy. Finding a recurring topic is like digging in your backyard with a fork and discovering a gold vein, because it shows you what you are naturally empathetic to as you think about it first thing in the morning. It may also become a pillar for your next design, as you know you will likely be interested in that theme and have a higher empathy toward it.

ARTIST'S DATE

This technique comes from the homonym book by Julia Cameron,[1] which I highly suggest reading as it takes a deep look at this tool. It's based on having a weekly slot of free time where you completely disconnect from your usual world and other people: phone off, no one knowing how to reach you, for that couple of hours you have to disappear from others; your job is to do something you really like by yourself, even better if it's something that you've never done but you think it's good. During this date, you need to document everything in a notebook—again, better with a non-digital one—not from a chronological point of view, but from an emotional one: what are you feeling? Where did that feeling come from?

An important part of this tool is your attitude: it needs to be playful, almost child-like; enjoy what's happening and if something goes wrong just laugh it off, because that's life, and you don't want an inconvenience to ruin your date. Just like if you were on a date with a person you always had a crush on, you wouldn't care about small inconveniences because you'd want to make the most out of the time you have, the same goes here: it's a date with yourself; be sure to enjoy it.

Once you have your date and have documented everything, as with White Writing, you can't read what you wrote for a whole month, not even to check for spelling mistakes. This serves a triple purpose:

First, it helps you rediscover your inner child, your capability of being playful, open to new experiences, and appreciative of what's out there.

Second, doing activities that you like and trying new ones, while documenting them, trains your emotive introspection, meaning you better recognise your emotions and what generated them.

Third, as for White Writing, it helps you find recurring issues that let you better understand yourself and your empathy toward those recurring topics.

Examples of artistic dates are writing a poem, playing with a dog (animals can be part of your date, only other people can't), trying a new restaurant, going to a movie theatre; but it can also be gardening, cooking, really anything as long as you like it and you do it alone—technically, it could even be climbing Mount Everest, as long as you do that in a couple of hours, keep notes on your emotions, and come back safe.

INTERNAL GAME DESIGN

Before telling you about this tool, I need to make a small premise: while this type of tool is very powerful, it can be very psychologically dangerous as it is very aggressive and destructive, on the contrary to the previous ones that are positive and supportive.

The Internal Game Design requires you to take a 30-minute session once a week, on your own, again with a notebook and a pen; for this technique you need to play the role of the bad guy, with an extremely critical and negative eye about your design, actively and aggressively trying to demolish your design, concept, and idea—it has a purpose I promise.

The goal is to have the "bad guy" ask complex questions that you—the designer—need to answer with a logical explanation in your notebook—again from one to three pages per session—demonstrating that your design/concept/idea is bulletproof; of course, they won't be completely safe, and this technique also allows you to spot the critical flaws.

You may be asking yourselves, "Why does it have to be aggressive though?" and there are two main answers:

On one hand, playing the role of your worst enemy is key to identifying problems: you ask questions you know are hard to answer, you know the weak spots of your design, and an aggressive attitude takes off the safety that usually stops you from being too harsh with yourself.

On the other hand, this type of interaction trains you for the worst-case scenarios: no one wants to have such a heated argument with a colleague, and most of the time you won't, but if it happens you need to be able to remain calm and explain your reasons, even if the other person is as red as a tomato.

As you might have anticipated, the notes you took can't be read for a whole month, and, again, once you read them you may find recurring themes to discover your empathy, other than analysing your answers under such pressure—and against a person who knows all the design flaws that you subconsciously try to forget about; as always, recurring themes in your answers are the key to finding your empathic engine, as talking about a topic multiple times under such pressure shows how truly connected you are to it. The last great insight this technique gives you is that your behaviour/mood while responding to the questions is, also, part of your engine: maybe you become aggressive, you feel threatened, or you lower your voice, those all includes moods and feelings you are naturally more empathic with.

This was the last one of the preparation techniques for emotional game design, and I'm sure you still have one question since the beginning of this part: why the physical notebook? Well, I'm the biggest fan of technology myself, but the movements of the hand when writing, the friction of the pen on the paper, the turning of the pages, are all elements that help bring the mind into a meditative state ten times more than writing on a tablet with a stylus or typing the words on a screen—you are like a conductor, moving your body to help emotions arise in time to the music.

EMOTIONS, FEELINGS, AND MOOD

All the tools you are reading about coming from emotional game design have a very specific goal, that is finding your empathetic engine: this is the set of emotions, themes, issues, and elements that motivate you and that you want to cover on a deeper level in your design.

Everything can be explored deeply: from sorrow to rage; just because people are more likely to experience one more than the other in their day-to-day life, it doesn't make the other less valuable. Note that, however, the more common emotion is, the harder it will be to explore it to a level that can impact the player: we all feel angry sometimes, so it's complicated to design a game that makes us truly *understand* anger rather than just live it to destroy places, shoot things, and things like that—don't get me wrong, I love to destroy things in videogames just as much as anyone else, but that's not what emotional game design is for.

Not all games can be profound—not that they should—but those that are need to be designed carefully, requiring a lot of research, planning, and, most of all, interest: if a topic isn't in your empathetic engine, chances are you won't be able to make it fit during the development, and you won't enjoy working on it as you lack the interest toward that topic. Knowing your engine lets you both predict what games you might be more drawn to and develop a sensibility or interest toward the issues that aren't in it at the time; it takes time to develop empathy, but this shouldn't discourage you.

Once you know yourself—aka your empathetic engine—there is one more thing you are missing to work with complex emotions: understanding the scientific theories behind them.

First things first, what *is* an emotion? According to *Wikipedia*, "Emotions are psychological states brought on by neurophysiological changes, variously associated with thoughts, feelings, behavioural responses, and a degree of pleasure or displeasure."[2]

For the *Cambridge Dictionary*, "[Emotion is] a strong feeling such as love or anger, or strong feelings in general".[3]

I could go on and list tens of other definitions, but the truth is that an objective one doesn't exist, just like for the definition of *game*; all we know is that emotions are physical reactions happening in our brain, happening after an interior and/or exterior event; they can have a different degree of intensity, physical influence, and much more, but we still aren't sure of what they are. This is the reason why there are many different scientific theories, created by different scientists, and while they often have common elements and similar outcomes, those results aren't the same.

Why should we care about all this scientific stuff? Because different theories give us different points of view useful to generate complex emotions, and we need to understand the science behind them to be able to handle them correctly—you really don't want to use a chainsaw for this job.

The first thing I think it's crucial to clarify is the difference between the following terms: emotion, feeling, and mood. It's important because what we normally use as *emotion* is composed of these three different things, and as designers, we need to know which one we want to target—it's also important to address elements with their right name to show yourself as a professional, where many amateurs could confuse these three words (Figure 15.1).

Emotion: an instant reaction, positive or negative, to an internal or external stimulus; this is the physical and chemical part.

Feeling: the subjective experience one associates with emotion; this is the interpretation of the emotion. Different feelings may have a very similar physical reaction, for example fear and anxiety are both connected to one's stomach and sweating, but their mental interpretation can be very different. Just know that

FIGURE 15.1   A simple representation of the "emotional loop".

Source: Author.

humans are terrible at recognising emotion and therefore at interpreting them, thus the resulting feeling is often wrong too—especially when facing new situations, our brain tries to recall the most similar event to know how to react, with the main problem that the two scenarios may be totally unrelated.

Mood: a sensation widespread both physically and mentally for a longer period of time as a reaction to the stimulus derived from an emotion; in simple words, something makes you laugh; you feel happy, and this happiness remains for the rest of the day. The mood remains even after the stimuli stop, which can be both good and bad for a person: if you get angry because you argue with someone, you storm out of the room and spend the whole morning angry, but the person who made you mad isn't near you anymore—this further proving how bad we are at interpreting things: you may keep thinking about the argument you just had, even if that won't change a thing.

These three elements are very different from one another, leading to very different uses in designs and different resulting games: a horror may be based on an anxious mood, therefore focusing over a long period of time, while others may focus on the emotions by using jump scares, meaning strong moments in a very little time. Games that talk about very complex issues often focus on the feeling: by working on how the player interprets the emotions, they rely on the person's capability to experience an event; someone with no sensitivity over the theme of that game may find it very boring, while someone opposite to them would experience it with a strongly different intensity. While the game is the same, the filters completely change the resulting feelings—if you have the best coffee in the world filtered by a water-purifying machine, all you will taste is water.

TWO FACTOR THEORY

This theory was created by Stanley Schachter, an American psychologist often considered the father of the modern understanding of emotions. He stated that emotion is the result of a complex procedure that involves the emotional response, cognition, and an initial stimulus.

The stimulus is an internal or external trigger that starts the process to get an emotion. The stimulus is followed by arousal: the emotional response to the stimulus. Then there is the cognition: the interpretation the mind gives to the arousal based on the context the person is in. The result of cognitive interpretation is what we call emotion.

It may sound like a complex process put this way, but it happens in a fraction of a second every second of your day: anything can be a stimulus, you may just not notice it or it may be too small to generate a perceivable response; even reading these words may generate different emotions in this very moment—you don't believe me? *Cake.* Maybe now you are slightly mad because I made you hungry, maybe you are happy because cakes put you in a good mood, or maybe you really don't care that much and nothing changed.

What if you hear a very loud noise?

Loud noise, adrenaline, it's your alarm: "I wanted to sleep more", and now you're sad.

Loud noise, adrenaline, it's an earthquake: "I need to get somewhere safe", and you are scared.

Loud noise, adrenaline, it's the timer: "My cake is ready", and you are happy.

Of course, all those three events have a very different sound, but they are all perceived as a loud noise before your brain further processes the sound; this shows how even the same stimulus can generate a completely different emotion based on the context you are in.

The cognitive interpretation is key to how emotions are felt: depending on how the player perceives the stimuli in your game, their experience could change completely, and by combining this knowledge with other design tools—praxeology to generate needs, self-determination theory to set one's motivation, and really any technique you need for that task—you can manipulate the player into feeling exactly the emotions you want—it's scary to think that you can even manipulate one's emotions, I know, but keep in mind that you can't force anything on the player: if they don't want to experience something more than they want to play the game, they can just close it at any time.

GROUNDED COGNITION THEORY AND EMBODIED COGNITION THEORY

These theories were born during the 20th century, inspired by aspects of psychology, connectionism, and phenomenological tradition: scholars from this last group were a key source of information toward proving that emotions and body are connected, as opposed to theories like the Cartesian dualism that were strongly believed in at the time.

The two factor theory in fact, while being crucial for the understanding and manipulation of emotions, didn't take the body into account, as if the interpretation of emotions was only psychological—which is, of course, false, creating a major flaw in the theory.

These two new theories, instead, highlight the fact that the process mentioned in the previous tool takes place in the human body, and its conditions do change the perceived emotion depending on many factors, from the level of hunger to the temperature of the room, from the space around them to the shape of the controller: a study[4] proved how being hungry when going grocery shopping can increase the amount of food a person buys, just because they are hungry at that moment—quick tip, have a meal before the next time you go to the grocery store. If basic needs can change one's experience doing an activity as common as shopping, imagine how more true this is for games where the player is exposed to incredible experiences and hundreds of possible triggers.

There are three main elements related to the body covered by these theories: the physical state of the body itself, the physical space around the person, and the state of their body's sensors: the sensors can drastically change how you perceive your surroundings, for example when hypothermia sets in someone might not even notice it, because their sensors are long gone to prevent them from feeling that huge pain.

The main two elements useful to game design are the first two, body and space; the master of these theories applied to games is *Nintendo*: their console has had strong physical elements ever since the *Nintendo Wii*, from controller tracker to hardware you stand on to play, making you use your whole body as a game interface. The Nintendo Switch allows you to separate the two controllers; the Nintendo DS series used a stylus as the core input, and the Nintendo Labo further pushes the use of the space as a gameplay tool.

Another field focused on one's body and space is the VR technology: VR devices often require a configuration of the room someone plays in for the very spatial element, tracking not only their body movement but their location across the room; as you may know, this has some risks coming with it, where players forget they are in a simulated world and walk into a wall in real life, or they get scared while playing a horror game and throw the controller to a nearby television—funny to see while scrolling your phone, not so funny when it happens to you.

Furthermore, VR games need a redesign of many gameplay elements because of the real movement the player has to do to perform an action: shooting an arrow with a mouse only requires two clicks, while in a VR game you need to stretch one arm and bring the other close to your cheek. It can also be tricky to communicate to the player how a weapon works: they don't just reload by pressing *R*; they need to grab a lever, flip a switch, press a button physically located on the weapon: this requires a very different prototype to communicate the item's affordance, and it's all part of the embodied cognition theory.

Of course, these two techniques don't apply exclusively to Nintendo products and VR ones, otherwise, it would be a very limited market compared to all the other gaming platforms out there: the design of any game, on any platform, should take into account physical elements like the position of the hands on the controller or on the keyboard and mouse, as well as the posture a player has while experiencing a game. Certain positions make people react slower, certain grips are better for specific games or events, and knowing which one the player will use is important to know both what they are expecting from the game and how they are living it: if in a horror game a person is lying down reclined on their chair, they are probably feeling less suspense than someone standing straight with their nerves all tense.

There are tons of different elements influencing a player's performance, and while some are part of one's personality—if Mark never gets scared, they probably won't have strong reactions to a jump-scare-based game—others can be "calculated": tiredness, for instance, is one of the most common "side-effects" in games, especially for sessions of multiple hours in a row or very intense gameplay segments; a tired player often reacts more aggressively to the stimuli they receive rather than someone full of energy.

Why should you care about this? Because it's crucial to set the pace of your game: if the player just experienced a boss fight, placing another battle right after is a very risky move, as they may just close the game and be mad at you for not respecting their space.

This is why, for instance, one of the golden rules of the pace design is to always have a cinematic after a big fight, for it lets the player take their hand off of the controller and relax their mind, and any other stimuli will most likely be perceived negatively—you wouldn't be happy if after running a 10k someone told you "Well, actually we added five more kilometres, so keep going please".

While you could get all this information about your game with surveys, the best way is to analyse the player while they are playing, taking note of their posture, facial expressions, reactions to events: did they grind their teeth? Smack the table? Throw the controller? What was their posture? Did it change after the fight was over? For instance, if they are still tense after the fight, you may be lacking feedback letting them know they can relax, or they may even not trust you and expect another enemy to come up out of the blue—maybe they are right because you tricked in the past, or maybe you still need to walk that extra mile to gain their trust.

NOTES

1 Cameron, B. J. (1999), *The Artist's Date Book: A Companion Volume to the Artist's Way.* Los Angeles: TarcherPerigee.
2 *Wikipedia: Emotions*: https://en.wikipedia.org/wiki/Emotion
3 *Cambridge Dictionary: Emotion*: https://dictionary.cambridge.org/dictionary/learner-english/emotion
4 Nederkoorn, C., Guerrieri, R., Havermans, R. C., Roefs, A., and Jansen, A. (2009), *The Interactive Effect of Hunger and Impulsivity on Food Intake and Purchase in a Virtual Supermarket*: https://pubmed.ncbi.nlm.nih.gov/19546869/

Emotional Theories

16

As you know, we don't really know how emotions work for sure, so various experts have suggested multiple theories and interpretations on emotions and their characteristics; the *right* one has yet to be discovered, so, in the meantime, you can use some of the most famous ones, extracting the pieces of information you find useful both for your designing style and the game you are working on—just like the player type's taxonomy, they all examine the same concepts with different lenses. Mastering all of them would take a very long time, so my advice is to take the key elements of each one of them to then further study the ones you think might work best for you. You will find common elements among multiple theories, making those more reliable pillars, while other ideas may be more hypothetical: it doesn't mean they aren't true, but they might only be applied to specific scenarios.

PAUL EKMAN'S WHEEL

Paul Ekman is an American psychologist and professor at the University of California who conducted many studies trying to understand emotions, from the biological correlation between emotions to emotion's resulting facial expressions.

This first theory divides the states a person can be in into six macro-groups where feelings and moods exist: excitement, tenderness, frightfulness, anger, sadness, and happiness. Each one of them has a series of declinations; for example anger includes irritation, madness, rage, and so on; happiness covers gladness, optimism, satisfaction, etc. The key aspect of this theory is that it provides a clear line about where a feeling or mood belongs in one of the six macro-categories (Figure 16.1).

There is, however, a state a person can be in that hasn't been included: neutral. This raises the question: can someone really be in a neutral state, or are they in a mood so mild that they don't perceive it? Maybe only in a deep state of meditation can one achieve true *nothingness*—but what are we once deprived of our emotions? I guess we need to wait for more research to find that out.

ROBERT PLUTCHIK'S COLOURS

Robert Plutchik, former psychologist and professor at the Albert Einstein College of Medicine, took Ekman's theory and expanded it by adding more macro-categories,

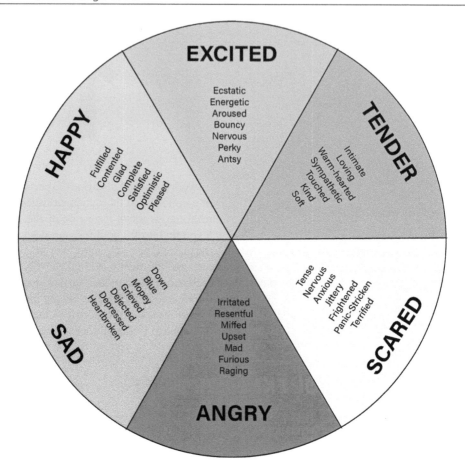

FIGURE 16.1 A representation of Paul Ekman's Wheel.

Source: Author.

bringing the count from six to eight: ecstasy, admiration, terror, amazement, grief, loathing, rage, and vigilance—as you can tell, their names changed too, but in the emotional range each name is referring to is the same.

By looking at Figure 16.2, you can have a clearer understanding of this theory:

The inner circle of the flower is composed of the eight archetypal states that a person experiences physically.

Each one of these includes a "basic" feeling—the second ring—for example the physical experiencing of *rage* leads to the *anger* feeling.

The third ring is the moods derived from one relative feeling: an *annoyance* mood comes from a feeling of *anger*—which, again, comes from a state of *rage*.

Last, the outer ring is made of complex feelings coming from the mix of two basic feelings or moods, therefore two different archetypal states: *annoyance* and *interest* generate *aggressiveness*.

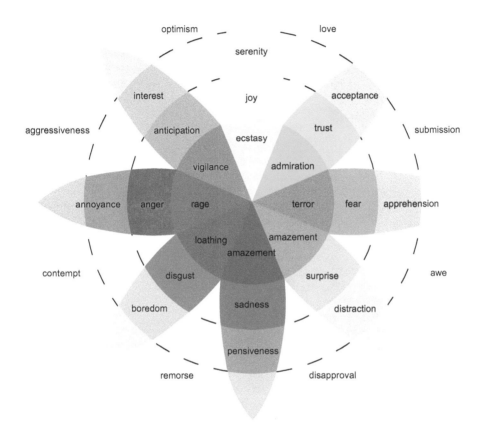

FIGURE 16.2 A representation of Plutchik's theory in the form of a flower. Each ring is a different level composing an emotion.

Source: Author.

Does this mean only the petals of emotions that are near each other in the figure can create a more complex feeling? Not at all: there are tons of possible combinations, as every feeling can be mixed with any other feeling, as shown in Figure 16.3. As you can see from that picture, even feelings located on opposite sides of the flower can be mixed.

This is fascinating because the theory introduces the concept of complex feelings, which aren't a consequence of the main states but of their combinations, meaning that when designing a game emotionally—thus with emotional game design—you shouldn't stoop to the simpler feelings that everyone is more likely to experience quite often in their daily life; instead you should aim to combine feelings people take for granted to make them live something deeper or ones they may experience a few times in their lifetime. This allows your game to get hold of the player's deeper level of empathy: most people live a routine-based life; the feelings they experience are usually the same bunch, meaning that there are many ones right there collecting dust, because they think they aren't influenced

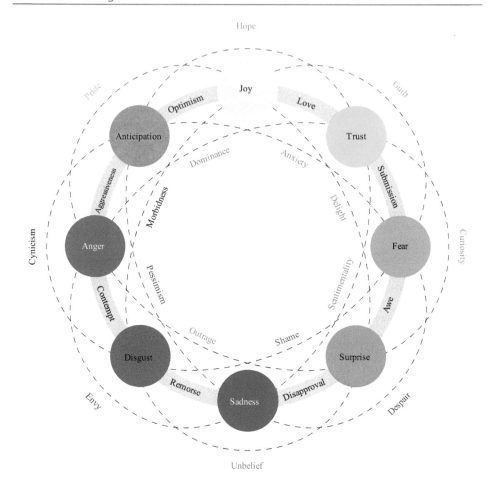

FIGURE 16.3 A representation of the possible combinations of first level moods generating second level moods.

Source: Author.

by certain emotions or they aren't empathetic toward topics related to those emotions. Maybe they are right, but maybe they are not: just like you develop your empathy as a designer, they too can discover new topics that they are interested in or experiences that move them deeply, as none of this can happen if your game stops at the first level of the players' feelings—you wouldn't stop mining because you found some coal when you could dig deeper and get some diamonds.

Combining this theory with Paul Ekman's Wheel lets you find different shades of every feeling, as each macro-category has multiple different declinations that affect what the player is experiencing: the sadness coming from mourning is very different from the sadness coming from a rejection, both for intensity and in how it feels in your body and mind; therefore, also the types of remorse generated from mixing these states with boredom will be different from one another. Just imagine all the possible combinations of feelings you can make the players experience just by combining different elements of these two theories, with different intensities and sources of the feeling—they are countless, and while some may be similar, others could be things someone never experienced in their whole life.

It sounds great, I know, but there is a catch: to generate a specific feeling, you need the physical causes of the two macro-groups that compose them, because they both need to be lived in the body for the brain to process them as the feelings you intended—one doesn't feel scared if their body doesn't tell them they are in danger, don't you think?

TWO-DIMENSIONAL ANALYSIS OR RUSSELL'S CIRCUMPLEX MODEL

James A. Russell is an American psychologist who, starting in 1980, developed a circumplex model based on human feelings, placing them on the Cartesian plane, on the X axis going from Unpleasant to Pleasant and on the Y axis ranging from Deactivating to Activating—as you can see in Figure 16.4.

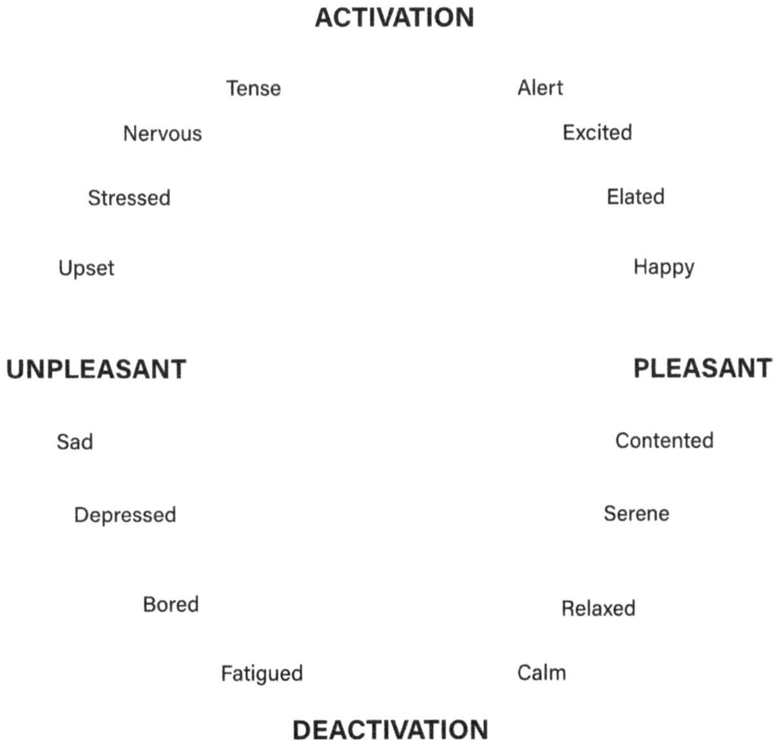

ACTIVATION

Tense	Alert
Nervous	Excited
Stressed	Elated
Upset	Happy

UNPLEASANT   **PLEASANT**

Sad	Contented
Depressed	Serene
Bored	Relaxed
Fatigued	Calm

DEACTIVATION

FIGURE 16.4   A graph of pleasantness and activation for emotions to be placed in.

Source: Author.

Placing the feelings experienced in your game on this graph allows you to understand the possible combinations of pleasantness and activation they bring to the player: unpleasant but activating may be *stress*, pleasant and deactivating could be *relax*, and so on. Feelings and mood, therefore, have the power to activate and deactivate the user no matter the environment: if the right triggers are there, they will experience that feeling as long as they are engaged with the game.

This information tells you whether a feeling is the right fit for your gameplay segment or if it needs to be changed by modifying the elements triggering it: if you have events triggering stress and tenseness in the player right before a cinematic, they won't enjoy it as they expect something "bad" to happen, because you told them that, in a way—you can't pull a fire alarm and expect everyone to be more relaxed than before.

It's important to manage the emotional pace of the game by paying close attention to what the players have to go through gameplay-wise, compared to what they experience emotionally: if those two aren't on the same page, the players will feel that something is off, just like reading a bedtime story to a kid but shouting it the whole time.

HOURGLASS OF EMOTIONS

This theory was developed by Erik Cambira, Andrew Livingstone, and Amir Hussain, published in 2012 in a study called "The Hourglass of Emotions".[1] Basing their studies on other emotional theories—Russell's circumplex model, Whissell's model, and others—they theorised that emotions can be represented on a "sentic vector", a four-dimensional *float* vector that can potentially synthesize the full range of emotional experiences in terms of pleasantness, attention, sensitivity, and aptitude.

Until now, the other theories portrayed feelings and moods as depthless, while, according to the Hourglass of Emotions (Figure 16.5), they have various intensities, creating a whole new possible mix of those feelings and moods that can be found combining the four main elements mentioned before: pleasantness, attention, sensitivity, and aptitude.

	ATTENTION > 0	ATTENTION < 0	APTITUDE > 0	APTITUDE < 0
Pleasantness > 0	Optimism	Frivolity	Love	Gloat
Pleasantness < 0	Frustration	Disapproval	Envy	Remorse
Sensitivity > 0	Aggressiveness	Rejection	Rivalry	Contempt
Sensitivity < 0	Anxiety	Awe	Submission	Coercion

This combination of feelings/moods can be represented either with a table or graphically on a Cartesian plane, using those four elements as the axis two at a time: depending on the two elements you pick, you will find four different feelings. For example, low attention and high sensitivity lead to rejection; high aptitude and high pleasantness provide a feeling of love. On top of that, they are represented in a circle composed of

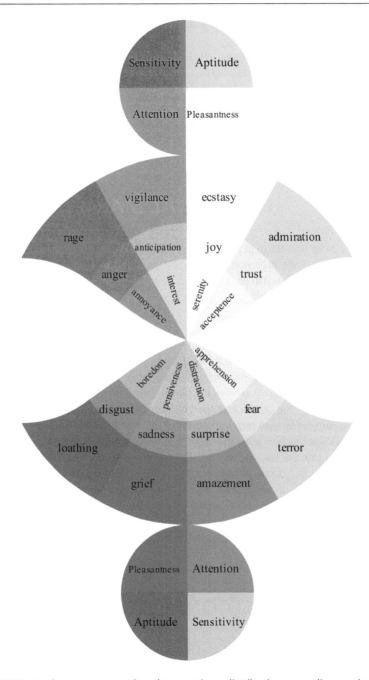

FIGURE 16.5   An image representing the emotions distribution according to the hourglass model in the form of an hourglass.

Source: Author.

three rings: these represent the different intensities of the feeling/mood in each one of the rings.

This was an extract of the theory—the full thesis provides the mathematical formulas behind the polarity defined in terms of the four affective dimensions, as well as the sentic levels of the hourglass model divided by their intervals—but it's a solid enough ground to use in your design. While you could take a deeper look at the formulas and principles behind it, the introduction of different degrees of the four factors presented by the theory is a crucial pillar of the emotional theories by itself, so be sure to lock it in your tool bag.

EMOTIONAL MAP

The Emotional Map was an experiment where UC Berkeley students asked 800 people to react to 2,185 gifs, then provided the feeling suscitated by each gif; the data was then represented on a website[2] where each gif was placed depending on the type and intensity of feel it aroused. On the website, you can see the gif, where it is located toward the possible feelings, the macro group that gifs belongs to but also the smaller groups located in between multiple feelings; each gif is marked with a letter, letting you know what feeling it belongs to the most, according to the people who took part in the test.

This is a fascinating source of information, as you can see what type of images are more likely to generate what feeling, and you can use the gif as a reference to generate that feeling in your game. Let's say you want the player to feel awkwardness when looking at an NPC during a cutscene: you can look at the gifs associated with awkwardness, analysing—for example—a movement and making the NPC move that way or even exaggerating it if you want that awkward feeling to be more obvious—think about a time when you wanted to shake hands with someone, but one of you was going for a simple shake while the other was thinking about a shake-and-hug: it happened so quickly that neither of the two knew what to do, so you ended up doing what looked like a breakdance move more than a handshake.

This was just an example using handshakes; now think about all the possible scenarios and feelings you can create with all the gifs analysed in this study, from disgust to romance, from admiration to anxiety, and all the shades of feelings in between.

EMOTIONAL ATLAS

The *Bodily Maps of Emotions*,[3] developed by Lauri Nummenmaa, Enrico Glerean, Riita Hari, and Jari K. Hietanen, illustrates, among other things, the maps of bodily sensations associated with different emotions: this is very useful combined with the grounded cognition theory, as, since many feelings affects the same areas of the body, it's one of the reasons why it's so hard for humans to identify a feeling without confusing it for another with very similar affected areas. For instance, drunkenness and vitality both affect the head, arms, legs, and slightly the chest of a person, so it may be hard to tell if, when you are drunk, you are really happy or just influenced by alcohol.

You can use this tool to analyse your players during a playtest, looking at their movements and reactions—did they touch their neck? Did they turn their head during a gruesome scene?—or you can ask them to check the areas where they felt something on a sheet. You could, of course, theoretically place a thermal camera pointed toward them during their session, but, other than being expensive to rent, it may make them uncomfortable and alter the results—it's hard to play it cool when you can see every single sweat drop on their forehead.

As for the Emotional Map, you can use the atlas as a reference to animate the characters, focusing on them touching their stomach when hungry, their chest when panicking, frowning their eyebrows when thinking, and so on. The degree of obviousness of these movements completely depends on the tone of your game and how subtle it should be: in an investigative game, a small flinch can be a great hint about when someone is lying, but make it comical and it completely breaks the tone of the game; on the opposite, in a game designed for kids, huge reactions can keep them interested and make it easier for them to understand those signs.

Before moving on to the next part of emotional game design, I think it would be helpful to recap the keystones of the previous theories:

Feelings have categories: there are many ways to look at feelings, some are completely different, some have common ground, so it's important to choose the right fit depending on your needs.

Feelings are linked to both internal and external elements of the body: while you already knew that games work on the internal side of a person, remember that external factors are very important too, from the music to haptic feedback, and as a designer you can ask the player to reduce undesired stimuli you can't control—for instance, "play this game using headphones", or "play in a quiet environment"; you can't enforce these requests, but the player will know that if they ignore them their experience might be ruined by those external factors.

Feelings have different degrees of intensity: the higher the degree of the feeling you want to generate, the higher the arousing elements for that feeling need to be.

Complex feelings are the result of the mix of simpler feelings: while the simpler ones are easier to separate from one another, complex ones may be interpreted differently by different players.

Feelings can prevent or cause actions: be sure that the feelings you want to generate in a segment respect its pace: for a higher pace, create an environment where activating feelings are likely to be experienced.

REACTION TYPES

This part is, by far, the most complex one of emotional game design, and it is explained after the emotional theories for that very reason: you need to have a solid understanding of how emotions are generated to work on ones that can last for time.

Reactions can be divided into three categories: visceral, behavioural, and reflective.

Visceral reactions are the physical response to a trigger. They can't be controlled unless you train yourself to change them, as they are part of the human instinct: the *fight or flight or teddy bear* response when facing a threat, the gag reflex when someone is sick next to you, and so on.

Behavioural reactions are the results of a series of stimuli used to change a behaviour: for example, the operant conditioning theory is based on this type of reaction—you still have it in your tool bag, right? Great, great, be sure to check it every once in a while or it may fall off.

The last category is reflective reactions: this is the principle for which humans think about an action they did even after some time; how many times did you have an argument with someone, and only hours later while taking a shower you thought of the perfect thing you could have said? How many times after watching a movie did you stop for one second and ask yourself "Wait, what did *that detail* mean?" This type of reaction is much harder to generate than the previous ones, and it's the one emotional game design focuses on.

There are many ways to get reflective reactions—or *reflectiveness*—but the two most common ones in videogames are via attachment or via the emotional context.

To generate attachment, you need to use the game's narrative: the story of any product has always been a key component of human beings, from taletellers travelling through kingdoms to cinematic multiverses mixing together different universes' plots. This works great especially with complex themes and moral dilemmas, as they push people into thinking about serious issues, making them reflect over and over again, but it's not very helpful to us as it essentially means "write a good story"—you didn't need to buy this book to know that a good story is a good thing for your game, but don't worry, attachment can be generated in another way.

What you can use is the social element: no man is an island, meaning that adding social aspects like competition or friendship creates reflectiveness, because everyone thinks about their relationships with others. It could be not to be alone, to find your soulmate, to make friends, to beat them at a challenge, no matter the case, if you are spending time with someone you think about how your actions impact that person and not necessarily in a good way: you could think about how crushing your opponent in a *1V1* match would ruin their day as a revenge to when they said *"GG EZ"*—I'm not here to judge, we've all been there.

A great example of how social elements are used to create reflectiveness is Hazelight Studios' *A Way Out*: two players cooperate to escape from jail throughout the whole game, talking to each other to coordinate their actions, until, near the end—**Spoiler ahead—** one of the two betrays the other, as only one person can survive. Having a tight collaboration—often between friends—then transformed into competition puts the players in a situation of reflectiveness where they wish there was another way, denying what is about to happen, until they realise there isn't, as the enforcer doesn't let the game progress until the betrayal happens.

This type of situation creates a very complex feeling, because the simpler ones they are made of are often in contrast with one another: betrayal is the combination of friendship and anger, the enforcer pushing the action provokes disgust, meaning that what the player is left with is a mixture of three different feelings that can't be put into any single category of any previous theory, generating a reflective reaction. The player now has to think about all those feelings they're going through, taking their time to break everything down and understand the origin of what they are experiencing—just like when you try a new food for the first time, and you try to isolate all the tastes to figure out the ingredients: sometimes it's easy, while other times they blend so well together that you may spend a whole day thinking about what that tiny note of aroma was.

If social elements aren't your cup of tea, or if they don't apply to the game you are working on, don't despair, you can still use the emotional context. It is based on three elements:

First, intimacy: you need to create a moment that *feels* intimate to the player; luckily, there are many ways to do such a thing: small spaces, close up shots of your characters, as well as tons of cinematography techniques. An example of intimacy comes from Thatgamecompany's *Journey*: as you ascend toward the final part of the game, a white-fade of the camera slowly takes place; fewer and fewer elements are presented to the player on-screen to allow them to focus on the feelings of that moment, rather than the gameplay, in fact reducing their agency—this works great, because if you don't need to think about the gameplay all your mental space can be filled with feelings.

Next there is vulnerability, which is very hard to create, but a good rule of thumb is to follow *Pixar*'s tenderness rule: The most empathic emotions are lived by the character projected on another character; this means that the emotion a character feels should be more visible on other characters rather than on themselves—you should use others as emotional mirrors pointed straight to the character experiencing an emotion.

Note that vulnerability is only referring to the emotional side of a game and not the mechanical one: using an armour that makes your character more vulnerable to melee attacks but increases their damage is not part of emotional game design, it's just strategy.

The last important element of reflectiveness is time: once a complex feeling occurs, you need to give the player time to think about it, or it's just wasted; this can be done with a low-paced area, a return to their base, a safe spot where no threat is present, and so on—emotions are like food: they need their time, just like fresh chicken breasts flavoured with lemon, soy sauce, and garlic needs to marinate before it can be grilled and eaten, otherwise no aroma will stick.

This is exactly the goal of emotional game design: generating strong feelings to then let them sink in for the player, reaching a level deeper than any other simpler event reached, and maybe even changing the person's perception of related aspects of their lives.

SUBTLE CONFUSION

This is the last game design theory covered in this section, and I decided to put it last both to let it sink in better for the reader and because it's a very strong but emotion-related technique: while others were closer to a cinematography or narrative point of view, this is much more game design based, reaching one of the peaks of manipulation of the player.

This theory is based on generating a state of confusion in the user, since confusion works as an emotional multiplier—just like stress does in the nudge theory; this tells you that slightly confusing the player—*slightly*—is a great tool to boost the emotional reach of a moment, that being narrative or gameplay related. This confusion, though, must be on an emotional level, not mechanical: if a player doesn't know where to go because there is no guidance, it's not going to work at all as an emotional booster—to be fair it would probably generate the opposite situation, with them getting frustrated because they don't know what's happening and what they are supposed to do—so be sure to understand the different types of confusion they experience playing your game.

An easy way to understand the emotional weight that choices have—which is the pillar of this theory—is the following example:

> Your player must pick one of two swords: *boring sword one* that deals 10 damage and *boring sword two* that deals 11 damage. They have the same moveset, look, size, name, and so on, so the choice is purely mathematical: *boring sword two* is the best choice; even if you added the "attack speed" value, the choice would still be completely derived by a formula that calculates the damage per second of each sword.

> What if they had the same stats, but one was called *the toddler-protector* and the other *the elder-saver*? It would now be completely up to the player's emotions: do they like toddlers or elderly more? There is no mechanical difference between the two, but some players might spend quite some time picking the one that suits them the most, making this choice purely emotion-driven.

Now that you have emotions involved in the choice-making process, you need to add the confusion factor, and what better way to do that than with a dilemma with no right or wrong answer?

This is best represented by the *trolley problem*: a train is following a track on which are located five people who can't move out of the way, so if the train follows that path they are going to be killed; there is a lever that can re-route the train on another track where one person is in the same situation as the previous five. Would you pull the lever? If you do, one person dies instead of five, but you would have killed them actively, if you don't, five people die but you didn't kill them, you would have just not done anything—as you may recall, according to praxeology not acting is, by itself, an action, thus potentially sticking you in an infinite loop of this confusion over what is and isn't acting.

There are infinite possible variations of this theory: five serial killers and a pregnant woman, five great people and your best friend, your five best friends and the person who will find the cure for cancer, and so on. The variables can change; your choice can change, but it would always be a moral dilemma, where no right or wrong exist: your logical side of the brain tells you that five lives are more important than one; the emotional side says that pulling the lever is actively killing someone, and it weights the choice differently based on who those people are.

There is another variation of the trolley problem that relies more on the physical action of, well, sentencing someone to death: the train is going on its tracks, you are on top of a bridge where you see five people tied to those tracks, and there is a person next to you:

do you push them down to stop the train before it reaches the five people? Note that all the variations mentioned for the previous problem can, of course, be applied here.

In this case the choice is even harder, because instead of pulling a lever, you need to physically push someone: this removes the virtualisation of the "bad" action—the lever—making everything more connected to your body and integrating the embodied cognition theory in the choice-making process. While in the first problem you could find excuses for yourself like "I just pulled a lever" and "pulling a lever doesn't kill people, otherwise lever wouldn't exist, *right*?", now you have to face the truth: "if I push him, he dies".

A great example of both removing virtualisation and the weight that the Embodied Cognition Theory can have is Hazelight Studios' *It Takes Two*:—**Spoiler ahead**—to kill your target, you and the other player have to spam-push a button, to drag them to the edge of a rooftop, and then kick them down until they freefall: it sounds brutal but not really confusing right? "That's the bad guy, they deserved it" you might think. Well, the thing is that the "bad guy" here is a happy and kind stuffed elephant, who did nothing wrong to you and begs you the whole time to spare its life. During this whole sequence you feel the controller vibrate every time the elephant gets closer to falling, when you tear off its ear, and so on: not only do you have the emotional weight of what you are doing but also a physical input to your body reminding you of the brutality of the action—you can't even keep your eyes closed during the sequence without having your hands prompting you of what's happening, making it less "virtual".

Now, this example was very brutal, and not all the gameplay segments related to subtle confusion need to be *this* strong; this scenario worked great on the physical level—meaning with as little virtualisation as possible—but lacked of the ethic/morale factor: as a player, you had no choice but to do what you did—it was enforced—but there are situations where the ethical factor is the core of the moment: many *RPG* and *CRPG* games often have missions where the player has to play the role of a judge, choosing what will happen based on their own ethic. Different combinations of virtualisation and ethics can create very different results, so, as always, be sure to find the right balance for your design.

Those two elements, however, aren't the only ones to consider when designing a situation of confusion:

Personalisation: as mentioned in the trolley problem, what if you had to kill someone you love to save five people? Depending on who the "sacrifice" would be, your scale of values could change completely.

Pressure Removal: what happens if all the forces pushing/forcing you toward a decision are removed? For example, in *Call of Duty: Modern Warfare 2* the player faces a level known as *No Russian*, where they enter an airport's elevator with four NPCs, with the goal of shooting everyone they see—of which they are reminded clearly multiple times. As the elevator's doors open, the NPCs start shooting, and most of the players follow their lead. The twist is that if a player decided not to shoot anyone, nothing would change in the mission, meaning that their decision to act was pushed by the other higher-ranked soldiers (the four NPCs). As the player finds out they didn't have to shoot, it has a strong emotional impact, because they thought that the NPCs were enforcing an action that, instead, was just pressure, generating subtle confusion.

While having that pressure can drive players, note that to generate confusion the action should not be enforced since the player could find excuses like "they told me to do it" to justify themselves, but if they then discover that they didn't *have to* do something, the confusion hits much deeper.

If in *No Russian* no NPC put any pressure on the player, their behaviour would have been different: some would have hesitated before choosing what to do, while others wouldn't have shot at all, making the situation much clearer and therefore generating no confusion—the same way it's easy to see your reflection in the waters when they are calm and hard when they are rough, it's hard to understand your emotions when there is a lot going on, which for us is an advantage.

This is a very strong type of manipulation, even worse than lying: when you lie the player can rightfully blame you and feel no guilt, but in this case they did everything themselves, no lies and no enforcement, making the guilt feel ten times worse.

This brings me to the next element: lack of reliable information; if you have all the data regarding a choice—whether that is the people on the trolley track or if you do have to kill the people in the airport or not—it is transformed from an emotional and ethical one to a logical question: "you don't have to shoot any NPC", or "humanity would be 5% better if you didn't pull the lever for the trolley" aren't choices anymore, those are certain answers.

Confusion heavily relies on uncertain information, and the best way to generate that is making every answer *vague*—you have to become a magic 8 ball only using the answers that no one cares about. Say your game has a sword and an axe the player has to choose from: the sword has 3 in damage and 10 in speed, while the axe has 6 in damage and 2 in speed: these are numbers that the player can process in a formula to find the objectively best choice, which is the opposite of what you need for this tool.

Transform "3" into "mild", "10" into "nimble", "6" into "moderate", and "2" into "disappointing", and now look again at the stats: the sword has mild damage and precise speed, the axe has moderate damage and disappointing speed. "Which is worse? Mild or disappointing?" the player is going to ask themselves. Surrounding them with all these types of vague information helps lead them into a state of confusion, because they won't know if they picked the right weapon, thus making them unsure about their feelings toward it; note that this scenario would create frustration in the player if the game is aimed to be a power fantasy or a classical RPG, as this technique can only work for emotional elements of a game—how can the god complex arise when the player is constantly doubting whether they are making any right choice?

Long story short, there are a lot of elements that can influence the state of subtle confusion generated in a player, and they are: ethics/morale, virtualisation removal, personalisation, pressure removal, and lack of accurate information. These are the pillars of this theory; as always you should test all of them and master the ones you like the most, of course combining them as needed.

There is, however, one last set of scenarios crucial for this technique, and that is the dichotomy element: creating contrasts between core elements of your game. There are many aspects to combine depending on the game, but since it would be impossible to cover all the possible scenarios, I picked four among the most powerful/common ones.

Mechanics vs *objective*: let's take a look at Brenda Romero's *Train*,[4] where each player has to fill a train cart with people as quickly as possible; the player who puts the most people in the cart wins. As the game ends, the players find out that the train is going to Auschwitz and that they were Nazis.

Brenda, by hiding the meaning of the objective, creates an extremely powerful dichotomy where the mechanics tell players to perform an action without thinking about it and not knowing what it is for, only thinking "the game is telling me to do it, so it's fine". Then, upon the discovery, they enter a reflective state, wondering if it was their fault for following the rules or not—this is a clear metaphor for the German soldiers who did what they were told, not wanting to know anything more to feel less guilt.

This technique, as you can see, is very powerful and relatively easy to use: create a reflective objective hidden at first, with mechanics guided by a strong enforcer, and let the player perform the action for a while; when your goal is reached, unveil the real objective to the player, and let their emotions sink in about what they did.

A great videogame example is the NPC *Socrates* in Ubisoft's *Assassin's Creed: Odyssey*: in a mission he asks the player to find proof of a corruption that would change the elections' result, then in one of the later encounters, he questions if a "good" person can become "evil" and vice-versa, implying the question of whether altering the elections was the right thing to do or if he—and the player—should have let democracy and beliefs run their course.

With every encounter, Socrates ask the player these ethical questions with no right or wrong answer, often making the player question their previous choices during the game; he doesn't do that to make the player feel bad but rather to genuinely make them reflect on the consequences of their actions, leading to the state of confusion you should aim for in a game—even though, if I have to be honest, every time I ran into him I was both fascinated and scared, fully knowing that an ethical dilemma that would have made me question my every choice was coming my way.

Morale vs efficiency: this is based on the ethical dilemma of doing the morally "right" thing or the most efficient one. For example, in 11 Bit Studios' *This War of Mine* you are facing the horrors of war not from the point of view of the soldiers but as the civilians trying to survive in a besieged city: during the game resources are needed to survive, but their finding often comes with risks such as the death of one of your characters. In an expansion called *The Little Ones*, children are introduced as possible civilians, coming to your door asking for help: the player can choose to rescue them—knowing that they don't provide any advantage, consume resources, and ask for more attention than adult characters—or to leave them out, sentencing them to death. From an efficiency level, you should ignore the children, but from a moral one you should rescue them: this decision, especially due to the serious mood of the game, is heavy on the player's heart, because they either save a life and risk theirs, or they let innocent ones die.

Character vs player: in this scenario, the player has doubts about the character they are playing as; the game that does this best is *Hellblade: Senua's Sacrifice*: the game creates a layer of ambiguity around Senua, almost as a fog not letting the player see her clearly, creating a blurry image of her past and her actions. The player can't firmly say whether Senua is "good" or "evil" until her past is unveiled, potentially changing their perception of her. While, similarly to mechanics vs objective, the truth is kept hidden for some time, in this case the state of confusion comes more from the process rather than the ending: giving hints of an unclear past, letting the player come up with hypotheses, questioning their actions while playing—the first one is like a cake recipe perfectly clear at all times, until you take it out of the oven and it turns out totally different, while the second one is a recipe that is ambiguous from the very beginning.

Ambiguity vs character: this is the case when what's happening isn't clear to the character, but it is to the player. You know how you scream "Don't go through that door!" to someone in a horror movie, because you know the killer is in there, while they don't? This is the same thing: the player has pieces of information unknown to the character, often communicated via cutscenes, different points of view in the case of multi-character games, or even meta elements—for instance, the trailer of the game shows an enemy not yet encountered by the character.

This is the rarest of the scenarios, and to be created the character has to perform, say, terrible or evil actions without knowing they are bad while the player knows it or hiding an important truth about the character, generating a state of reflectiveness in them.

In Frictional Games' *Soma*, the player knows that the character is a robot and not a human being, that he doesn't *teleport*; instead his memory is being transferred to another robot, and so on; this slowly grows the desired reflective state that finds its peak when the character faces the truth that the player already knew. The difference from a "classical" plot-twist is that, in this case, the player doesn't focus their emotions on the twist itself but rather on empathising with the character as they see *him* process that information, with all the emotions that said processing involves—receiving bad news feels terrible, but seeing someone you care about go through that path hurts even more. This is well done by *Pixar Animation Studios* where, in their movies, you can see a character's emotions projected on another character, creating a feeling of vulnerability between the two of them—also thanks to their eyes, which are a key way Pixar communicates emotions and, most of all, the intimacy that opens the doors for those vulnerable moments.

This brings me to the last keystone of emotional theories, which is the theme: as I said in the beginning of emotional game design, it's important to pick a theme you are empathic with, meaning it has to be part of your empathic engine. Only this way you can create scenarios, metaphors, and worlds with a deep impact on the player's emotions, because you understand that topic so well that you know how to twist it to bring the best possible outcome according to your design's goal: it could be to move the players, give them a new point of view on a underestimated issue, or open their mind toward a sensitive topic you care about—if you don't care about something, after all, how can you make other people care?

Wow, what a tough section this was! There were so many tools scattered all over the place. *What?* You picked them up? That's great, I'm glad they didn't go to waste, and even if you missed one here and there, fear not, you can always have another, more careful, run—it feels just like finding all the objects and secrets in a game, doesn't it?

I know your tool bag is getting pretty heavy by now; have a break if you need to, but remember that every single one of those tools may come in handy any moment, so it's very important that you learn how to use them, not just by reading: join a game jam to test them one at the time, or have a small project to try out the one that sounded really complicated. The more you use a tool, the more it becomes part of your design process and part of how you think: what sounds complex today might be the very framework that will help you create your best game tomorrow—you may become the one giving me tips on how to best use it, in a few years.

Once you have tested—integrated in your design process—all the design techniques in these pages, you won't even need to open this book again once: you may keep it as a memory, use it as a doorstop, or pass it to someone who is be entering the lands of game design in that very moment—there are no dangerous creatures, that's true, but having a map to follow showing where all the tools are hidden is a great start. Worst case scenario, if you do use it as a doorstop, it will be a great conversation opener for when you have guests around!

NOTES

1 Cambria, E., Livingstone, A., and Hussain, A. (2012), *The Hourglass of Emotions*. Berlin Heidelberg: Springer-Verlag.
2 *Emogifs Map*: https://s3-us-west-1.amazonaws.com/emogifs/map.html#
3 Nummenmaa, L., Glerean, E., Hari, R., and Hietanen, J. K. (2014, January 14), 'Bodily maps of emotions', *PNAS*, 111 (2): 646–651: https://doi.org/10.1073/pnas.1321664111
4 Romero, B. (2009), *Brenda Games: Train*: http://brenda.games/train

SECTION FOUR

Documentation

Introduction to Documentation

17

After having read so much about brainstorming techniques, research tools, and design frameworks, you should be filled with knowledge about all those aspects of the design process, so it's very important to find a place where you can put all these things safely, or you may lose some pieces along the way. Until now, you probably wrote everything in a text file, a notebook, or random pieces of papers, but they now need to become documentation: being able to create and maintain a good documentation is one of the most important skills in this field, because it's the way a designer talks to others—I'll get to that in a second, don't worry. Documentation doesn't necessarily mean a written document, as it can be any physical—thus not spoken—way you can convey knowledge: a document—of course—a picture/video/gif, a physical paper prototype, and much more. Finding the best possible way to communicate information is very important for a designer, even if it means writing it with a permanent marker on the wall—that's not a scalable way, but I won't judge as long as it works for you.

This section is divided into three main parts:

Introduction, which you are reading right now, where I talk about the reason why designers need documentation.

Golden Rules: a series of guidelines that, no matter the type or the goal of a document, should always be followed to create high-quality documentation.

Documents: a list of documents that every designer needs to know how to create for any project that they will work on; note that while you may find the same type of document with different names and formats, the use and goal are the same—as you know, game design is 50% art, meaning that there is no mathematically right way to create a document: finding the best way to express the data in each different situation is part of a designer's art.

Earlier I said that documentation is the way designers talk to others, but what does it mean? You may know the Latin phrase "*Verba volant, scripta manent*", which means that spoken words are forgotten, while written ones stay forever. This is the first main reason why documentation is needed, as no matter the project or the team, eventually everyone will forget at least one tiny detail of the design: they could remember the value *11,254* instead of *11,245*, forget the goal of an old design, or completely remove a decision taken months before from their mind.

Why does this happen? Can't designers just *remember* stuff? Well not really, because it's natural to forget: a project generally lasts years, tons of decisions are made, concepts change, and designers are human, so it's impossible to remember every tiny element of

DOI: 10.1201/9781003229438-21

their job, especially when they have to work on five different things at the same time—do you remember what the first word of this chapter was? Me neither, and just a few minutes have passed, so you get how hard it would be to remember it for *years* and for hundreds of words.

A document, in fact, keeps every piece of information in a secure state, as it doesn't get lost over time and only selected people can modify it, often providing a "log" of who modified even a single word—it may sound overkill in a professional environment, but you'll see why it's best to have it, just in case.

The second reason why documentation is so important is that every piece of information needs to be communicated: for instance, if I design a wall-run mechanic, other game designers might need it to design related movement mechanics; level designers use it to manage the distances between walls, their lengths, and so on.

You may think that the best way to exchange information is talking face to face, but it's not really so: face to face is the quickest way, with a *good* efficiency level, but it's far from perfect; how many times has someone told you something while in a hurry or while being stressed, and you misunderstood part of what they said? Or even worse, did someone ever introduce themself by saying their name, and five seconds later you already forgot what it was? Now multiply this risk for the number of people in a meeting: *Jerry* talked about his design for a mechanic, *Mary* about hers for a level, *John* about theirs for the narrative; all looks great and you close the meeting; a couple of days later, when you need to work on something related to the protagonist's story, you need to call another meeting to ask John about that little detail, or Mary misunderstood a sentence Jerry said and now the level is upside-down.

Verba volant, it can be misunderstood or forgotten very easily; talking is a very quick way to communicate, that's true, but its not-perfect efficiency makes it unreliable: you could even say "Jerry told me the dash should be five metres long" on purpose when he told you it was two metres, so a "she said, he said" situation that could last hours takes place, and how could your team know who is lying? Or did they just misunderstand something? These scenarios, with documentation, are very less likely to happen.

On the other hand, documents take time to be created, but they will keep every word, image, or table there forever, also keeping track of who wrote what. It's sort of a last resort for when a member is "secretly" altering the design, and while it is one of the worst-case scenarios you could face, it's not an impossible one:

> Some time ago, while working on a project, I tested the implementation of a design I worked on and it was very different from what I had designed, so I went to the programmer and asked them why it wasn't matching the document at all; they told me they had no idea what I was talking about, as the code *did* match what was written on the design document. "Maybe I made a mistake while typing" I thought to myself, as I opened it: the programmer wasn't lying, the code did exactly what was written in there, but the text wasn't at all what I originally wrote. I opened the chronology of the document, only to find out that a member of the team was secretly modifying the design to make it follow his personal vision, hoping no one would have noticed until the end of the production—as you can tell by this outcome, it wasn't the brightest of the plans to begin with. This person was, then, of course, removed from the project: as I said in the first

few pages of the book, *your ego won't fit*, and this usually means accepting and following someone else's vision.

Now, it's true that documents take more time to make than simply telling someone the design by voice, but what if you work with 20 people, and all of them keep asking the same question? Assuming that the answer would be 3 minutes long, you would spend one hour each day just to say the exact same thing, which means 20 hours every month. Say, instead, you spend 2 hours writing a document with the answer to the most probable questions: you just saved 18 hours from being wasted every month—so yes, documentation takes more time to be created, but way less time to be distributed.

The last main reason for which documentation is crucial is that spoken information often disappears and becomes *tacit knowledge*, and tacit elements are very dangerous in any part of the design process: you and another designer may know that piece of information, while a new colleague who just joined your team doesn't, even after reading all the documentation, because it wasn't *documented*, it was just *said*. They may work being completely sure to know what they need to know, producing the design of the whole open-world side of the game, only to find out that it's completely wrong for the vision because of that tacit element they couldn't possibly have known about. This leads, of course, to their frustration, as they spend time and resources working on something that may go straight into the trash can, maybe even making a bad first impression of them with the team through no fault of their own.

These were all very bad scenarios, I know, and lack of documentation does not always lead to the end of the world, but they are all more than possible, further proving how critical this topic is for a professional and efficient working environment.

Golden Rules

18

INTRODUCTION TO GOLDEN RULES

The concept of Golden Rules is very important in our field, because there are tons of different types of documentation, and also because, being part of the 50% art of every designer, every director may impose a format that better delivers their vision: for instance, no borderless images, no coloured text, no double-spacing, and so on.

While no perfect "document archetype" exists at the moment, what you can do is follow this series of guidelines that put you on the right track for creating high-quality documentation: some will be big *dos* and *don'ts* that could save your document from killing whoever is trying to read it—metaphorically speaking, of course—while others are smaller tips to show your proficiency with the tools, avoiding minor mistakes, and all sort of things that a colleague would point out to you if you asked them for a feedback about the structure or readability of the document. These are smaller tools that every designer needs to have, not small because they are not important but because, compared to wide topics like praxeology, these can be learned in almost no time—they won't provide you with *perfect* documentation, but it will be high quality at least, even the first time you use that type of document.

Before getting to the actual rules, you need to understand two main concepts regarding documentation:

The first one is that every document depends on its goal—aka the type of project, the person who will read it, and the task for which the document was created. Even inside the same team there are very different documents: the one you write for a programmer is totally different from the one you give to an artist, as the first one needs the technical side of the information of, say, the shooting system they have to implement, while the second needs the dimensions, colours, and reference for the gun used to shoot.

The second one is *technical writing*: as you know there are many different types of writing, such as narrative, academic, informal, etc; each one is very different from any other one, for instance the one I'm writing in right now is very different from the one I use for a design document, because the purpose of this book is not the purpose of a document, and the reader is different as well.

In every design document, technical writing has one main goal: to be as clear as possible, in the shortest possible amount of time/space; this means writing in a form shorter than a summary, literally removing any non-essential words one by one.

DOI: 10.1201/9781003229438-22

Technical documents don't need a flow, *"for examples"*, or words that make the reading pleasant: as long as it's clear, it only needs to be quick to read; designing games is hard, but, above everything else, it's a race against time, as there are so many things to do and only so much time. Everyone in a team—artists, designers, programmers, etc.—has a ton of tasks, so you can be sure that no one will care about a *pleasant* or a *nice* read, they all want—and need—a *quick* and *clear* read—you surely could travel to the opposite side of the world by car, foot, and boat, but if you care about time you will just get on a plane.

That being said, let's now move on to the golden rules of documentation.

SHOW, DON'T WRITE

It may sound antithetical: I'm talking about documentation and the very first rule is about not writing? Well, think about it this way: if you can show in a chart what would take you 100 words to explain, go with the graph. A gif instead of three paragraphs? Absolutely. A gif instead of two whole pictures? Even better. A *less is more* mentality is crucial to developing high-quality documentation. "A picture is worth a thousand words" they say, and in this field the saying applies to any transmedial element: how hard is it to describe a boss fight, conveying all the emotions and feelings, the boss' movements, their deep and scary voice, the majestic soundtrack playing in the background, and hundreds more details? It would take pages and pages, while the right video can convey the same information in a few seconds, minutes tops. The same goes for, let's say, when you are asking a sound designer for a specific sound: it's hard to describe in detail something you are not expert in; it's a lot easier to link them an audio reference saying "similar to this, but with a violin instead of an ARP"—it's not your fault for not knowing an effect's name or how to describe it with the right terms, but it's your duty to be as clear and concise as possible when communicating what you mean.

BOX 18.1   AN EXAMPLE OF HOW SHOWING SOMETHING CAN BE FAR MORE INTUITIVE THAN ITS DESCRIPTION, IN THIS CASE WITH THE COVER OF THIS BOOK

Think about a hexagon; inside this hexagon, there is a sword, a pencil, a heart, and a few other shapes. Outside the hexagon there is a PS1, a smartphone, and some other signs. There is text too: some is inside the hexagon, some is outside, some is over it.

What am I talking about? And, most of all, how did you picture it? Now, close the book.

It was a description of the cover: you probably understood it quite soon, but what if you had never seen it? Maybe you were close, or maybe your mental image was completely off: this is the perfect example of why showing something is far more effective than describing it.

This rule is applied to anything, music, sounds, videos, etc., because every designer has access to the biggest archive that ever existed: the internet. No matter how unusual or random something you are talking about is, I 99% guarantee that there will be something about it online: a dog baking a cake? A t-rex riding a bicycle? An alternative version of the Hearth where people are hot-dogs? There *must* be at least a post or drawing somewhere out there, and if there isn't, it only takes five minutes to edit a picture that shows the concept.

Now, just because you *can* use pictures and other media, it doesn't mean you *have to*: if it's done to make the reading faster and easier go ahead, but don't fill your document with elements that convey no information or, even worse, can distract the reader from what's really important—images are like magnets on a fridge: sure they make it look less "boring", but if I asked you to look for a specific magnet on a fridge filled with 100 of them, you may just wish it was left empty instead.

BRIEF AND SHORT

Sometimes there will be concepts that need to be described with words, and when those times come you will need to be as brief as possible: no one has the will or time to read your documents, but it's crucial that they do for the success of the project—*Verba Volant*, remember?

How can you convince your co-workers to open and read your document? First of all, including multimedia elements—the first rule—and, second, keeping them short and *concise*: get rid of any unnecessary sentences and improve the ones you want to keep.

The following example is a 130-word description of Jakub Koziol's *Little Alchemy 2* mechanics, written by a first-year game design student:

> The goal of the game is to craft as many items as you can. Every item is distinguished by an icon and a name. To craft an item you simply have to combine two other items. Not all items can be combined and some items can be combined with a copy of themselves. Every item can be duplicated indefinitely just by tapping twice on the item. Every discovered item can be obtained again using the "library" (an alphabetically ordered list of items) suitably located at the right side of the screen. At the beginning of the game you are given four starting items (water, air, earth, fire). There are over 720 items that can be obtained. Few important items can be unlocked by obtaining a certain fixed number of items.

The same concept can be conveyed with the following paragraph:

> Goal: Craft the maximum number of items by combining two items at the time; items can be duplicated, combined with themselves or other specific items, not all items can be combined. Discovered items are stored in the *Library*, used to recover them. The game starts with four items: water, air, earth fire.

As you can see, the description dropped to 52 words, less than half of the original amount; this means that a person would have spent less than half of the time reading the document, to gain the same amount of information. Now multiply that saved time by the number of people in a team, the number of documents produced by that team, and the amount of time saved by optimising a sentence, and you just saved the team what would probably be weeks of unnecessary work, which can instead go toward other elements of the game—again, in a race against time every saved minute counts.

It will be very hard to write in a technical way at first, taking you more time than writing in the way you would talk about something in person, but the more you do it the better you become, then saving you and your team countless hours during the development of a project. Your co-workers will also find it easier to understand everything in the document, because no unnecessary/time-wasting information will be present: they read exactly what they need to know, no possible subjective interpretation or written equivalent of small talk. It's also a form of respect toward your team, as, by taking only the time you really need from them, you are acknowledging that they are just as busy as you, and their time is just as valuable as yours. They, in the same way, read your documents because they respect your work and time that went into it, and it's for this mutual respect that these rules are so important: it's very important to always have in mind your colleagues when behaving in a professional environment, from a document you write to the way you talk to them. We should all remember that everyone around us worked hard to be in that spot, in the industry that they hopefully love, and no one has made that many sacrifices to be treated poorly by a colleague.

THE RIGHT TOOL FOR THE RIGHT JOB

As you already know, documentation isn't about writing a text document only, even if filled with other media, as many different tools can be used to convey information: spreadsheets, slide presentations, wikis, paper prototypes, and many more, each one tuneable in different ways, with colours, animations, links, and so on. There is no right answer to the question "What document should I use?" as it changes based on what you need to document and who it is for, for instance an art-related document may be best presented as a mood board, a core loop as a flowchart, a complex narrative with multiple linked characters as a wiki.

The right tool for the right job, meaning that you need to understand which tool best fits your needs, even if you will need to create a new one from scratch—before slide presentations existed, someone used to convey that same information on a text document, until they realised "there *must* be a better way".

Think about Quantic Dream's *Detroit: Become Human*, a narrative-based game with multiple choices for the player to take during each sequence: at the end of each sequence, a screen shows all the ramifications the story could have taken, highlighting the one resulted by the decisions the player made—Figure 18.1. This could easily be a production document: imagine how hard it would be to list with plain text all the possibilities: "*segment 7 branch 4 choice 5, which is only available if in segment 3 branch 2 choice 1 was taken*"; that's just madness, no one would understand a choice they are referring to without having to go back to another document and read what it was about; now picture a format like the

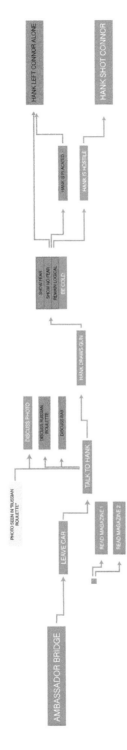

FIGURE 18.1 A representation of the logic behind *Detroit: Become Human*'s choice tree.

Source: Author.

screen used in Detroit: *"this arrow points to this branch, each choice points to a different ending"*; it's a hundred times easier, don't you agree?

Of course, a document like that couldn't possibly include all the information regarding each choice, but it's a great map to avoid getting lost in that sea of possibilities. This makes it easier to visualise a part of the production instead of having to picture it based on words only: exactly like a map, why spending hours describing the shape of a country with all its curves when you can just show it? A single map can't show you *everything* about a country, or it would be too messy to understand, but you can use the type of map that you need for a specific task: one shows the urban density of each city, one shows the height of the mountains, one only the roads, and so on.

It may takes some minutes to understand which tool is the most efficient one for that task, but it's worth the time, because working for hours with the wrong tool won't just feel right, both for who writes the document and for who reads it—nothing stops you from using a hammer to tighten a screw, but chances are it won't work as planned, and you may even get hurt, so why not just use a screwdriver?

IMPLEMENT VISUAL LAYERING AND SEPARATION

This is the concept often used in architecture—thus in level design too—of implicit and explicit space: when creating a document, any type of document, there are countless implicit and explicit spaces that you generate without even knowing it depending on where you place text, images, and even empty parts.

Separating and visually framing the content is crucial to communicating to the reader what to read, in what order, with what relevance, and the connections between different elements. For instance, a table of 50 rows with the same colour and style tells you they belong to the same topic, while two tables with an empty line between them communicate the end of a section and the beginning of a different, potentially unrelated one; this is done, among other tools, with spaces.

One of the most powerful tools in a document is an empty line: you are dedicating a whole space intentionally left empty to communicate the separation between two elements, which the brain reads as a signal to stop, breathe, and prepare for the new part—just like you stopped for a second when the previous paragraph ended and this begun.

This is an example of what I mean by that.

As you can tell, your mind gave far more importance to that sentence compared to the previous paragraph, because it thinks "if it is so separated from the rest, there must be a reason", paying more attention to those few words.

Implicit spaces are also very important for tables and frames to signal the belonging of a piece of information, other than increasing the visual appeal of a document: to avoid feeling like a punch in the eye, documents need to look good, and to look good an element needs to be symmetrical or, at least, respect an ordered logic:

MECHANIC	STATISTIC	VALUE	UNIT OF MEASURE
Run	Speed	4	metres/second
Jump	Height	3	Metres
	Gravitational Acceleration	9.81	metres * second-2
Dash	Max Distance	5	Metres

As you can tell from this table, it's immediate that the stats *Height* and *Gravitational Acceleration* both belong to the mechanic *Jump* as it occupies two cell spaces, while speed and dash only have one parameter—of course this is a simplification. Furthermore, the bigger dimension of the Statistic column makes you pay more attention to that, while the first row written in bold indicates that it's the heading of the table; as you can tell, there are tons of ways to communicate the function and meaning of an element, with space being one of the most crucial among many others. Note that this doesn't make any other tool less important, but others may have more limited applications, meaning you need to understand them all to then quickly identify what the best tool for the job is.

Tools can of course be combined, and if you are wondering how to know when you are using too many of them at the same time, don't worry, the next rule is all about that.

AVOID JUNK: LESS IS MORE

As a designer, the "less is more" mindset is very important to maintain as few elements as possible, making the most out of the ones you have and avoiding junk. The same mindset needs to be applied to documentation: there are thousands of possible combinations of different tools you can use, but just because you *can* doesn't mean you *should*. Before making any change in the format of the document, ask yourself if it's really needed, or if there is a better way to show that same element, which means a strict no-nonsense policy: do you really need to change font? And that colour? Are you sure you want to highlight that sentence in purple? The general rule is that if something doesn't either bring a clearer understanding of the concept or the use of fewer words, you shouldn't change it.

There is a huge difference between a harlequin paragraph with ten different tools used and one with a black plain text with a single word different from the others—if everything is special, special is the new normality; notice the difference between the following two paragraphs:

This is an example of a very confusing paragraph, there are tons of different tools trying to grab your attention, *making it very hard to focus here* <u>and most likely distracting you</u> **or even making you focus** on the wrong thing ~~such as~~ **<u>this</u>**.

This is an example of a plain paragraph; there are only two tools used to grab your attention, making it very easy to focus **here** and most likely letting you immediately know not to focus on the wrong thing such as this.

First of all, I apologise for making you wish you never read that first paragraph; besides that, however, you can see how you didn't know where to look at first, because every part of that sentence was screaming "look at me!"—if you are at a concert and you heard people shouting at the top of their lungs, you wouldn't really care about them because everyone would doing that, but if that happened while at the doctor you will most likely jump on your feet for the fright: the same thing is going on here.

In the second sentence, however, you knew that the core of the paragraph was the word *here*, because it was the only one different from all the others: I'm not saying you should only use one key word in your documents, but the fewer there are the bigger their impact will be.

NO WEAK LANGUAGE

When writing a document, in 99% of the cases, you are communicating your design/analysis results to other people, and there is no space for *maybes* or uncertainty: terms like "I think", "it could", and, of course, "maybe" show that you are not sure about what you are talking about, which is a problem. People reading a document that exudes insecurity often think it's a request for feedback, help, or a meeting to discuss the issue; this isn't *always* a problem, for instance if you wrote a design idea and want to have your colleagues' opinion, but if you bring a document that should be final to a co-worker who needs that design to go on with their work and it's full of uncertain elements, they won't be able to do their work and, furthermore, they may spend even more time designing an alternative version to what you wrote about in a weak way.

Other than that, weak language increases the amount of words—thus time—required to read something; take the following as an example:

> All the comments I read about tanks or jobs like Machinist, Samurai doing too little damage, I think can be considered minor problems that require balancing or upgrading their damage.

This is another abstract from a student's analysis, and by removing the unnecessary and uncertain parts it can be shortened in the following sentence:

> Comments regarding tanks/jobs dealing insufficient damage are considered minor problems requiring balancing.

What changed? Let's break it down, step by step:

> "All the" could easily be excluded, since not specifying the portion of the quantity equals the whole quantity. "I read about" is weak because they are implicitly saying that someone else could find comments that contradict their analysis—I'm not saying it's not possible, but saying that something isn't true when a valid antithesis is found is obvious and doesn't show confidence in one's own work.

The examples aren't needed since they provide the condition behind the issue—the low damage.

> "Too little [damage]" can be shortened into "insufficient".
> "I think" again shows uncertainty, as well as "[they] can be [considered]", which becomes "are [considered]": an analysis document draws conclusions starting from a set of data and the interpretation of the designer, meaning that whatever is written in that document is stated by them considering both the data and the interpretation as valid. Of course it can potentially be refuted, but if even the writer isn't sure about their thesis, how can they convey that information to other people?
> Last, "that require balancing or upgrading their damage" both mean "balancing".

As you can tell any word that isn't needed got cut, and while it took more time to explain the mistakes rather than just reading the original version, that person will now be more careful not to repeat those same mistakes—you know what they say, "Give a man a fish . . .".

CHARTS AND TABLES SIMPLIFY THE DATA

As you already know, showing a piece of information instead of writing it is very important, but charts and tables are so important that they needed a rule of their own. They are incredible tools: picking the right chart or table format can completely change both the visual appeal and readability of your document. To choose the best one, of course, a basic understanding and knowledge of the most used types of charts and tables is needed—don't worry, this part is exactly about that, and you will find some practical examples as well.

Flowchart

A flowchart is a formalised graph used to show a logical sequence, and it can be used for many different topics: coding, designing, describing a loop or player journey, etc. There are many different versions of the rules that should be followed regarding the meaning each shape should have—for example rectangle means an operation, a rhombus equals a choice—but that's not the point: as long as you and your team decide on a set of rules regarding each shape, you can even use shapes that aren't normally used for this chart: the important thing is that everyone understands the same thing while reading it (see Figure 18.2).

Cartesian Diagram

First of all, different from flowcharts, the other types of graph have a more formalised structure, meaning that you should follow the format in which they are most commonly used—*i.e.* you can't invert the X and Y axes in most cases, or you will get a result that either doesn't work or that may mislead the readers who don't notice the inversion.

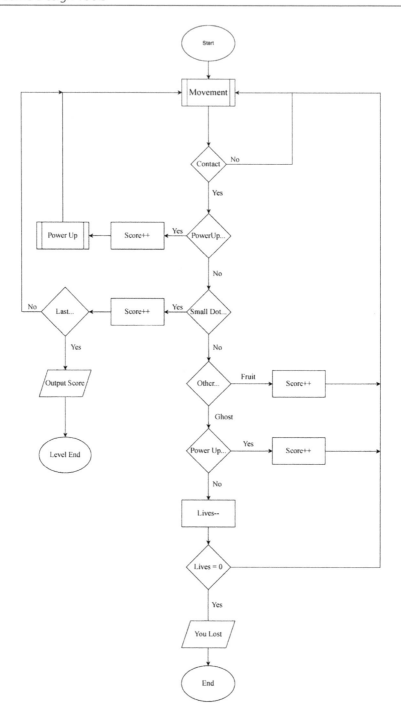

FIGURE 18.2   An example of flowchart used to describe *PacMan* games structure. The ovals are the beginning and ending of the process, the rectangles are the instructions, and the rhombi are the choices.

Source: Author.

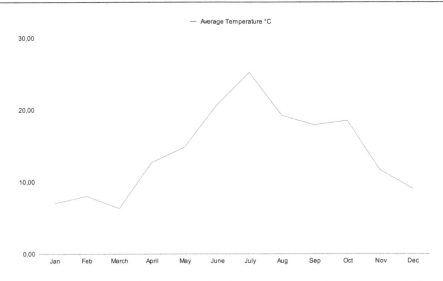

FIGURE 18.3   A Cartesian diagram showing the average monthly temperature in Rome in 1987.

Source: Author.

The Cartesian diagram shows the correlation between a value x and a different value y, represented on a Cartesian plane according to either a set of values or a formula from which the values are calculated (Figure 18.3).

Line Chart

A line chart (Figure 18.4) is the representation of the changes—trend—of a value compared to another value as a line, where multiple lines can be present in the same chart as long as they are based on the same two type of values: if you are comparing the amount of gold earned in each area by the four players who tested your game, you have four different lines, but all of them are based on "area" and "gold", distinguishing the player using a different colour and a key somewhere on the chart.

Stepped Line Chart

A stepped line chart (Figure 18.5) is similar to the line chart, displaying the correlation between two values at each data point, with the main difference that this chart is used for sudden changes that then stay stable for a set amount of time, thus displaying the impact and not the trend of the curve.

Bar Chart

A bar chart displays the absolute frequency of the listed elements: the vertical axis shows the frequency, while the horizontal axis only works as support for the chart. It allows you to compare different items to each other in the same category. It can also be used to

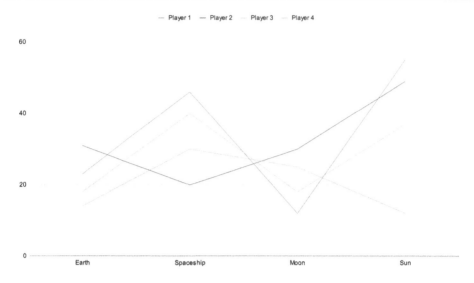

FIGURE 18.4   A line chart of how many gold coins were earned in each section of a hypo-thetical game by four different playtesters.

Source: Author.

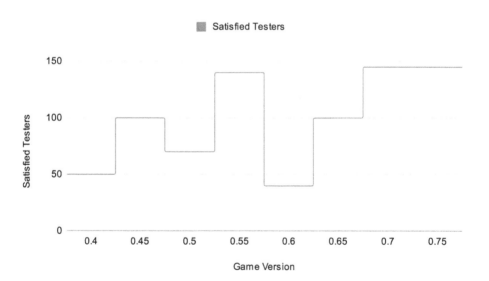

FIGURE 18.5   A stepped line chart of the number of playtesters that gave positive feedback over each version of a game, focusing on the impact of the curve rather than the trend.

Source: Author.

display multiple elements for each item, still measuring their frequency; it sounds very complicated, but as you take a look at Figure 18.6 you will immediately understand how it works—that's why you *show, don't write.*

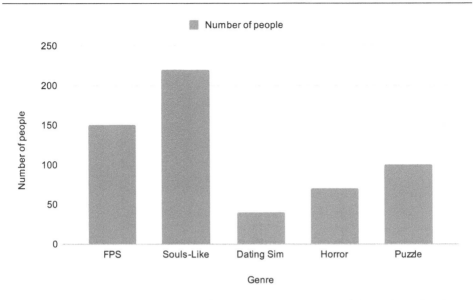

FIGURE 18.6   A bar chart displaying the favourite videogame genre of a hypothetical audience.
Source: Author.

Stacked Bar Chart

The stacked bar chart works the same way as the bar chart, showing the frequency of multiple items over the same metric; the main difference is that, in this case, you can stack multiple bars on top of each other, where each bar represents a different element with a different value from the ones it is stacked with. An item can have multiple—potentially infinite—elements stacked on top of each other, and with this chart type the axes are exchangeable to display the bars horizontally (Figure 18.7).

Histogram Chart

A histogram chart has a similar appearance of a stacked bar chart, but instead of comparing categories, it compares the distribution of data in a single category: taking the previous example, instead of having men, women, and non-binary players divided into age groups, in the histogram only men or women or non-binary players can be displayed at a single time, analysing their distribution over the age (Figure 18.8).

Pie Chart

A pie chart is a circular graph divided into slices, each one of which indicates a numerical proportion of the relative element: it visually represents the dimension of each group compared to the total size of the dataset.

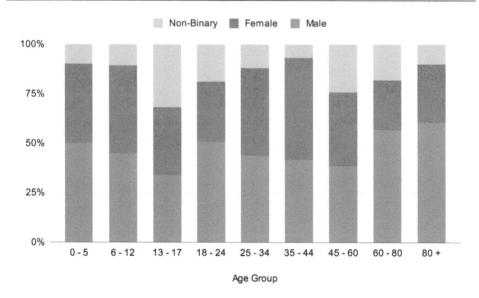

FIGURE 18.7   A stacked bar chart representing the number of men, women, and non-binary players of a game divided by age groups. Each age group can have a different percentage of each category, displayed one on top of each other.

Source: Author.

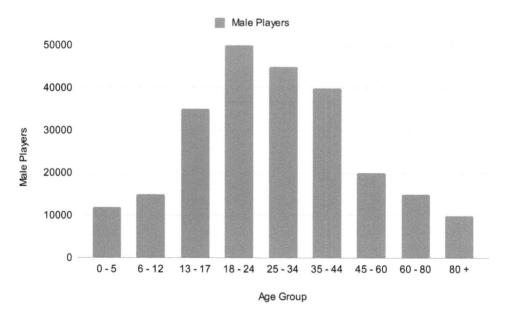

FIGURE 18.8   A histogram chart representing the same dataset of the stacked bar chart but only for one of the categories, focusing on its distribution over the amount of players per age group instead of the percentage.

Source: Author.

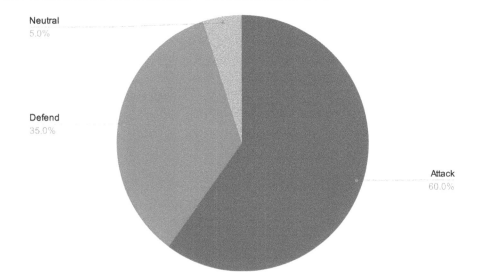

FIGURE 18.9   A pie chart showing the types of actions performed in a game divided by their goal (attack, defend, stall) colour-coded to communicate affordance.

Source: Author.

This is one of the most basic charts, with a great instant affordance that can further be increased by colour-coding each slice of the pie to match the group it is referring to: for instance, looking at Figure 18.9, you can see that the number of *attack* actions is coloured in red—generally associated with offence—the *defend* actions slice is blue, and the *neutral* in grey for that same common association.

Pie Chart with Intensity

A pie chart with intensity indicates the percentages of each item just like any other pie chart, but the external expansion shows the intensity of that same item: each slice shows the mechanic that a group of players likes the most of a game, and in a standard pie chart the red and yellow groups would have no difference; thanks to the intensity parameter, instead, you can see how the yellow players have a way more intense liking of that mechanic, letting the designers know that, for instance, by increasing the presence of that mechanic in the game, the players belonging to the yellow group will be more involved than what any other group would have been if it was their mechanic's presence to be increased (Figure 18.10).

Area Chart

The area chart is very similar to the regular line chart, with two main differences: the section between each element's line and the X axis is coloured in a specific tone according to the key reported on the chart, and the X axis must be zero. This chart shows the trend of different groups compared to the same element, for instance time or, as shown in Figure 18.11, updates.

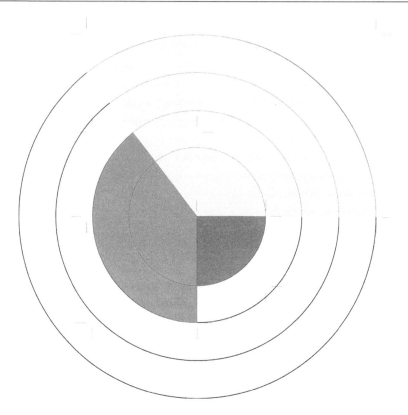

FIGURE 18.10   A pie chart with intensity displaying what mechanics a group of players likes the most of a horror game. Yellow is *breath holding*, red is *sprinting*, and orange is *hitting*.

Source: Author.

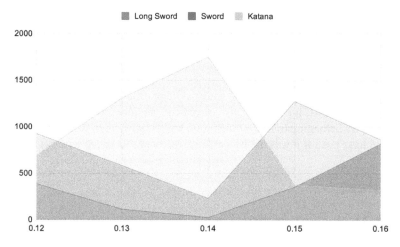

FIGURE 18.11   An area chart showing the amount of players using each type of weapon—long swords, swords, katanas—over each update.

Stacked Area Chart and Percent Stacked Area Chart

The area chart has two main variations that you should know of:

The stacked area chart works the same way as the previous area chart, with the exception that multiple data sets are, of course, stacked on one another, and each data set's starting point is the end of the following data set.

The percent stacked area chart, instead, works just like the area chart, but instead of using absolute values it uses percentage values (Figures 18.12 and 18.13).

Scatter Plot Chart

The scatter plot chart uses a Cartesian plane to display plots' positions; in this case, you are not looking at the correlation between the axes elements but rather at possible clusters formed by the plots' distribution (Figures 18.14).

Clusters are very helpful because, while the plots should normally be distributed in a more-or-less uniform way, they are instead grouped in specific areas, for countless possible reasons: as for every chart, it doesn't tell you *why* something happens, it just tells you that it is happening; to find out the cause of a chart's content, you need to analyse all the elements that may be influencing the represented data—even if they are elements that are not displayed on the chart itself.

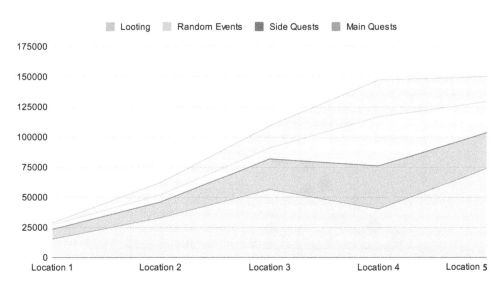

FIGURE 18.12   A stacked area chart displaying the sources and amounts of in-game currency for each area of a game.

Source: Author.

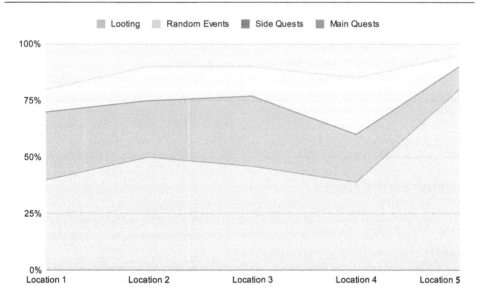

FIGURE 18.13 A percent stacked area chart showing in which area players spend what percentage of the play time, performing which activities.

Source: Author.

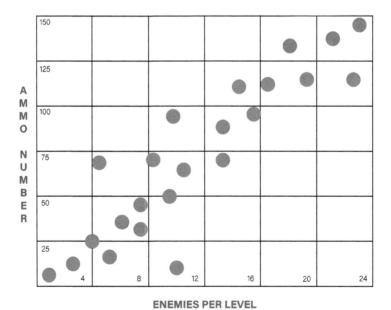

FIGURE 18.14 A scatter plot chart displaying the ammos bought in a FPS game over the number of enemies in the level.

Source: Author.

Bubble Chart

The bubble chart shows the correlation on a Cartesian plane between the X and Y axes, with the addition of a third element of comparison: the size of each bubble; it illustrates the correlation between X and Y with a qualitative element.

For example, a bubble chart illustrating how much people liked (size of the bubble) a recipe for a cake with three different amounts of milk (X axis) and chocolate (Y axis): the bigger the bubble, the more they liked that version of the recipe. Each bubble has a different colour in order to understand which version it was—as shown in Figure 18.15.

Think Outside the Chart

The bubble chart was the last of the charts covered in this book, for a very specific reason: while most charts—excluding three dimensional ones and such—work on only two axes, there are many tools you can use to communicate more pieces of information: the colours of each line, the size of each column, the texture, the shape, and much more—just like the size of the bubbles. These tools can be used both to add an element

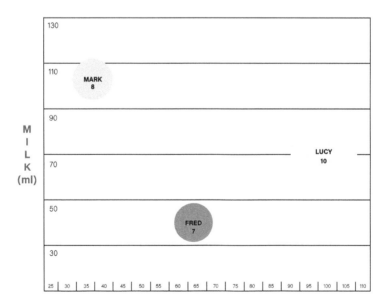

CHOCOLATE (g)

FIGURE 18.15   A bubble chart illustrating people's favourability toward three versions of the same cake, each with different proportions of milk and chocolate.

Source: Author.

to the comparison—like the size of the bubbles—or to facilitate the readability of the chart.

Think about a dishwasher's energy chart—Figure 18.16: it's just a bar chart oriented vertically, but the colour—and letter—of each bar lets you immediately know if it's good or bad; imagine the same chart but with no letters nor colours: sure you could still figure out which class the dishwasher belongs to, but it would take more time to count the bars to know the exact class—*one, two, three, four,* so A, B, C, D, *it's a D.* But what if the chart doesn't start with A but rather with A+++? You don't buy the item because you think it's a D, when in reality it's an A—and this was just a dishwasher, imagine what would happen with a similar mistake in a meeting with tons of money at stake.

An energy consumption chart, with seven bars in different colours captioned from G to A. The lower bars, G, F, and E, are longer and on the red spectrum of colours; the middle bar, D, is coloured between green and yellow; the upper bars are the shortest and are on the green spectrum.

One last example of how to customise charts to help you deliver their purpose/content is the one shown in Figure 18.17: cakes are used to show the possible combinations of ingredients for a cake and their amount; if you remove the cake, it's just an ordinary stacked bar chart, but that drawing instantly lets the reader know what the topic of the chart is—even more, a chart like that is not something you see every day, making its read more interesting; of course, if all the graphs have a strong customisation—recalling the less is more philosophy—they become counter-productive, taking the user more time to read them and creating documents that look like a graphic design paper rather than a design document.

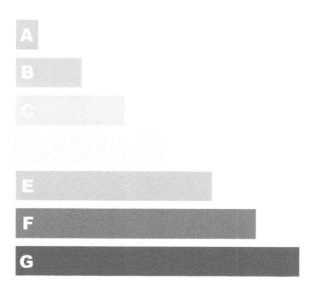

FIGURE 18.16   A bar chart used to illustrate an item's energy chart. Colours and letters are used to better communicate which class the item belongs to.

Source: Author.

When you think that a customisation of a chart would help deliver a piece of information, without impacting its readability, feel free to adjust it as you please. As I mentioned before, there are many elements you can change in a chart, but here are some more advanced ones: shapes, colour intensities, iconographies, perspective, opacity, overlaps, outlines, and line treatments; these aren't *all* the possible changes though, they are just a good place to start: once you get used to charts, you can really modify anything—you may need specific software since certain features may not be included in the most common suits, but if it really would make the difference don't let a software limitation stop you.

A good beginner tip is to create a checklist with all the elements you can think of that can be changed in a chart—colour, shape, opacity, and so on—then running them one by one by asking yourself "If I change the colour, does it make the chart easier to understand?" *Yes* = change it/*No* = don't touch it. Do the same thing for each element on the list, and, by the end, you should have the most readable chart you could have—as always, don't overdo or you will have the opposite effect.

That should be it for the charts, but what about tables? There is a very specific reason why this golden rule was placed after those other ones instead of being on top of the list, and it's because everything you have read in this chapter, both for text and graphs, applies to tables: a table is a table—not considering three dimensional ones, just like for charts—so there isn't really much to say about it, because it all depends on what it's needed for;

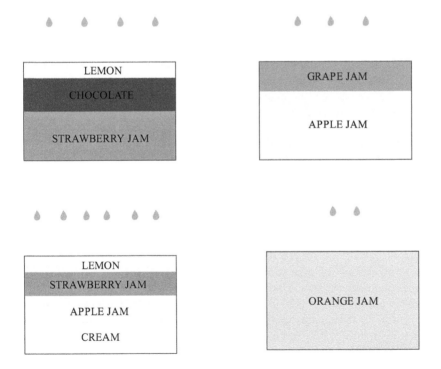

FIGURE 18.17   A stacked bar chart displayed in the format of cakes, to better communicate what the chart is about.

Source: Author.

I could show you how I create a table for a specific job, but chances are you will never face the exact same issue: "what if I need more columns? And those two rows have to be merged together! My boss told me not to use that colour". Tables contain data, and finding the best way to express that data is both your job and part of your art; the more documents you will write, the more table-related tools you will experience, surely making mistakes but learning from each one of them: "The table was too big and a new page was added to the document with an empty line at the end without me noticing it; a colleague told me about that empty page, and since then I always check where the document ends". This is just one of the most common examples I've seen among my students; I could go on for hours but I'm sure you would just forget about half of them, because it's not something you can learn from one reading and then you're good to go; you need to see them yourself, both while writing your documents and while reading people's ones—just know that as long as you follow the golden rules, you won't make any *big* mistake; it will all be about polishing your table-making skills.

Now, let's get back to the other golden rules; you have just read some of the most important ones, but they aren't over—you don't want your tool bag to be half empty, *do you?*

Colours

You already know a lot about colours, as you remember from the *No Weak Language* rule, so you recall that, since colours are so powerful, they must be used sparingly.

The best colour combination is black text on white background, both because everyone is used to it—even if you use a dark theme everywhere, you probably spent a big part of your life reading black words on a white sheet of paper—and because it makes it easy to read without disturbing the eye as much as, say, purple and yellow would do.

It's very important to know that colours can have different meanings depending on the culture you are in, so you have to know what they mean beforehand: for instance, Red represents love and passion in America and Europe; it represents fear, love, marriage, and beauty in Indian cultures; but, in China, it means luck and fertility, while in Thailand it also means *Sunday*. Imagine creating a document with a red background—in 99% of the cases, don't do it—which should communicate love and passion, but part of your team reads it as fearful, and another part thinks it's about some gambling mechanic for half the document.

Once you are sure of what each colour means for your team, the next rule is not to use strong colours: by "strong" I mean fluorescent colours, ones with high intensity, a high contrast with one another, or that, in general, are tiring to read for the eyes—pastel colours work very well for these very reasons.

If you really need to use colours, use them wisely—*no junk*, remember?—and know that they are used to group, divide, highlight, or give meaning to a paragraph or word; if you think about it, the **bold** style is just a blacker black with a slightly wider font.

Last thing for colours, they work great with tables, especially soft/pastel ones, as you can fill a section of a table with a colour to better convey its meaning or separate it from the other ones.

Beautiful Documents

This is more of an artistic golden rule, and, to be fair, it's a bit of a hook: "beautiful" is both an exaggeration and a meaningless word, because it's totally personal, so let's use "visually appealing" instead.

As you know, no one on the team really has time to read documents, while things that are pleasant to look at, on the other hand, are more enjoyable, because they fulfil the natural beauty-seeking instinct that make them perceived as more worthy of time/resources; now, put those two things together. If your documentation is visually appealing, people will be more willing to read it and they will have a less negative experience while doing so: instead of thinking "*Oh no*, I have to read three pages of document about a gun", they will think "I have to read three pages of document about a gun, *well*, it could be worse"—no, no one will ever be happy about it, but at least they won't be *that* bothered.

In a professional work environment, however, this rule isn't true, because people are paid to—among other things—read a document, right? Wrong. The "other things" are something like 100 different tasks, depending on their role. Just count the number of pages of this book dedicated toward research, analysis, and design tools, and then count the ones used for documentation; the first three are the vast majority of the book, because the vast majority of your time and resources will go toward those very same things. Sure, you will have to write documentation very often, but documents are the way you *convey* your work, not the way you do it—there is no document to write if no mechanic has been designed.

This beauty rule is even more true when talking to an outsider, for instance a publisher: if your *pitch deck* doesn't look good, the chances that the publisher will be hooked by your presentation are extremely thin; you are there to sell them your game when the game doesn't even exist yet—you need a great presentation to sell what's currently nothing, don't you agree?

BOX 18.2 A BRIEF DESCRIPTION OF A PITCH DECK, ITS USE AND STRUCTURE, FURTHER COVERED IN CHAPTER 19

A *pitch deck* is a presentation used to support your pitch and give a brief idea of the game's vision to a publisher. As such, pitch decks must have the best possible visual appeal, no errors, and a meticulous attention to detail—a good deck doesn't guarantee you an investment, but a bad one is guaranteed not to make you get it.

Just like documents, pitch decks don't have a standard you need to follow: they change based on the project, the publisher, and the type of pitch. Shorter ones, such as the *elevator* pitch, may not have any video to avoid wasting precious time, while longer ones could let you spend a few seconds looking at a video or listening to a piece of soundtrack to show the mood/style/direction of the game—don't worry, I'll talk more about this type of document in the next chapter.

It may sound like I'm exaggerating, but the rule of beauty constantly affects your life; you bought this very book because it looked good, or, at least, it didn't repel you: what if the text was centred with an offset of 1cm to the right? Or if half of the page was upside down? What about an empty white cover, with just the black title written in Arial? I'm pretty sure that unless someone *really* recommended it to you, what would have happened is the following: you pick it up because the title sounds interesting, you realise the cover is awful but hope that the inside is better, so you open it, you then see the upside down off-centred text. You close it, put it down, and never touch it again—did I get it right?

But here you are reading it, why? Because someone in the editorial staff centred the text, someone designed a visually appealing cover, someone checked that everything was perfect, because visual appeal is a key element of marketing and selling a product—and also because they wouldn't have let me publish a book that requires you to turn it upside down every 20 seconds, but it's probably for the best.

Since everyone is surrounded by visually appealing products everywhere and every day, it's very easy to see what makes something—like a document—*ugly*, because the more you try to look at it the more it hurts your eyes, but it's much harder to find what makes it look *good*—I like this new phone's design, but is it the cameras? Or is it the body? Or the colour? Your documents will have tons of these tiny elements that could potentially make it perfect or ruin it, so remembering to keep it simple also makes it easier to adjust them all.

Making everything harder, however, is the fact that what worked once may not be the right fit the second time, while something that would ruin the document now could be perfect the next time around. Luckily there are some guidelines that put your document on the right track to look good; I'm sure you remember all the rules about colours, junk elements, and a *less is more* mindset, but there are some more useful ones:

> Symmetry is key for good documentation; if the spaces occupied in the document are the same, as well as margins, it's already a step toward visual pleasant-ness—and, rule of thumb, don't leave any space to be wasted: half-empty page on the bottom? Add an image, or a paragraph to say something you thought couldn't fit in the document.
>
> Another rule is not scaring the audience away: use short paragraphs to avoid cre-ating a *wall of text*—no one is there to read a novel, they want the abstract of the abstract at best—and use images that are easy to read, without too strong colours or shapes.

A great way to know if your document is visually pleasant is looking at it from a distance—or zoom out, around 25% of the original size. You don't need to read any word; you will just see how spaces are distributed, which colours are used the most, the presence of walls of text, and much more—sometimes it's very important to change perspective: you will spend so much time looking at something zoomed in to the very smallest of the detail that you may forget about the bigger picture.

By fixing what doesn't look good from a distance, your document will gain a lot of pleasantness that an external person would notice instantly, but for you who worked on that document for hours in a row it became invisible—there is a whole rule about this later, don't worry.

"How beautiful does a document need to be?" or "How much time should I spend making a document look good?" you are probably wondering, and the answer is *not much*:

with the right amount of time and effort you could turn a document into a work of art, but it would be a huge mistake. A document isn't meant to be a masterpiece, it's meant to be a document that delivers as much information as possible in the shortest possible amount of time. It belongs in a workspace, not in the Louvre.

Making a document that looks good for the sake of looking good is, quite frankly, an end in itself. You need to make your work just appealing enough not to repel people to make sure they read it, not to have it auctioned—every further effort would be just a waste of time which, just to remind you, you won't have.

One last way to make sure your document looks good is to flip it upside down: this is just another way to change perspective and break the previous conception you had about it. Looking at something in a way that doesn't allow you to *read* it lets you *see* it for what it is, not its content but just its form. It's the same thing that happens when someone opens it for the first time, with no idea of what it says: they won't know that "the third sentence is very important" or that "it contains important pieces of information": if the appearance is repelling them, they will never know any of that. It's part of your job to make sure that each document encourages and drives the reader toward the content, not that they go on because they *have to* find the important parts.

Knowing Your Target Audience

As you should already know by now, there is no such thing as the "perfect document", and each one needs to be structured differently depending on who will read it: a document that shows a mechanic to the director is very different from the one that shows it to the publisher, which is different from the one that goes to the programmer, and so on—there are so many different people involved in the production of a game, with so many different skills and duties, that you are lucky if you can use the same document twice.

The version that goes to the director is a design-technical document, as they easily understand all the design terminology and frameworks you used and they are interested in design topics like loops, motivational drives, aesthetics, all the other tools you've read about so far, and much more.

A publisher wants visually appealing material, based on bringing them the desired feeling of a mechanic, without any technicality but rather with information about how the player is going to feel, concept art that makes them think "*That's cool*", and elements that can be used for the marketing of the game to hook the right target audience. They won't care about the details of your progression system or an inflation-free currency system, even if they are perfectly designed—not because they are *bad* but because it's just not part of their job, just like you won't care if a programmer writes a code that runs 0.1% faster: it's great, but there isn't much you can do with that information.

Speaking of programmers, they would need a document that focuses on the technical aspects of the mechanic, the variables you need to be able to tune later and their names, a flowchart for the logic of the mechanic, and so on—something very different from what was contained in the other two documents.

These three examples can't—and *shouldn't*—be a single document, or everyone would receive ten pages of stuff that only concerns them for about 30%. While skipping the parts they don't need, they might lose the ones meant for them, or they may keep getting notifications when something was changed on the document even when it was a section that didn't concern them—more on this issue in a later part of the chapter. These must be three different documents, with three different structures, and three different data contained in each one of them—if someone asks you for a hammer, why should you give them the whole toolbox?

Knowing your target audience means one more thing, which is that you have to get used to how someone wants their documents: any team you join most likely has a way to communicate with one another that comes from months of trials, errors, fixes, and optimisation of the workstyle—including documentation—and you need to learn their way, even if it's very new to you. Surely you may find spots for potential improvement, allowing you to work on a better version of their own model, but you can't improve something if you have no idea of how it works, so you need to learn it first.

Furthermore, you may find people reluctant to change, imposing their style even if it's flawed; it's a shame, I agree, but you really don't want to step over your director—one of the goals of this book, to be fair, is to form designers with an open mentality toward change and new ideas, to avoid these very issues in the future and make this industry a better environment for everyone, especially future designers.

Ownership

The concept of ownership is very important in a production environment because a document is just as valid as its content; if even a paragraph isn't true anymore, the whole document isn't true. Productions, in fact, have the idea of *owning* your documents: you are responsible to keep it up to date, changing whatever is outdated and adding what's new, and you are responsible to discontinue it if needed. Since you are the owner, your job is making sure that everything in there is always true, or, if you terminate it, you still have to make sure it's written clearly somewhere that the document isn't a reliable source anymore, and where that new design knowledge is located—*aka* a link to the new relative piece of documentation.

It's easy to update the documents that are strictly connected to a change that was just decided, but there are tons of documents created during the development of a game, so it's quite impossible to remember which others may now be outdated and which not. This is why a good way of managing the documents you own is to pick a day and every month on that day—or every week, every six months, every two months, it depends on the environment you are in—you go through all your documents and update whatever is old or discontinue ones that are too old to be updated and write new ones to replace them.

It sounds like that day is going to be mostly dedicated to this task, and it may be, but you have to remember that those documents have your name written on them, *literally*. Someone may use an old document that you forgot to change, ending up with a lot of wasted time and something not needed anymore.

It doesn't matter *whose* fault it is, you should never care about it—the only important thing is to create systems that prevent such mistakes from happening again, never ever focusing on the fault—but it's your *responsibility* to make sure the documents are correct. Sure they could have asked you if the data was correct, but it should have been correct anyway, so you could decide it's both of your fault and have a bad day or say it's no one's fault and pay more attention the next time.

You may be wondering why I'm giving so much relevance to the "there is no guilt" thing. Well, you will have thousands of problems during the development of a game—I'm not exaggerating; you are lucky if you don't get into five figures—and among all of those problems, the ones you need to avoid the most are human ones. Technical problems? There is a mathematically better solution. Design problem? Do some research and decide based on how the results relate to your vision. Human problems? No easy fix, you need a conflict resolution session—if not multiple ones—that may last for hours, and the scenarios where each part wins are not that easy to achieve. If the team members start blaming each other, people will be scared to make a mistake because of other people's judgement or of getting fired, and both cases create a hostile working environment for everyone.

I'm not saying you should go wild with mistakes, making ones that could easily be avoided by a professional designer or purposely not caring because "there is no blame"; what I'm saying is that if everyone is doing their best, for every problem that arises there will be 99 other potential problems that have been fixed or avoided. And when something unexpected does happen, the team sits down, talks about it, understands how to fix it and how to prevent it from happening again, and moves on.

Decant Your Documents

Just like you can't drink a bottle of good wine right after opening it, you can't send a document as soon as it's finished, because you are probably missing something.

After finishing a document, checking it from a distance, flipping it upside down, and checking it again just to be sure it's ready, leave some time in your document-production routine to let it settle—or *decant*—before submitting it; it may be an hour or it may be a whole day. During this time, do something totally different, and when the hour or day has passed, check it again: I guarantee that you will notice at least one thing that can be improved—*at least* one.

This technique comes from art, especially drawing and painting: when you are drawing something, your brain isn't just *reading* what it sees, but it *interprets* it, because your mind knows what your vision is, what you *want* to see rather than what you are really seeing. Decanting the drawing and doing something different, however, unplugs your mind from that topic and lets all the temporary information disappear—just like turning your computer off erases everything in the RAM, because no energy is keeping that data active. This is also one of the reason why multitasking is a terrible idea: you aren't really doing multiple things *at the same time*, you are just emptying and refilling your mental RAM very quickly, so quickly that it didn't have the time to be completely dismissed, meaning that in the mental space that should be filled with one topic, you are stuffing multiple different things all compacted together—and since that space is limited, you remember a bit of everything but not much of anything.

Doing one thing at the time and then decanting it, on the other hand, allows you to focus completely on that one thing. After taking a break, when you look at that drawing—or document—again, you see it without interpreting it: you are just looking at it for what it is, with all the problems you were too *zoomed in* to see before.

You have no idea how many times I've written an email, sent it right after it was finished, and suddenly had an *oh no* moment: maybe there was a typo, maybe I forgot to attach a file, or maybe I realised a sentence could have been misinterpreted. Luckily, many email providers let you cancel the sending of an email for a couple of minutes after you press the "send" button, to let you attach that document or rewrite that sentence, but why use a last resort when you can easily prevent such mistakes?

Compare the amount of data, paragraphs, or images in a document to the ones contained in an email, and it should be easy to see why the decanting time for a document is a minimum of one hour but better one whole day—you can't check everything in your document in those two minutes, so any mistake would probably stay there.

Pivotal Documents

19

After reading so much about how to write good documents, from the visual appeal to the technical language, it's time to talk about some of the most common and pivotal ones. *Pivotal* not because you can't develop a game without them—I'll get back to this in a moment—but because they are among the most commonly used in the industry, meaning that no matter which studio you apply to, you need to know these types of documents, even if called by a different name.

First things first, none of these is ever completely exhaustive: there are a thousand different documents that have the same goal as each one presented in this book. One may be more suitable for bigger teams, another one includes more detailed data, a third one may be more minimal but needing more singular other documents, and so on. Remember that each document is tailor made for its audience, team, project, and purpose, just like a suit: sure you can use a generic one bought at the store, and it will still work as any other suit, but the sleeves may be too long, the shoulders too tight, or the colour too bright. If all you need is a generic suit go ahead, but if you need to wear it every day for the next two years, maybe it's better if you invest resources into making sure it fits you perfectly.

This brings me to the second point: none of these documents should be used as a "template" that you can just fill, because it's probable that your team—or project—has different and specific needs that aren't included in the "base" version of the document—these are just practical examples. The golden rules you've read about before have this very goal: customising a document, *any* document, for your necessities while keeping it aligned with the quality standard of the industry.

To highlight how important this non-template perception of documentation is, just think that one of my former game design students, who was also working as a manager at a videogames-unrelated company, asked me if he could use one of the production-oriented documents outside of the design environment at his workplace. I was quite confused at first, so he told me that such a document could increase the efficiency of his unit for reasons X and Y, and it made perfect sense, so I agreed with his idea. I also told him, however, that the document couldn't be used just like that: he would have had to change it a lot, because the needs of a game development company are very different from the one he worked at.

This is just to show how powerful it is to be able to adapt a tool to different needs. For a project you may need to add a column, for a second project you will need to change the order of some elements, for another one you could even take half of this document and half of that other document; those are all things you can do, because you have all the tools you need, and because mastering one tool is far more efficient than learning the basic of three different ones.

DOI: 10.1201/9781003229438-23

During your career, you will face tons of different documents: you will adapt some, drastically change others, or even create brand new ones never seen before—which I hope you do; I can't wait to try them out myself. It's also very probable, however, that you won't use a lot of them at all: this one doesn't suit your company, that one doesn't work well with the current project, a third one is hated by the director, etc. No matter what the reason is, it's perfectly fine to do so, the same way you may stick to a document's structure to avoid any mistake as it's the first time you have used it. It's your tool bag, and you can use each tool however you want, but remember to change it whenever it doesn't work for you. game design isn't an exact science, and part of your artistic freedom is doing things differently even when they don't make any sense to others: they just need to make sense to you and your team.

DISTRIBUTED DOCUMENTATION

As you know, this book isn't meant to teach the history of videogames, but, when talking about documentation, looking at the past gives you a great example of what not to do: if you look for the game design documents—*aka* GDD—of older games, such as the first *Deus Ex*, you can see that they were huge text documents, with hundreds of pages and who knows how many words, that contained everything of the game—let me repeat it, *everything*. They described every little detail of every major area of the game: mechanics, UI, levels, progression, characters, and so on. All of this in one, single, huge text document that no one has ever read except maybe a couple of fans of the game. I can safely say that not even the developers have read the whole document, so one question arises: *why*? Why have such a document?

In the early days of videogames, developers created games the same way they created software: following a production system called *Waterfall*. According to this system, the design team would imagine every little detail of the software—in this case, the game—in their mind, then transcribing everything they pictured on these big and seamlessly infinite walls of text. Then, they would hand this tome to the production team, leaving them to transform their words into the actual product.

As you can imagine, this system never worked, for thousands of different reasons, but the main ones are the following three: first, no one can have a perfectly detailed vision of a product from the start without facing the production reality. Second, games are an interactive medium, thus requiring an iterative production process—every game is born ugly: it doesn't work as you wanted, the controls are slippery, the gameplay is quite a mess. But then you adjust it a bit at a time until it becomes less ugly, then mediocre, decent, good, and eventually great. Third, this process is full of human errors, which makes a lot of sense considering that as you finish *page 475* of the GDD, you have no idea of what you wrote back on *page 023*.

On a more practical level, these documents were a mess to use too: you would get a notification every time something was modified, even if it was in a section you didn't care about because it was all in that one document. It may not sound so bad, but remember that tens of people would work with that document, generating just as many notifications every day. You would either check every single one of them, spending countless hours even just to check what was modified, or disable them all and have no idea of when a change that concerns you would occur, thinking "I'll just ask another designer", to then have them spend hours updating everyone else about everything that was changed—do you now see why earlier I talked about having different documents for different people?

Long story short, it just didn't work. Even the very software developers that created this system are moving toward better production-oriented methodologies.

So what happened to the documentation? It became distributed: instead of having a document with 400 pages, you now have 200 micro-documents of two pages each. A modern document only describes one element or detail of the game or multiple elements seen from a wide point of view—then linking each element to its very own document or set of documents, but don't worry, there is a tool for that too.

For instance, the *jump* mechanic may have a *jump* folder, containing *GD_Jump*, *TD_Jump*, *ND_Jump*, and so on, each one describing the same mechanic but from a different point of view: GD_Jump talks about the game design elements of the mechanic, its dynamics, aesthetics, the loops it is part of. TI_Jump is focused on the technical implementation aspect, with the variables needed for tuning, a flowchart of the code, etc. ND_Jump regards the narrative meaning of the jump and its role in the story—I could go on for hours, but you get the idea—of course, each one of these documents would be different from the others, because they would have different audiences and different goals.

One big advantage of this type of documentation is that each document is created and updated based on the current needs of the project/team: the whole *Jump* is outdated? You know that everything in the *Jump* folder is outdated, and you either update it or create it brand new, without having to look for the *Jump* section in a 400-page document manually.

On this note, creating many small documents is also perceived as an easier task by a team than creating a single big one: "Write 600 pages within the next year" sounds way worse than "write 2 pages every day".

Last, if you completely mess up a 2-page document, worst case scenario you only need to write 2 pages, but if you mess up 600 pages, mistakes could be literally anywhere.

COMPENDIUM

The first type of document you should know is the Compendium, sometimes called Wiki, Design Bible or Game Document. It is a tool that contains the links to every other document created in every phase of the development of a game, from the very first one of pre-production to the very last one of post-production.

The list of documents follows a fixed order decided by the team, also keeping track of additional information that allows one both to find and to know the status of any included document.

Originally it was a text document, but designers started to use different media depending on the project, like wikis or *Confluence*—a production-oriented online tool used to track every item of the development. It doesn't matter which medium you use, as a compendium only needs to respect its function and not a format; what matters is that it works for your team—as you've just read, templates are the archnemesis of a good designer.

Since modern documentation is distributed across hundreds or thousands of mini-documents, isn't it counterproductive to have to scroll through a whole list of these documents, just to find the one you need? Yes, you are right, but this is avoided by using a constant and reasonable nomenclature—or naming system—like *DocumentName_SystemName_ProjectName* and by correctly setting up your compendium.

A compendium—*any* compendium—is composed of multiple sections, used to divide the work into smaller chunks: for example by department—art, design, coding, sound—or by level—level 1, level 2, level 3—or by production state or whatever works for you (Figure 19.1).

Each section contains the document name, a link to access it, a short description—not more than one line—a date, its status—outdated, dismissed, work in progress, up to date, and so on—its owner—whoever should be contacted for any uncertainty or error—and when it was last modified. Each one of these elements serves a very specific purpose, and I highly suggest including them to avoid potential mistakes—for instance, if you don't know when it was last modified, how can you be sure it's up to date?

Again, this is not a template, meaning that you can add as many other elements as you need or potentially remove ones I suggested if you have another tool to provide that same information, but remember that if you saturate a tool too much it becomes counterproductive, so it's worth spending some time to understand what your team really needs to work at its best. Nonetheless, you *must* have a compendium, no matter its medium or format, because it's the map you will be referring to every time you feel lost in the huge sea of documentation.

One last reason why this tool is so important is that it allows a transparent environment, where everyone can see what's been done, what the current vision is, encountered problems and much more—not that everyone *has* to check every document listed inside, but if they want to they can.

HIGH VISION

This document is very unique, because it's usually made by one or a group of directors of the game—sometimes even the CEO is in that group—and not by a junior or even a senior designer. It has to be made by directors because it describes the *vision* of the game, written by those who will lead the team toward it.

Vision is a very important word in this field: it is the objective of your game, the arriving point of years of production and thousands of hours of work. It describes not only the mechanical scope of the project but also the players' one: how will the game affect them? Is the game conveying a meaning? Are you trying to change the world? As always, there are no wrong answers to any of these questions as long as they work for you, because no game is objectively wrong—but beware, the more you go toward sensitive topics the more controversial your game will be, as you recall from the players' polarisation from the Big Five model.

How do you write down the vision of a whole game? Would it take tens of pages with all the key points that your project should hit, like a roadmap? Not at all. On the contrary,

Compendium

Status Legend					
To Do	WIP	Done	Outdated	Iterative	Discontinued

Production				
Game Design				
System	Name	Owner	Due Date	Status
MC Movement	GDD_Walk	Mark	13-Jan	
	GDD_Jump	Mark	13-Jan	
	GDD_Dash	Clare	15-Jan	
Enemy Movement	GDD_Glide	Clare	20-Jan	
	GDD_Run	Mark	20-Jan	
	GDD_Walk	Lucy	20-Jan	
	GDD_Teleport	Lucy	22-Jan	
Level Design				
Area	Name	Owner	Due Date	Status
Castle	LDD_CastleLayout	Lucy	14-Jan	
	LDD_CastleReferences	Mark	14-Jan	
Art				
Topic	Name	Owner	Due Date	Status
Buildings	Art_AssetList	Mark	25-Jan	
	Art_BuildingsReferences	John	31-Jan	
Main Character	Art_MCConceptArt	Steve	07-Feb	
Final Boss	CDD_FinalBoss	Steve	15-Feb	

FIGURE 19.1   An example of what a compendium may look like. In this case, it is made of a table in a text document, and a colour-code is used to indicate each document's status.

Source: Author.

this document should be no longer than two pages—or it can be created as a presentation with a high visual appeal; in that case it will be longer—because of the micro-documentation principle of modern design that you have read about before.

I know it can sound counterintuitive that such an important document has to be so short, after all this sounds like the only map your team has in a raging sea, but remember that isn't about the path, it's about the *direction*. A path tells you all the turns you have to make in the perfect order to get to your destination, where a direction—or a compass— tells you where your goal is, no matter if you took an unexpected turn.

This is very important for developing any product, but it's even more true for games: following a path would give you the product you imagined, sure, but what if it doesn't work? No one can imagine every single detail of a project, but even if they could it may not be right, so there sure will be things that don't work as intended, and ignoring those problems to stick with your perfectly planned roadmap will give you a game no one but you will enjoy. game design is all about finding the best possible compromise among a hundred different things—time, money, vision, players' satisfaction, etc.—and a good designer isn't someone who brings you to the original destination six months late, with half of the crew gone and ten million dollars over budget. A good designer is someone who gets you to the closest possible place to the destination on time, on budget, with everyone still alive—and hopefully happy enough to get ready for the next adventure.

A high vision document works great because it gives enough guidelines to know what you can and can't do but not enough to make you feel like you are just following a checklist. To better explain all the parts comprising this document, I'll follow each one of them with one example of a real game. In this case I'll use FromSoftware's *Elden Ring*, since I'm playing it at the time that I'm writing this chapter.

First off, you have the title of the game—*aka* what the outside world calls it—or of the project—what your team calls it internally. Those two may be different, especially in early production phases, and sometimes the internal project name may be used outside of the company until an official name is announced.

As an example, this would be *Elden Ring* as a game title, and something like *Open World Souls* for the internal project name.

Then there is a *concept brief*: no more than a paragraph used to describe the concept of the game, its heart and soul, both mechanically and narratively.

Elden Ring concept brief: explore an interworld of different worlds in a challenging open world adventure with RPG elements, discovering the story of a decading universe and with a strong verticality thanks to a mount and the jump used to travel around.

Next off, *key elements*: usually three, those are the main elements of your game, also called *pillars* or *key pillars*. They are the foundation of your whole game; everything in the project sits on these pillars, so it's crucial to define them correctly. Every single element you add during the development needs to support one of these pillars, and, if it doesn't, that element is just a *nice to have*: you only do it if everything else is done, because it doesn't push the project toward the vision—I'll get to that in a minute.

You may even design something that goes against one of the pillars—also called *Opposite Design*—creating a huge risk that may create inconsistency in the game, ruin the players' mental model used until that point, and much more. You could purposely do such a thing to create a *wow moment* in the game or for a section that you want to confuse the players, but be very wary of the risks coming with that decision.

Elden Ring key elements:

Submerged narrative to unveil—also called *Iceberg narrative*.
Hard game with no complete mechanical explanations: strong enemies, challenging moments, some mechanics have to be discovered by the players.
Non-linear progression: open world, different possible paths, the player chooses where to go.
Then you have *primes*, also called *objectives*, which are divided into four categories: mood, emotions, objective, and metaphor/meaning.

The primes are like pillars, but applied to the players instead of the game: these are the elements that the player should perceive while playing the game.

Prime mood is, of course, the mood the player should be in during their playthrough; this is covered in the emotional game design part of the book, so if you have any doubt I highly suggest taking a look back at it.

Elden Ring prime mood: desire to explore, fight colossal dragons, discovering every inch of the world.

Prime emotion follows the same concept but applied to emotions instead of moods: I'm not referring to the most satisfying emotion, or the strongest one, but the one that is felt most of the time during the playthrough.

Elder Ring prime emotion: challenge—fighting tons of enemies—and Fiero—killing that very strong boss after 20 tries.

Prime objective is the players' objective: what goal does the game instil in the player? Defeating all the bosses? Unveiling the twisted story of the game world? Completing every single quest? The players' objective is like a lighthouse, casting light on everything they need to do to reach their goal, working as a guidance: is "killing the *ultimate final overpower* boss with a chopstick" under that light? Yes? Then they will do it.

It's crucial to keep this lighthouse in mind, because if you spend half of the production time designing secondary quests that you think are great but the players' objective is to kill the main villain as quickly as possible, they won't do any side quest no matter how good they are—sometimes it's not about something being *good*, it's about it being *right*.

Elden Ring prime objective: the game tells the objective early, "find the Elden Ring and become the Elden Lord". From the very beginning, the player knows that to win the game they have to do whatever is on the path to become the Elden Lord—also, having a clear objective in an iceberg narrative works great, because every time you think you have found the answer to a question, two more questions arise, increasing the perceived depth of the world and thus its story/lore.

Prime metaphor/prime meaning: this is the concept that the game is a whole big metaphor, either hidden or clear, toward a bigger issue such as violence, life, or—like this book—cakes. Not every game has a prime metaphor or meaning, of course, but some of the ones that do work as a metaphor are often heavily based around it—every element of the game works toward better delivering the desired meaning; therefore the designer needs to always have a clear picture of what they are trying to convey.

In the high vision document, this metaphor should be summarised in no more than one line: you don't have to explain it there—that requires one or more specific documents—you just need to note it down, so no one forgets about it.

I haven't finished *Elder Ring* yet, therefore I can't talk about its metaphor, so here are a couple of other famous examples:

The Old Man and the Sea, by Ernest Hemingway, talks about every person's own battle, the difficulty one encounters along the way, the sacrifices, and how they can sometimes lose it in the end.

Pan's Labyrinth, directed by Guillermo del Toro, shows the importance of disobeying in a world of dictatorial rules, to follow a human morality and compassion toward others.

This concludes the "standard" part of a high vision document, meaning it concerns the whole team, and that is why it is often written by the directors together.

Now, moving on to the design part, which changes based on the department it is made by, there are four elements to define: must do, must not, nice to have, unique selling points—or *USP*—the target audience, and, if needed, a narrative/setting brief.

Each department must have their version of this section, and each one should have different content: sound designers have different concerns for the project than game designers, artists and programmers don't care about the same issues, and so on. Including everything in the same document, while possible, would go against the Distributed Documentation pillar that modern game development is based on.

Must do: These are a series of features that you want to be the core experience of the game, so core that if one of them isn't respected when the deadline comes, the game doesn't get released. They are not something you wish to include or that you think would be important; they are something you *know* is going to be in the final release, because they define your game for what it is.

How many *must dos* should you have? You could have potentially infinite ones, but they would lose relevance and become *nice to have*, leaving you with no clear direction about what the true core of the game is. My best advice is to have a maximum of three must dos, because the fewer you have the easier it will be to follow them—imagine telling someone "You have to drink a glass of water every hour for the next 6 hours"; it's not very hard to do that, right? They set a timer, and every hour they drink a glass of water. What if you add "Every 23 minutes you also have to jump two times, every 7 minutes do a twirl, and every 48 minutes and 12 seconds high-five someone"? There is so much to keep track of that eventually at least one of those tasks will be forgotten, or the person will be too tired or already busy doing something. The same happens with too many *must dos* in a production—and I'm pretty sure you don't want people twirling and giving high-fives all around the office.

Must not: At first glance, a *must not* may look like the opposite of a *must do*: if your must do is "linear progression", a *must not* would be "non-linear progression", but that would be wrong—or, to be more accurate, it would be redundant. A *must not* comes from research: with the tools previously covered in this book—or with other techniques as well—you can find the reason why games similar to the one you are developing failed, for instance one of your competitors performed badly because it was too challenging for the target audience, so a *must not* would be "recurring challenge aesthetics". It's all about finding which areas you should avoid to keep your audience as satisfied as possible with the game—it's not about what you or your team like; remember that a game only comes to life when someone plays it.

Taking as an example the souls-like genre, *Lord of the Fallen* received much criticism because of the excessive slowness and heaviness of the gameplay. If you were to make a similar game, one of your *must nots* should probably be exactly this: "slow and heavy gameplay feeling". Of course, this would mean performing an extensive research aimed at understanding what made the gameplay perceived *slow* and *heavy*, as those are subjective terms and need the data that shows what they really mean. For instance, "animations were 12% slower than the ones used in other souls-like games" or "the average movement speed of enemies was 1.34 metres/second while the audience better responded to 1.62 metres/seconds".

This doesn't mean that you can't have slow weapons or slow enemies; *Elden Ring* has tons of both, but they are not so slow that the audience gets frustrated by that slowness, or for really slow weapons there are visually appealing VFX and animations that give a sense of extreme power from the upcoming attack.

Long story short, a *must do* comes from the team; a *must not* comes from the audience; you have to find that sweet spot where your vision and what the players want meet.

Nice to have: the *nice to have* are additional objectives that will be reached if everything during the production goes according to plan—rare, sure but not impossible. They are anything that doesn't necessarily push the product closer to the vision, but that would be appreciated by the audience and that would improve their experience with the game. They also have, however, the objective of being the first thing to cut if the time starts to run out: "Levels from A to E are our must, level F is a nice to have. We only have time for five levels? We cut level F". This may sound obvious, but it saves the time that would go toward researching and analysing which level to cut because, by vision, level F was never really intended as a core part of the game—furthermore, you know that no one in the team will oppose that choice because everyone knew that it was an extra feature when the high vision document was created (Figure 19.2).

Unique selling points: These are the really unique elements of your game, what makes your game different from all the others out there—not *better*, just different. There should be three of them, not more and not less: too many and you won't be able to develop them at a good level of quality, too few and your game will be too generic. A USP can come from anything, that being a vision, a new technology, or a hole in the market: if no one has ever tried a specific combination of element it could be both your great opportunity for success or a product that wouldn't sell any copy—in this case, ask yourself some questions, like "is it too hard to develop such product so no one has tried before, or is it just a bad idea?" To avoid taking the wrong road, use your data: find some people belonging to the market slice you want to target and pitch your idea, or have a focus group with them, conduct an interview, and so on.

Having the USPs since the pre-production of the game is very important because everything you design and develop has to sustain at least one of them, otherwise they are either half-implemented "nice to have" or *gimmicks*.

It may seem hard to find three unique elements, but USPs are what makes your game itself, just like all those features that make you yourself, different from anyone else in the world—if you think about it this way, it should be very hard to limit yourself to just three features, don't you agree? Think about those games where their USP allowed them to get that boost to surpass their competitors; for instance, *Hades* is different from any other roguelike not only for its in-depth narrative, but also because its dialogues and story change based on what the player did in the previous runs, so no two people will have the very same narrative. If it wasn't for this system, would it have failed? Surely not, but maybe it would have missed some great opportunities.

BOX 19.1   A DEFINITION OF "GIMMICK" AND ITS DIFFERENCE FROM A USP

A gimmick is a fake USP, a feature that may make the game better or unique at first glance but really doesn't affect anything. For example, I could tell you that I just created the first *Super Mario Bros* videogame with a unicorn instead of *Yoshi*: it would be different from any existing Super Mario Bros game, but the gameplay wouldn't change at all; it's just a graphical change.

Gimmicks don't have a real gameplay impact; they only provide the illusion of uniqueness.

Amazing Game - High Vision

Concept Brief
A squirrel falls into nuclear waste, finding out he has the power to control appliances with his mind. He now uses them to fight the mole people who are trying to conquer New York City.

Key Elements
Appliances Control: toaster shoots bread, washing machine shoots clothes
Easy to understand narrative, but hard to predict: plot twists are core
Linear progression (spatial and mechanical)

Prime Emotion	Prime Mood
• Simulationism • *Easy fun*	• Nonsense: "How did they think of this ?" • Escape from reality

Prime Objective	Prime Meaning
• Experience the next big crazy thing	• Not everything has a meaning: randomness

Must Have	Must Not
• Mechanics based • 3rd Person	• Real physics based • Complex AI

Target Audience
16 to 25 years old, primarily male players. Students / workers with not much money. Killers: chaos and visceral stimuli; Achiever: love to progress.

USPs	Nice To Have
• Unpredictable story • Common objects with a mechanical twist • Chaotic and "random" environments	• Mini-bosses (mole people) • Crafting system

FIGURE 19.2   An example of what a high vision document may look like. This does of course change based on the team's needs.

Source: Author.

Target audience: The target audience used in the high vision document is your perfect player, the one that will love the game from the bottom of their heart, the one that talks to everyone they know about how great the game is—an *evangelist*. This player can be expressed with any of the tools you have read about in the previous chapters, or other ones that work for you, but it's very important to use more than one tool: don't just use Bartle's archetypes; cross that result with the Big Five model, add the Quantic Foundry taxonomy and so on; the more the better.

Knowing who the perfect target will be is a great vision tool, because whenever you have a doubt you can run a research on the issue and compare the results to this ideal player. Something like this would happen:

> Should we add *emotes* in our PVP game? Research tells us that most of the generated aesthetics would belong to the Killer player type, and the emotes would increase the frustration perceived by the player according to the Big Five model. Our target audience belongs to the achiever player type and has a very low tolerance of frustration: we shouldn't add emotes to the game.

Once again, it's not about doing what the team likes, it's a matter of satisfying the audience's needs and following a constant direction—the perfect target audience doesn't change, so you won't spend any time chasing shifting interests in niches.

Last, narrative brief/setting brief: this is only required for games with a strong narrative value or setting. It should be no longer than one paragraph, just like the concept brief but purely focused on narrative or setting only.

ONE PAGER

First things first, let's make it clear: this document must be one page long, no exceptions. If it takes two pages, you are doing it wrong.

Now that that's out of the way, a one pager is a "photograph" of the project, with all the main characteristics unrelated to vision, that goes to insiders, and not the press or the public. Most of the information contained in this document can be found elsewhere, because this is just the overview of the overview of the game (Figure 19.3).

It is composed of the game objective—or *logline*—game setting/narrative, core mechanics/core systems, aesthetics, USPs, and other technical elements if needed.

The game objective is a paragraph—no more than two lines—describing the player's objective for the game and some of the most important game mechanics. A good logline should answer all the five Ws—who, what, where, when, why—and "how", this last one because it allows you to talk about the interactive part of the game and relevant mechanics.

Elden Ring game objective: the tarnished—who—explores the open world and fights many enemies and unique bosses in the land of a high fantasy world—where, what, and when—while finding new and upgradable equipment to defeat the enemies—how—to reach the Elden Ring and become the Elden Lord—why.

The game setting/game narrative is similar to the narrative/setting brief, so it still needs to be no longer than one paragraph, and it's not always needed. Differently from the brief, this one is unrelated to vision, therefore it can be more of a catchy sentence rather than a goal for the team to accomplish.

Elden Ring game setting: a vast intraworld with high verticality, fallen from the greatness of a glorious past that the player will unveil.

The core mechanics/core systems are the main three mechanics or systems that comprise the heart of the game, which best describes the core loop of your experience. This should be described very briefly, mainly to give a quick comprehension of the element and avoiding possible misunderstandings.

EldenRing–OnePager

Game Objective

The tarnished **explores** the open world and **fights** unique bosses in the land of a **high fantasy world** while finding new and **upgradable equipment** to reach the Elden Ring and **become the Elden Lord**.

Game Setting

A vast intraworld with high verticality, fallen from the greatness of a glorious past that the player will unveil.

Core Systems	
Combat System:	Evolution of *Dark Souls* combat system, with a jump mechanic to add verticality.
Exploration System:	Open world with free roaming, only specific gates enforce the golden path.
RPG System:	Character values defining their statistics, from damage dealt to HP.

Unique Selling Points
80+ bosses and minibosses, most of which with open progressions and solutions.
Open world souls-like with multiple vertical levels for each area.
Iceberg narrative, multiple endings depending on the choices taken during each run.

Aesthetic

Gothic/medieval fantasy style:

- Dark swamps, ruined castles, rotten enemies.

Holy/sacred style:

- Bright wide spaces, yellow tones, elegant enemies.

Additional Info

- Developed with Unreal Engine 4.2X.
- No more than *152,826* polygons should be present in the camera at the same time (<u>benchmark</u>).
- The world is written with the collaboration of George RR Martin

FIGURE 19.3 A fake one pager for *Elden Ring*, listing the main points that anyone in the team should know as soon as possible.

Source: Author.

Elden Ring core systems:

Combat system: an evolution of *Dark Souls'* combat system with a new jump mechanic sustaining the game's verticality.

Exploration system: an open world with free roaming, with the exception of certain gates used to enforce the designed golden path.

RPG system: characters' values defining their statistics, from chance of dropping items to damage dealt to enemies when combined with the weapon used.

The aesthetic section, in the sense of artistic style, is whatever tool best conveys the art style of the game: from a mood board to show the direction of meshes and textures to a collection of soundtracks for the sound side of the project.

The unique selling points are the same as the ones used in the high vision document, three elements that make your game unique and that the team will always work around during the production of the game—once again, make sure they are not gimmicks.

Other elements you might need are technical details that need to be kept in mind, for instance "The game has to run at 60FPS on PS5" or "It is developed with Unreal Engine". These should include any critical information for the team, not the player—remember, this document is for insiders. Think about a one pager as the document you hand out to the new entry of the team, to give them an idea of the project as quickly as possible—then they will explore all the details reading the other, in-detail documents.

DESIGN DOCUMENT

The most important thing you need to know about any design document is that it's extremely malleable, more than any other document out there: there is no "design document archetype", because it's completely up to what the document is about: a mechanic? A system? A level? Or a character? Each one of these would be very different from the other; even two documents about different mechanics may have very different needs and therefore formats.

This type of document can be customised so much that it takes the name of the department it is used in: game design document, level design document, character design document, and so on. I will focus on the game design document more, while briefly stopping at a couple of other ones you will need, as long as you respect the golden rule there isn't that much of a difference among any of them—remember, however, that they serve different purposes, so an *LDD* may need a map where a *GDD* could only need pictures as a reference.

GAME DESIGN DOCUMENT

GDDs are fairly simple compared to other documents; here is what their key elements are—but, again, you are more than free to change any of them as you need:

Mechanic/system name and description: no more than two lines used to describe the mechanic or system, its goal and its feel. The goal is to have a general idea of the mechanic or system, with the mechanic, dynamic, and aesthetic expressed in a less formal way than an MDA.

If the mechanic or system is part of the core loop, be sure to specify it here. You can also add an image or a flowchart to better illustrate how the loop is structured.

Let's take, once again, *Elden Ring* as an example: the counter-attack mechanic takes place after blocking an attack with a shield, creating a window for a heavy attack. The goal is to offer an attack opportunity to players with a defensive style, and the feel is strategic: "I let you hit me so I can hit you back".

User case: this part may be called in many different ways—user case, use case, scenarios—and it's composed of three descriptions of how the mechanic or system is used in the game. Note that they shouldn't be mechanical descriptions, rather they should look like narrations.

One example from *Elden Ring*: the player is facing the lizard boss; it attacks with the tail but the player blocks it with their shield: a brief animation triggers exposing the lizard's weak point, and the player casts a heavy attack with the weapon in their right hand dealing critical damage.

Research: a GDD needs a place to list all the research related to a design, from frameworks used to analyse similar mechanics in other games, to studies that highlight how a competitor needed that element but didn't include it in the game. Any tool you used to create the foundations of this mechanic or system goes here, with links to quickly access the in-depth research and analysis documents—remember that a GDD should be short, so you can't bring all the research in here: link any specific research document in this section, so that if someone is interested they can access it in no time.

Versioning: the versioning is a brief description of the mechanic depending on its state of development, with the different objectives each version has. For instance, you may plan a Version 1, Version 2, and Version 3:

Version 1 is the test prototype of the mechanic or system; it just needs to have the characteristics that let you know if it can be done and work as intended—worst case scenario, you only spent the resources needed to develop V1, recognising the problem early on. This version can be made by the designers, because it doesn't need fancy effects or polished animations.

Elden Ring V1: blocking an attack triggers a timer called *counter window*, if you attack the normal attack animation triggers, but the damage is different.

Version 2 is the minimum viable product—or *MVP*—meaning the first version that you consider to be shippable, the "safety-net" version—it's not beautiful, but it doesn't ruin the experience.

Elden Ring V2: blocking the attack triggers the counter window, a VFX starts, if the player attacks an animation triggers, which is different for every category of weapons, and tuneable damage is applied to the enemy.

Version 3 is the "perfect"—more accurately, the *high quality*—version of the mechanic. "Perfect" because it's very unlikely for a designer to consider something perfect: there always is that little detail that would improve the players' experience by 0.0001%, and if it wasn't for the deadlines you could keep working on it forever.

Elden Ring V3: each weapon has a different custom animation for the attack, and different enemies have different poses for when the opportunity window opens.

Each version may have a different name depending on the studio you work at: someone may use V0.1, V0.5, and V1; or V0.5, V0.1, and V1.5; and so on. It really doesn't matter what the name is, as long as everyone in the team knows it—just like document names, what matters is that they are used correctly.

Intersystem interactions: if the mechanic or system interacts with any other mechanic or system or if it does so in a specific way, this is the section where all that detail goes.

Elden Ring: this mechanic works as any other heavy attack, but its critical damage can be tuned separately from other critical attacks.

Framework: using any framework that works for you, this part is aimed at defining how the mechanic/system satisfies one or more needs of the audience and how it sustains one or more pillars of the vision. This may sound obvious, but remember that each mechanic and system should maintain the coherence with the vision and the needs of the players or that part of the design will feel generic, vague, or even counterproductive—you can always use the opposite design on purpose, but be wary of the risks.

Elden Ring block attack satisfied the need of more-defensive or less-skilled players to have opportunities to attack an enemy, with a slower and more strategic gameplay while keeping the challenge aesthetics, just in a safer form.

Input system and controls: this part is used to describe the input systems used for the game and how they should be used by the player. You may need a whole separate document if you have many different input devices or custom ones, like a whole new type of controller or a custom one specifically made for that game.

Elden Ring: hold L1/LB to block and press R2/RT to attack during the animation.

UI/UX—user interface and user experience: include any description or specific UI/UX element and describe how the UI enhances the players' experience.

Elden Ring: when the opportunity window occurs, a small VFX and sound are played to let the player know they can perform the attack.

Then you have a free section, where you can add anything that is important for the team or for a specific mechanic/system: it may be a note, a link to a whole other document, a chart, etc.

Imagine a GDD like a set of modules, where you can add new ones and remove the ones that don't work every time you write a new one. In fact, you don't always need to have all the ones I just listed, and you will most likely have ones that I didn't include here. The core of this type of document is to let you add or remove anything depending on all the possible factors involved, from the team's style to the specific element you are talking about: you may add flowcharts, pictures, charts, and really anything, as long as you respect the golden rules.

It's also important to keep in mind that the document should be as brief as possible, so instead of adding a whole section with the parameters used for tuning, consider linking it to a paragraph saying something like *atomic parameters here*—the programmers who need to implement them know where to find their description, while people from the art department don't have to read something they won't care about.

Last but not least, if your mechanic is inspired by something specific, your GDD should have some references here: a gif from that other videogame, a picture from a movie, maybe even a quote from the book—it doesn't matter what it is, it just needs to convey that feeling, that art style, or what is important from that reference.

LEVEL DESIGN DOCUMENT

Now, moving on, there are the level design documents: they have a bigger visual impact compared to GDD, in fact a map is often present to show the level with a bird's-eye view, in a more or less detailed way depending on the state of production—it doesn't *have to* be in bird's-eye view, that's just the most suitable perspective most of the time.

The map describes the golden path and any important element: to complete the level, the player has to do *this*, then go *there*, fight *him*—the best examples of level maps are the ones used in guides, as they usually contain everything relevant to the players. Sometimes it should be a scale map, but it depends on the production state: there is no need to have a perfectly scaled brainstorming map where any area may be cut the next minute, but, on the other hand, before bringing all the elements in-engine it's useful to know how big everything should be.

Some LDDs also have a storyboard: a sequence of drawings used to show the core moments the players will experience in the level. This is very helpful for games with an important visual aspect, like a very specific camera shot or movement, as the storyboard helps in picturing spaces, positions, lighting, and much more—it may be a collection of concept arts made by the artists, sketches made by the designers, or speed levels made in-engine.

You may also include technical elements such as the colour code for the level, the style of the architecture, the possible interactions noted on a separated map, and anything that may help the reader understand the level design for that area.

NARRATIVE DESIGN DOCUMENT

Next up is the narrative design document: it is just like the previous ones but obviously focused on the characters, story, or world setting of the game. Note that each one of these groups has tons of different elements to be covered, so you will probably need many of them, especially for a narrative-based game. For instance, a character design document talks about the character's clothes, archetype, the way they speak, how they move, and anything that distinguishes them from any other character—something like an identikit of each character.

Narrative design documents are very pliable, even more than other design documents, because each game has a different narrative value for each department: if the game is very narrative-based, these documents may be the first ones to be written, or the narrative may be an environmental one with a lot of presence in the level design; both of these options require very different documents and formats.

To write the foundations of a narrative design document, as a rule of thumb, take some parts of a GDD and some of a LDD that concern the narrative side, conveying the focus on the plot, world, or NPCs, depending on the game—a document about an explicit story-focused narrative game will be very different from one about a game with an iceberg narrative, so finding a good way to present both of them is part of the job.

TECHNICAL DESIGN DOCUMENT

Last, technical design documents are the documents that don't care about *why* something is that way, rather they focus on *how* it works. GDDs and LDDs focus on the needs that you satisfy in the players, their user cases, and what happens. TDDs, instead, come from the previously covered design document, but only looking at how to make something happen. Sure that mechanic is well designed, but what are its values? Should it deal damage or multiply the one you normally inflict? How many enemies should spawn? Where? How?

As you can tell, there are many different questions that need to be answered from a technical point of view, and that is also why these documents should have a simpler form than the other design documents: they need the variables, the values, any particular element to script to accomplish the design, and then they are good to go.

Technical documents are sometimes used by the designers, sometimes by the programmers, and generally by anyone with an interest on the practical side of that mechanic—again, without caring about why it works like that. Many technical design documents about tuning, game economy, or progression are made on spreadsheets with thousands of values, formulas, and charts: while it may look overwhelming at first, a spreadsheet is the best way to work on so many values when thinking about the *how* instead of the *why*. Imagine writing a paragraph to explain every number in a spreadsheet of 1,000 by 1,000 cells: most of your production time would go there. Instead, you may explain each range of numbers defined by a study of the progression, and, as long as each value is in the range it was designed to be in, everything is as it should be.

VERSIONING DOCUMENT

I'd like to start this document by saying that it may be an outdated tool, as versioning systems are included in different tools used in most workflows; however, it's still important to know how it works.

In the game design document subchapter, you have read about versioning applied to each mechanic, with different versions meaning different steps of the production: the same happens with the whole game.

Each version describes a specific state of the game, for instance V1 is the minimum shippable version, V1.5 is the high-quality and polished version, and V2 is the game with DLCs; it always changes depending on the team and the project.

Dividing the game into different versions lets you know what should have a higher priority for each step of the production: if V1.5 needs a mechanic that isn't listed in the V1, that mechanic isn't so core to the experience, or it's not needed anytime soon. That is why having a list with what needs to be done for each version—and its priority—helps to form a clearer picture of the game; it may be a *Roadmap* created by the producer, a list used in Scrum, or any other agile framework used by the team—that is why this document itself is outdated, but its concept is still part of the development of a game. Note that a roadmap includes the versioning and the time factor, but not vice versa: I always suggest defining the versioning first—thus the objectives—and then the roadmap—aka the production times; a good versioning document/system is a great first step to creating a roadmap if you are inexperienced.

On a practical level, this document should include the feature's name, its version, a brief description of how it works, the deadline, and the criteria to consider that version ready—does it have to be approved by the publisher? The directors? The CEO?

As you now know, the function of this document can be found in tools that integrate multiple tasks of a production so that you can track the team's production speed and the version of the game all in one place, alongside many other tools. While I would love to dig into the details, production is such a wide topic that it would require a whole book by itself; that is why in this book you only find the fundamentals—who knows, though, maybe one day it will have one.

DESIGN LOG

The design log—also known as snapshot document, design snapshot, feature shot, and other similar names—is a very particular document: it's the ugliest one of all, as it needs to be done quickly and no time should go toward making it look any less ugly. It is a collage of copy-paste from other documents—thus with different styles—or even a screenshot from the game engine with some notes all around it.

A design log is almost a note document, where some ground knowledge is contained to give you a quick update on each feature: the feature owner, its version with a link to the versioning document, its current state—does it work? Is it broken? Does the owner know it's broken?—any known bug, and any relevant note to understand what's going on with that element. You may find a screenshot from the engine with a note saying "all the grey boxes are 10% too big" or "if you parry and dodge at the same time you become invincible", and it's completely fine, because whoever is in charge of that feature knows that. Someone who doesn't have this document may test the game and panic as the character falls under the game world, so they may start calling meetings and rescheduling the tasks for the project. With a design log, however, they will just fall under the world, check on the log if it's a known issue, and, seeing a note saying "You may fall forever, don't worry about it" they will relax and get back to what they were doing: no panic, no problem.

It's also a great tool for big productions, where you may be working on a feature for a while to then be put in charge of something else, and when you get back to the first feature two months later you can check what its state was and maybe find a note you left yourself like "Remember that to change X you first need to disable Y"—it would be hard to remember those little details for months; I think that's clear by now.

The same goes for when multiple people work on the same element, so maybe they fixed the "Disable Y to change X" problem, but now "If you set X to 4,13 the game crashes", so when you resume working on that you can start by fixing this new bug—and, once again, you won't panic.

I know that this "don't panic" thing will sound like an exaggeration, but trust me: panic *is* a big deal. When you or your team panic, all the priorities, the critical mindset, and sometimes even the professionalism disappear: problems start to seem bigger than they are, time seems shorter, and issues pop into your head even if they have nothing to do with what's wrong in that moment: "The jump doesn't work? Now we have to change all the textures!"—spoiler: no, you don't.

All these documents, other than creating a professional workflow built around the team and project, help you to avoid such situations, because when the panic starts to arise you open the related document and read Paul's note saying "It's broken, I know"; now, since the environment is professional, you know that Paul is taking care of the issue, and if it was something that should have concerned you, you would already know by now.

The production of a game really is like navigating the sea, with waves crashing on your ship, rocks making you adjust the route, and tons of things going on at the same time, but as long as you follow your compass, adjust your roadmap, and keep the sails under control, you will get to shore—and documents *are* just like sails: they do what they are set up to do, so it's better to take good care of them from the beginning.

PITCH DECK

What is a *pitch*? If you are new in the industry you may have never heard of it, and if you are a veteran you sure know what it is, but, in any case, I'm sure you have experienced it in your life multiple times—even if you didn't know it was a pitch.

Pitching is the act—or *art*—of presenting something, that being an idea, a tool, a product; in a broader way, however, it's the act of talking with the goal of convincing someone: convince your friends to try that new restaurant, convince your boss to give you a raise, or even convince yourself that you really need the latest version of a phone. As you can see, it doesn't matter what the pitch is about; the goal is always to receive a positive answer from the person—or people—that you are talking to.

In the game development industry, pitching is a fundamental skill because, as you remember, game design is 50% science and 50% art: this means that even the most experienced designer in the world doesn't have the absolute certainty that their idea will work. It's not like they aren't sure about it; they *can't* be sure, because while their 50% science may be perfect, the 50% art is subjective, so it might be perfect in their head to then be seen differently by the players—if someone tells you that their idea will 100% work, it's either copy-pasted from another game or it's their ego speaking; remember: if design was a certain world, machines would be doing it instead of us.

Designers, especially in bigger studios, often need to give a pitch about a mechanic or system to their colleagues before it can go into development. Since design is partially subjective, it generates questions and doubts in the people who see it, because they have a different point of view: someone may be concerned about the generated aesthetics, another designer thinks about the mechanic's accessibility, a more experienced co-worker worries about the feasibility of such mechanic in the short time the team has left, and so on. This is exactly where the pitch is needed: the designer needs to have the ability to convince others that their idea is valid—not *certain*, just *valid*—because no matter how great a team is, if everyone understands and believes in what they are doing, they will work better and more happily—understanding the goal of each new design is very important to understand where the game is going, avoiding feeling like you are just following instructions blindly.

Note that smaller teams, or ones with a high level of trust between the members, may not require anyone to pitch an idea, because they all respect each other and know that they will work to make their design suitable—if you have been working with the same 3 people for the last 20 years, it's probable that you either trust them or fear them enough to avoid asking for a pitch.

When pitching in most teams, however, a designer doesn't just show their idea, they sell it: the concept, the experience, and the development need to sound so great that people want to work on them, because the pitch portrays a picture that pushes the vision forward and improves the gameplay for the players but also stimulates the team. Each team can, of course, be stimulated in a different way: one may shine when facing a challenge, another one loves to work on the same genre because they are the best at doing it; most of the time, however, you won't know what really motivates your colleagues, so it will be up to you to find it out.

Pitching isn't just internal to the team, though: it also means to present an idea to a publisher, usually with the goal of receiving funds to develop the project. Just like with internal pitching, some teams may not need to pitch to a publisher because of a long professional relationship, or maybe the team has made award-winning games that automatically make them trustworthy enough in the publisher's eyes to not need to pitch, but most teams—especially new ones—need to give a great presentation, showing great slides and catching the publishers' interest.

To give a pitch, you need something to show while you talk, and that is called a pitch deck/document. A pitch deck is a collection of slides that is used in the presentation someone gives to either their team or a publisher, while a pitch *document* is any type of media used for that same purpose: while the documents previously discussed in this chapter are used to help understand a design or keep track of its development, a pitch document has the goal of convincing other people to believe in your idea and develop it. It may sound like there is just a small difference between "understanding a design" and "believing in a design", but in reality it's quite a radical one: a design document has to be clear in all its details, otherwise it's not solving the problem it was made for, while a pitch deck can potentially be vague on purpose. It's a risk, sure, but sometimes it's more about selling than explaining: think about half of the scams out there, they sell you the idea of getting rich, fit, good-looking, etc., but how it works is often unclear. "Use this lotion for a month and you will have a perfect jawline" or "Buy this course and you will get rich in just a few months": how does a lotion improve your bone structure? How can a ten-hour course tell you the secret to becoming a millionaire that no one else is taking advantage of? It simply doesn't; how the *magical product* works is kept vague because it's not magical at all, but what convinces people to spend money in these scams is the outcome, and the pitch is so convincing that people forget about the laws of physics or common financial knowledge. Those that manage to lure the audience into the scam, despite being unethical and everything, are great pitches, and they should be considered the new quality standard for your future presentations: if it makes people forget about how physics works, it's a good pitch—word of advice, though, only aspire to the pitch and not the scam itself: other than being unethical and everything, a pitcher's goal is to have the other person take a deeper look at their work, including researches and documents, so they would only gain a bad reputation if the game didn't really exist.

If you look at successful pitches from around different industries, from tech to cars, from the latest multi-millionaire corporate's announcement to the guy selling vegetables in your local market, you will note one key common element: they are all great at presenting their product. It doesn't matter if it's about the brand new phone or one pound of lettuce, they all manage to grab your attention and portray a scenario that you now need to live, that being the latest *ultra-sharp image AI-refined camera* that takes perfect pictures from three miles away or what will give you the best salad of your whole life—you didn't care about it before, but now you do.

Pitching, therefore, requires excellent presentation skills, because if you don't show that you believe in your idea, it's very hard to make others believe in it. Luckily, it's a virtuous cycle: you learn how to pitch by doing it, but you also learn to do it by creating convincing pitch decks, meaning that the more you try, the better you will do the next time. It also means, however, that you have to do it; you can't sit around and wait for the pitching skill to reach you out of nowhere; sure, someone may have a natural talent, but practice beats any unborn ability someone may have—as they say, "you don't have to be great to start, but you have to start to be great".

Following that train of thought, the first step for a good pitch is to have a good deck— or document—to show, and, while you should customise it according to your needs and target, here are some of the most important and common sections composing a good deck:

> The first slide should always be a cover art or any other audiovisive media that positively catches the audience's attention, that being a concept art, short trailer, gameplay shot, etc. This slide needs to be visually appealing, very refined in the details, and convey how the player feels when playing the finished product.

BOX 19.2   THE DEFINITION OF "COVER ART" REQUIRED IN PITCH DECKS WHEN POSSIBLE, WHY IT IS SO IMPORTANT AND WHERE THE NAME COMES FROM

A cover art, when talking about a game, is a concept art—created by an artist—that illustrates a key moment of the game and sells the fantastic world that the character will live in: do they ride cyber-dragons while shooting their enemies? Do they bake cakes in a moving truck with everything rolling over the improvised kitchen? Show it: what would take precious time to be told can be quickly seen in an image—it's still a document, and, as such, it needs to respect the golden rules of documentation.

The idea—and origin of the name—is that the cover art is so great at showing a core game moment that it could be put as the cover of the game: just like covers on shelves, yours needs to be more appealing to your audience than the other 999 games in the store.

Then there is the *logline*, also called game concept or overview, which is a short description of the game, but, differently from the one you have in the design document, this needs to be written not for design purposes but for marketing ones. It needs to sell the essence of your game, what makes it *cool*—I'm using a generic term intentionally, because marketing doesn't really care about design specific words. Players will hear the logline and they should think "I need that game".

Just because it shouldn't be a design definition of the game, it doesn't mean you shouldn't add pieces of information about its mechanics, especially if those are what make it unique: if it has a brand new movement system, or if it aims at revolutionising a genre, be sure to include it in the logline.

To compare a logline with a mechanic description—what you would write in a GDD—here is an example of both of them for *Elden Ring*:

Mechanic description: a third-person action-adventure experience, with RPG elements, an open world, and souls-like mechanics where the player can choose their progression order for the quests.

Logline: become tarnished after the shuttering of the Elden Ring in this new third-person open world; explore the vast world with powerful enemies, improve your character, and rebuild the Elden Ring to finally become the Elden Lord.

Depending on the state of the production you are in, you may now have a brief section displaying cool pictures, gifs, and videos to keep a high attention level around those you are pitching to: the concept art of a giant dragon shooting black flames from its mouth, the character walking through a gloomy swamp, or even a short display of the prototype of your new combat system.

This part isn't always necessary, because the project might be very new and there was no time to develop such material, or maybe you focused your resources elsewhere, so don't worry about not having it.

You then have the core loop/game overview: what are the expectations for the game? What is the prime mood and prime emotion? How does the system you are talking about fit into the bigger picture? Feel free to grab what you have already written in the high vision or in a GDD to answer any of these questions, just be sure to put it under the *coolness lens* first—a tool that transforms technical terms into cool phrases that intrigue the audience. If you show the combat system, don't focus on fighting the small and generic enemies, let them instead picture the character fighting a colossus as big as a whole castle or an enemy that gains power the more time the player spends fighting it—again, make it *cool*.

If your game can be seen as the mashup of different products—games, movies, books, etc.—be sure to include some references in a slide around this point. If the game has the gameplay of *Dark Souls*, with the art style of *Borderlands* and part of the mechanics of *Destiny*, it's not an issue to take inspiration from other games, as long as you are making something new out of it—remember that being creative is about combining things in a new way rather than inventing something from scratch. Showing these references is very helpful for others to imagine how the final game should look and feel: remember that while you have a clear vision in your head, other people only know what you tell them in this pitch.

The next topic should be the narrative: a couple of paragraphs/slides with all the information needed to contextualise the mechanic you just showed, again not seen with the eyes of a designer but with that same coolness lens of before.

You then have the game's unique selling points, which you can take from your high vision document but rewritten for a more catchy sound. For instance, if a USP of the game is that the projectiles you shoot have a chance to spawn an enemy, you could phrase it something like "Be wary of your own guns, they may betray you", to then briefly explain what may happen and why.

If you are pitching a game to a publisher, you should then talk about its business model: is it *freemium*? Does it have DLC planned? Is it completely free and you hope that the players will donate money to support your studio? None of these is mathematically better or worse; it all depends on who the publisher is, what the goal of the game is, or who the players are.

If your model is an already known one, don't spend much time explaining it—a publisher probably knows how these models work better than anyone—but if it's a whole new and never seen before model that improves, say, the players' retention, be sure to highlight it in this part of the pitch.

Assuming you did your research on the audience you want to target, you can talk about that too in this part.

Never ever, though, talk about your sales forecast during the pitch—aka your expectations on the game sales. No publisher wants to hear "This game will sell ten million copies because that other game sold that many". It's not because your game will never sell that many copies—trust me, I really hope it will—it's just not a good idea to make such a comparison with two different products and most likely not enough data to back that assumption up.

Now the listeners' attention might be starting to lower again, so here goes the user case: tell that great gameplay moment you thought of or that user's boss fight during a playtest that made them feel like a real pro. The user case doesn't care about the design itself, it rather focuses on the best moments coming out of that design:

> The player is exploring the dark swamp with a torch in the left hand and a sword in the right one; they see an object and decide to get closer. As they are picking it up, the flame of the torch illuminates two hands on the floor, next to the character's feet: the hands close around the ankles, and a giant skeleton charges their attack toward the character, marking the beginning of a boss fight.

That same example could have been said as "A trap holds the character in place when interacting with items in specific spots, to then trigger a boss fight", but it has way less appeal, because stories allow people to empathise with the protagonist: you think about how *you* would feel exploring the dark swamp, how *you* would react to that trap and how *you* would get out of that situation while fighting that huge skeleton—it's more likely for you to remember this example than any of the other 100 cake-related examples I've made so far, because, while cakes are great, you can't really empathise that much with them.

Since your great story got everyone's interest to the roof, you should now get to the more production-related elements, this being your timeline, action points, or "call to action": this is your plan if the publisher agrees to develop the game, so it's important to keep it as simple and short as possible. Rather than focusing on the perfect values to tune the character's movement speed, talk about what you will accomplish in what time:

> In six months we will deliver a polished ten-minute demo. In one year we will have the intro, the first level, and the first main boss. In two years we will bring the whole three levels and bosses, marking the end of V1 for the game. The next year will go toward the two DLCs to reach V1.5, also following our business model.

You may spend some more time to explain where the resources—the publisher's money—will be going, to make the project more transparent:

> 65% of the budget goes toward salaries, 15% pays the rent for the studio we use, 10% is for an hardware upgrade, and the last 10% is for emergencies such as a computer breaking down, or the studio catching on fire making us pay the deposit for a new location.

If you are pitching to a publisher, there should be a part about how cool and great your team is: did the team win any award? Does your last game have 99% positive reviews, or does the studio have an extremely loving and loyal community, so much that they would buy the game just to make you avoid failing? If it does, you should talk about it in this section.

After showing how great the game is, how cool the members are, and anything like that, it's time to close the sale: if you haven't done it before, say what you need—Money? Time? Maybe just the marketing?—then thank everyone for their time, put your contacts on a slide, and be sure to have a closing image just as refined as the cover art.

I know it might sound bad to be talking about *selling* your game, but sales pitches gained a negative connotation they don't deserve, at least not in this field: the publisher wants a game, while you have a game but need a publisher; everyone wins. It's not like you are selling them your 40-year old car that barely moves without letting them have a test drive because you know it would fall into pieces—as long as you are honest about the game and its timeline, you and the publisher are making a two-way deal.

And that concludes your pitch, or at least what you will say. *How* you will say it, unfortunately, can't really be taught. Don't get me wrong, there are countless books, videos, and techniques out there to improve your pitching skills, but the big difference comes from experience, just like riding a bike—or, totally random example, baking a cake: it doesn't matter if you read the physics behind how egg beating works, you have to grab a whisk and go for it.

If you do need an exercise before your first pitch, however, a simple but effective beginner's technique is pitching to yourself in the mirror, because it allows you both to pitch and hear your pitching: you can see your level of confidence, how you move, and even if you turn tomato red after talking too much without taking a breath.

As you know, there is nothing certain in game design, but pitching is about making it feel like it is, even if it's for just a second, because the images you show, the sentences you say, and the way you say it are so great that whoever is listening *wants* your idea to be perfect—it probably is a romanticised vision, but this is what it means to me, because how can finding yourself in a new unexplored world not be romantic, after all?

SECTION FIVE

Conclusion

Games, Cakes, and Love

20

So, what is game design? Take your time; think carefully about the answer.

BOX 20.1   A SPACE FOR THE READER TO WRITE DOWN THEIR DEFINITION OF GAME DESIGN

What is game design for you after reading a whole book about it?

....

....

Once you have it, compare it with the one you gave in the introduction chapter—do you recall what it was?

Impressive, isn't it? I haven't read either of them, but I'm sure something changed: did it become more technical? Once again, there is no wrong answer, because that sentence is the way you see game design; not just what it is or what it can be, but how you see it: *it is the mirror of each designer's soul*, remember? How you talk about this passion is truly just yours, and it says way more about you than about game design itself. This does fascinate me to my core: we all do this job that—hopefully—we love to do, knowing very well that no two people live it the same way. Even if they use the same process, with the same data, team, framework, time, and everything else, they will end up having two different ideas. There might be a huge difference, or a very small one, but there will always be one. And despite knowing this, we all work together, push games further, and experiment to bring game design to new heights.

All the tools you have found scattered through these pages, the tips on how to use them, ideas for potential new ones you will create, they are all truly yours: sure, any of them may be helpful to a colleague, but even with the same one, no two identical results will ever be created.

The same goes for the reason behind your calling toward game design: maybe you were on the bus and saw a kid playing happily or games were what allowed you to hang on in life and you wanted to help out others; maybe you ended up on this path by a coincidence, but if you have read a whole book about it, I'm guessing you decided to stick around. No matter the case, each one of us has a reason to do what we do, and I'm sure there won't be two identical ones.

DOI: 10.1201/9781003229438-25

For me it's all about making people live experiences that they could or would never want to live in real life: riding a dragon while throwing lightning spears down the sky? You just can't do that, sure there are other animals that you can hop on, and sure that's a great time too, but it's not a dragon.

The same goes for situations people don't want to experience in their lives, such as running from a serial killer, losing a son to cancer, or being betrayed by someone you love: these are all, unfortunately, very real and possible scenarios, but as long as you are living them through a game they will never hold nearly as much power as they would if they really happened. It doesn't make the pain you feel any less real, but when you close the game no one gets hurt: those are all situations you experience, that will be part of you forever, and they may have almost no impact on you, or they could completely change the way you see similar situations.

This is the main reason that brought me here, I've always had this creativity that I didn't know how to express: I tried through drawings, music, dancing, and much more, and while I liked a lot of those things, none of them felt really right for me. Then I tried with videogames: I had the chance to let the player be the architect of their actions, having them pull a trigger, choosing their favourite character as partner, deciding what to do with the evil guy who took away so many lives, etc. Don't get me wrong, non-interactive media are as great as games, but I haven't found in them that string connecting me to the user in a special way.

The game industry right now is led by people just like me, who started for a love and passion for games. Not just a love for games themselves but also for designing creative things; the same goes for many people across different departments: the character artist has a passion for creating characters, but an even bigger one for creating characters specifically for games. The programmer loves to code, but they love coding games more. The concept artist, the sound designer, the localisation specialist, the UX designer, and so on, they all find a plus in their job when it's applied to games, each one for their own special reason or calling.

This is something I'm really fond of, and it's also one of the reasons why this industry is one of the easiest to make new friends in no time: "I see you have an action figure of Mario on your desk, I love him too! What about a *Mario Kart* tournament with the office during lunch break?" People start talking about their favourite games during lunch and end up playing *Dungeons & Dragons* together each weekend, creating new bonds in a way that is quite rare, especially considering how hard it often is to make new friends as an adult.

The industry, however, isn't flawless. There are many of them, from the incorrect use of crunch time to unprofessionalism, from smaller issues like unorganised documentation—which can be fixed relatively easily—to crucial ones like harassment episodes. Why do such problems happen? Partially because bad apples are unfortunately present in every barrel, and partially because the industry grew up too much and too fast:

> In 1972 *Atari* was founded, marking what we can consider the birth of the videogame industry. 50 years have passed, and look at how much we have grown: it has become the biggest entertainment field in the world, more than movies, books, and music combined.
>
> To give you a clearer understanding, the Lumière brothers created the first movie in 1895; 50 years later there were still very simple projections compared to what movies are now; sure they were successful, but half a century later, that industry

was still in its early stages. An even clearer picture is visible when thinking about music, dance, or books: those have been around for thousands of years; they had time to grow and let people understand how to manage them. Now think about games again, and 50 years will look like a glance.

Other than being an interactive media, games are much bigger than movies or albums or books: a AAA game costs hundreds of millions of dollars, with hundreds if not thousands of people working on it and taking several years to develop.

This necessity to satisfy the market, push games further, and find out how to do everything while doing it didn't give most studios the right space to grow, having them sacrificing professionalism, personal time, or the desire to share and improve their techniques: instead of sharing that new methodology they just discovered, they'd rather keep it a secret, fearing that a competitor may cut them off with their next game—this creates *tacit knowledge* that often doesn't leave the team itself.

The tacit knowledge also comes from the lack of professional training: many people who lead the industry are self-taught game designers coming from other jobs, meaning they experimented with techniques until they found the ones that worked for them. While it's great to try new frameworks, this created imperfect tools that worked for that time and that studio, but that aren't meant to be iterated anywhere else or on a different project.

Sure, there are events aimed at sharing new discoveries with others, but they are often very limited, and a single tool isn't enough to change a colossal environment like this: this is one of the reasons for this book, joining my colleagues who wished to make information more accessible, both for experts and newcomers. I wanted to add, however, a practical direction for the readers to follow, not only regarding the hard skills but also reaching the soft-skill side of this job, hence why I've talked about professional behaviours and respect for your colleagues, other than the tasks themselves—these are also some of the reasons why I plan to write a second book, focused on the strategical/operative production of games.

I know that changing such a big industry is a big goal, but it's the very reason why I teach and I join every conference I can: forming the first generation of designers willing to share their experiences and learn from others, as well as helping people who already do this job, means a better environment both for games and for people. If the industry becomes more effective it becomes more efficient, meaning a better experience for anyone who works there: fewer mistakes, fewer burnouts, more money, more professionalism, and better games.

That being said, thank you for taking the time to read this book; I hope you found it helpful. Now you can start working on that great idea you had or tell a co-worker about the tool that is just what they needed the other day. Feel free to open the book anytime you need, as some tools are heavier to pick up, so you may need to check it again in the future. If you ever get lost, think about the reason why you started this journey; that will be your compass: it doesn't matter if you take a different route from the one you planned or if you have no route at all, because it's about following your very own direction—you can always have a break and bake something. I wonder, what will it be?

The Cake Is Real 21

During these pages I've mentioned food countless times, especially cakes: it wasn't intentional at first, but I discovered that they make great examples for game design topics. As a reward for completing this book, I want you to have this recipe for a cake, so that when you need to decant your document, take a break to unravel that one problem, or want to have something to eat for your *Mario Kart* party, you know what your go-to food will be.

TORTA PARADISO RECIPE

This recipe is for a *Torta Paradiso*—the Italian paradise cake—an easy and cheap first cake to bake.

PREPARATION	BAKING	SERVINGS	DIFFICULTY	COST
15 Minutes	45–55 Minutes	6	Low	Cheap

INGREDIENTS

- 6 Large eggs
- 150g Flour
- 1 Yeast for cake envelope (8g)
- 1/4 teaspoon fine sea salt
- 300g sugar
- 300g unsalted butter + a slice to grease the pan
- 150g potato starch
- 1 teaspoon vanilla paste
- 2 teaspoons vanilla extract

DOI: 10.1201/9781003229438-26

PREPARATION

1. Separate the egg yolks from the whites, place 6 yolks in one bowl and 4 whites in another bowl—you won't need those 2 extra whites. Cover both bowls with plastic wrap to let them reach room temperature.
2. Preheat the oven to 350°F.
3. Take a 9 or 10 inch springform pan—or similar—and slightly grease the bottom and the sides. Then, cover the bottom and the sides with parchment paper. Now lightly butter the paper too, and set the pan aside.
4. In a medium-sized bowl, take the flour, the potato starch, and the salt and sift them all in that bowl, making sure they mix evenly. Set it aside.
5. Take a stand mixer with a paddle attachment, and beat the butter until it's creamy, then pour in half of the sugar, all the vanilla pasta and vanilla extract, and the zest of the lemon.
   Beat everything for around 6 minutes on medium speed until it's creamy and pale. During this process, scrape the bottom and the sides of the bowl a couple of times.
6. Add the yolks one at a time while continuing to beat, scraping the sides and the bottom of the bowl.
7. Switch to a large bowl with a hand mixer; whip the whites until they hold barely soft peaks. Decrease the speed of the mixer to low, and very slowly add the remaining sugar one tablespoon at a time. Be sure everything is mixed together before adding the next spoon. Once all the sugar has been added, increase the speed to high and whip the whites—ideally—until stiff. If they aren't stiff after some time don't worry, you can stop there and go on with the recipe.
8. Get the yolk mixture of step 1, add the flour mixture with the paddle speed on low, and mix the flour in. Keep scraping the sides and bottom of the bowl. Add 1/4 of the egg white mixture and, quickly but gently, mix it with a spatula.
9. Add the remaining egg whites, and combine everything together. When they are evenly mixed together, scrape this bowl into the pan from step 3, and smooth the top.
10. Bake it until it's golden brown, and the cake tester put in the middle of the cake comes out clean, after around 45–55 minutes—if you don't have a cake tester, you can use a toothpick. Be sure to rotate the pan after around 25–30 minutes if your oven doesn't cook evenly.
11. Move the cake to a cooling rack and let it cool for around 25 minutes: remove the cake from the springform pan by releasing the sides and using a cake lifter to place it on the rack, carefully removing the parchment paper from the sides. If you are using a regular pan, place parchment paper over the pan, quickly flip it onto the parchment, and flip it back on the cooling rack.
12. Let the cake cool completely.
13. Once it's cooled, sift powdered sugar on top of the cake. Transfer the cake to a stand or plate.
14. Enjoy while being crashed by your friends on *Mario Kart*.

Index

9 781032 134789